Using Analytical Frameworks for Classroom Research

Collecting data and analysing narrative

Edited by Susan Rodrigues

Routledge
Taylor & Francis Group

LONDON AND NEW YORK

D0227796

First published 2010
by Routledge
2 Park Square, Milton Park, Abingdon, Oxon, OX14 4RN

Simultaneously published in the USA and Canada
by Routledge
270 Madison Avenue, New York, NY 10016

Routledge is an imprint of the Taylor & Francis Group, an informa business

© 2010 Susan Rodrigues for editorial material and selection; individual
contributions, the contributors.

Typeset in Galliard by
Keystroke, Tettenhall, Wolverhampton
Printed and bound in Great Britain by
TJ International Ltd, Padstow, Cornwall

British Library Cataloguing in Publication Data
A catalogue record for this book is available from the British Library

Library of Congress Cataloging-in-Publication Data
Using analytical frameworks for classroom research : collecting data and
analysing narrative / edited by Susan Rodrigues.
        p. cm.
     Includes bibliographical references.
   1. Action research in education—Case studies.   2. Classroom
management—Case studies.   3. Education—Research—Case studies.
   I. Rodrigues, Susan.
   LB1028.24.U74 2010
   370.7'2—dc22   2009033505

ISBN10: 0–415–55306–7 (hbk)
ISBN10: 0–415–55307–5 (pbk)
ISBN10: 0–203–85799–2 (ebk)

ISBN13: 978–0–415–55306–3 (hbk)
ISBN13: 978–0–415–55307–0 (pbk)
ISBN13: 978–0–203–85799–1 (ebk)

Contents

Figures

Tables

Contributors

Mary Ainley is Associate Professor in the Psychology Department at the University of Melbourne. She has considerable experience teaching undergraduate students and supervising graduate student research. Her research interests involve investigating the experience of interest and exploring the psychological processes that are involved when students engage with (and disengage from) achievement tasks. The goal of this research is to understand how to support positive educational experiences for students of all ages.

Charles Anderson is Senior Lecturer in the School of Education at the University of Edinburgh. Much of Dr Anderson's research has centred on learning and teaching in higher education (guided by a socio-cultural approach to learning). He has a particular interest in exploring talk and texts in educational settings. A central and enjoyably challenging area of his teaching is qualitative research methodologies and methods.

Keith Bishop is Senior Lecturer in the Department of Education at the University of Bath. Dr Bishop's research interest is the exploration of how the concept of 'accomplishment' might be defined within the context of science teaching and the implementation of curriculum change in sub-Saharan Africa. He also acts as a consultant to the AstraZeneca Science Teaching Trust. Currently, he is in the process of launching a new undergraduate degree in childhood, youth and education.

Sarah Buckley is Research Officer at the Australian Council for Educational Research. Dr Buckley's Ph.D. thesis examined the effects of affective factors, like motivation, and peer networks on adolescent mathematics anxiety. Her research interests include exploring social-contextual factors on students' motivation and achievement.

Lindsey N. Conner is Associate Professor and Associate Dean at the College of Education, University of Canterbury, Christchurch, New Zealand. She has a specific research focus on the teaching and learning of socio-scientific issues. She also has several projects in partnership with schools where they are investigating the alignment of pedagogy with purpose.

Paul Denley is Lecturer in the Department of Education at the University of Bath. Dr Denley's main area of research is in science education, particularly the initial and continuing professional development of secondary science teachers with a focus on knowledge bases for science teaching. His current research includes work for the AstraZeneca Science Teaching Trust, evaluating projects to support primary teachers in science and a DfID-funded project in Africa exploring the use of ICT to support science teaching. He teaches units in the department's MA programme on learning, curriculum and research methods, as well as supervising research students.

Rod Fawns is Senior Lecturer in Science Education at the University of Melbourne. Dr Fawns is a science educator with a commitment to pre-service teacher education that extends back 37 years at the University of Melbourne. He has been the principal supervisor for over 100 masters and 30 doctoral theses. His research contributions have been in social psychological and historical studies in science education and teacher education.

Bev France is Associate Professor of Science and Technology Education in the Faculty of Education at the University of Auckland. Her research focus is in biotechnology education and as a consequence she is interested in finding out how scientists and technologists work by asking them to tell their stories. These narratives provide information about how different groups of people talk to each other about biotechnology.

Divya Jindal-Snape is Senior Lecturer in the School of Education, Social Work and Community Education at the University of Dundee. Dr Jindal-Snape's research interests lie in the field of educational transitions and inclusion. A significant proportion of her work has been with children and young people with additional support needs, especially children and young people with visual impairment, autism, learning difficulties, emotional and behavioural needs. This has also involved developing social interaction through drama techniques and other forms of creative arts education.

Joseph Krajcik is Professor in the School of Education at the University of Michigan. He develops classroom environments in which students find solutions to important intellectual questions that subsume essential learning goals. He has authored and co-authored over 100 manuscripts and makes frequent presentations at international, national and regional conferences that focus on his research, as well as presentations that translate research findings into classroom practice. He is a fellow of the American Association for the Advancement of Science (AAAS) and American Educational Research Association (AERA), served as President of National Association for Research in Science Teaching (NARST) and received guest professorships from Beijing Normal University and the Weizmann Institute of Science. In 2009, Ewha Womans University in Korea named him a distinguished fellow.

Christine Redman is Senior Lecturer at the University of Melbourne, in the area of science, technology and ICT education. Dr Redman's research interests include enhancing the effectiveness of classroom science teaching through sound pedagogical uses of a diverse range of ICT. By examining teacher's practices and what factors informed their choices and effective uses of ICT, she hopes to better understand how to motivate and sustain deeper engagement in science learning experiences.

Susan Rodrigues is Professor of Science Education at the University of Dundee. She is the programme director for the Professional Doctorate in Education, Social Work and Community Education. She also contributes to the Professional Graduate Diploma of Education (PGDE) (secondary) teacher education programme. She has research projects exploring the effectiveness of context, teacher pedagogy and the use of information communication technologies in science classrooms.

Pauline Sangster is Senior Lecturer and Deputy Director of post-graduate studies in the School of Education at the University of Edinburgh. Dr Sangster's current research is on language learning and teaching (particularly on listening and its development within the socio-cultural contexts of classrooms), trainee teachers' developing reflexivity and reflective practice and the linguistic demands of national tests and examinations. She teaches on both general research methods courses and on courses where the key focus is researching language.

Namsoo Shin is Assistant Research Scientist in the School of Education at the University of Michigan. Dr Shin's interests are focused on the impact of constructivistic learning environments on student learning, especially everyday problem-solving skills, among K–12 students. She specialises in using quantitative and qualitative methods to document the effectiveness of instructional materials and learning technologies. She is currently a principle investigator of the National Science Foundation (NSF) project 'Developing an Empirically tested Learning Progression for the Transformation of Matter to Inform Curriculum, Instruction and Assessment Design'.

Shawn Y. Stevens is Research Investigator in the School of Education at the University of Michigan where her work focuses on assessing and improving student and teacher learning. In association with the National Center for Learning and Teaching Nanoscale Science and Engineering (NCLT), she is developing a learning progression for the nature of matter as it relates to nanoscience. In addition, she is characterising how new elementary teachers develop pedagogical content knowledge for science teaching, which is funded by the Center for Curriculum Materials in Science (CCMS).

Keith Topping is Professor of Educational and Social Research in the School of Education at the University of Dundee, where he mainly researches peer learning. He has published over 130 peer reviewed journal papers, 40 chapters and 17 books. His work has been translated into 11 languages.

the quest to explore language, talk and discourse usually results in a search for methodologies that allow us to focus on specific aspects of the communication process.

In Chapter 9, I use facets of Halliday and Hasan's work to show how classroom talk can be analysed. I show how the notion of register, coherence and cohesion can be used to illustrate and interpret classroom interactions, whether they are dialogues or monologues. I use transcripts from various classroom studies to show how classroom talk can be analysed in terms of its influence on the negotiation of meaning and its influence on shaping the nature of learning in classrooms.

Similarly, Christine Redman and Rod Fawns show how talk can be analysed with regard to a specific aspect of communication in Chapter 10. They show how Harré's positioning theory can be used as an informing analytic approach when considering what they call 'data sets that are gathered in the lived moments'. Christine and Rod describe how positioning theory has informed the development of pronoun grammar analysis as an objective coding tool for the fine-grained analysis of talk. They discuss how they analysed their teacher talk data through the window of positioning theory to illustrate the concept of 'oughtness'; they suggest that oughtness shapes why and how people determine what they *should* chose to adopt. Christine and Rod describe how positioning theory can help a researcher develop a deeper understanding of a community's values and practices, as well as help identify the community member's relations with these values and practices.

The final chapter, Chapter 11, revisits some of the key ideas and considers elements that help to ensure the data are trustworthy.

This edited book of chapters, addressing particular forms of analysis, is intended as a sampler. It is an introductory guide for those who are interested in the theoretical underpinnings of some commonly used analytical approaches. Each chapter identifies an approach, outlines some of the theoretical assumptions and constraints that underpin the approach, signals the traditions in which these approaches are located and provides data to show how this analysis manifests when deployed in educational research. Thus I believe that the book will be relevant to teachers, researchers, academics, postgraduate students and other academic professionals who conduct their research in educational settings or support others in doing so.

Chapter 1

Understanding educational achievement and outcomes

Person, process and context

Mary Ainley and Sarah Buckley

Introduction

Finding answers to educational problems is a complex undertaking. Whether awareness of the problem arises as a result of classroom observation, the reading of learned journals or armchair theorising, there is always a range of perspectives that can be brought to bear on a problem. In this chapter, we explore a number of models and analytic approaches that can be applied to investigate specific issues that are part of the complex mix of person, process and context that feature in education at all levels.

In the first part of this chapter, we take the basic components of person, process and context as described by a prominent theorist in developmental psychology and examine how they can be used to describe the basic components in a wide range of educational research. In the second part of this chapter, we describe some of the quantitative analysis tools used in educational research and show how different types of analyses pose different basic questions; questions about how variables operate and questions concerning combinations of variables, identified as personal profiles or as developmental trajectories. Using a variety of educational research examples, we intend to demonstrate that these are complementary approaches; each approach provides a slightly different lens on the educational issue driving the research. The approaches we describe are not limited to educational research but represent perspectives that are currently being applied to find answers to a wide range of behavioural questions.

A model of person, process and context

Urie Bronfenbrenner's (1979) ecological theory of development, which in later formulations becomes a bioecological model (Bronfenbrenner, 2001), has had a major influence on modern developmental and educational psychological thought. One way these models have influenced thinking is through the conceptualisation of a child's developmental contexts as a multilayered system. At the core are the microsystem processes in which the child is actor. Surrounding layers consist of more indirect, but no less important, influences on the child's development. The relationship between the home and the school manifests itself in issues such as: attitudes and expectations concerning homework; the influence of parental employment arrangements on family life; and the overarching cultural norms and community legal system providing both affordances and constraints on family interactions. Although not the only theorist to draw attention to this complex network of interacting systems, many of the insights from Bronfenbrenner's perspectives on research into children's development provide useful ways of looking at research into children's educational achievement and development.

Awareness of the multiple layers and interacting systems flows through to consideration of the different components or levels of analysis that are adopted in research designs. Bronfenbrenner (1986) outlines a useful way to understand the structure of specific research investigations. He describes three analytic models or paradigms, which he refers to as: a 'social address model'; a 'process-context model'; and a 'person-process-context model'. Each model provides a general schema for conceptualising the elements of a research question or a research design. At the same time, the specific questions, which can be addressed within these general paradigms, offer a wide range of possibilities for investigating and understanding aspects of the education process. One of the examples cited in Bronfenbrenner's paper demonstrates the differences between these three models. The example is from the developmental literature and concerns early attachment processes between infant and mother. This is not unrelated to a number of questions considered in the early childhood education literature where it has been shown that early secure attachment status is predictive of children's early school adjustment. A study by Crockenberg (1981) reported that in a sample of middle-class and working-class mothers the level of social support the mothers received from their social network at the time their infants were approximately three months old was a significant predictor of the mother–infant attachment relationship at 12 months of age. There are a number of contextual factors operating here, including the social address defined as social class membership (i.e. middle-class and working-class families) and the mother's membership of a social network.

At the process level, the study has identified the significance of specific interactive processes within the social network, namely, social support defined as help and support from 'husband, extended family, other children, friends and neighbours, and professionals . . . an assessment of the affective and material assistance experienced by the mother in her mother role, relative to the stresses experienced by her' (Crockenberg, 1981: 859). The outcome variable is also a process variable in that attachment status defines a particular pattern of interactive behaviour between mother and infant. However, it was also found that the beneficial effects of social support processes were related to the infant's temperament (a person variable). The strongest effects of social support processes occurred for mothers and infants where the infant was identified as having an 'irritable' temperament, while effects were described as minimal for infants with a 'calm' temperament. In this investigation the child behaviour of interest (attachment status at 12 months) was predicted by a network of interacting variables that included input from the broader social network, the patterns of interaction between the mother and her three-month-old infant and the temperamental style of the infant.

As Bronfenbrenner suggests, consideration of all three components – social address (context), process and person – acknowledges the complexity of factors associated with developmental outcomes for children.

The position taken in this chapter is that this framework for understanding the structure of research questions and designs offers one very rich way of understanding the various models that underpin research questions and investigations. In the next section we examine how social address (context), process and person components feature in current educational research.

The social address or context model

The social address or context model perspective is adopted in many of the reports that emerge from large-scale national and international surveys. The students' country becomes the social address, and variable and systematic differences in observed educational outcomes are linked back to features of the educational experience or the socio-political system. Many of the Programme for International Student Assessment (PISA) reports are of this type. For example, profiles of students' achievement in different areas of science, attitudes towards science, engagement and interest in science and intentions for future participation in science are reported according to students' home country. Different social arrangements for schooling, such as levels of public and private participation in the funding and the management of schools, have been analysed in relation to students' performance in science (see OECD, 2007).

Social address can also be conceptualised at a number of finer-grain contextual levels where comparisons are made, for example, between experience and outcomes for students from rural and urban schools or between schools or students distinguished on the basis of indices of socio-economic advantage and disadvantage.

Researchers from the Longitudinal Studies of Australian Youth (LSAY) have adopted a social address model for their investigation of patterns of movement of young people on completion of high school (Hillman and Rothman, 2007). The dominant pattern of migration from non-metropolitan areas to the cities was related to study plans. The most common reason for movement was to participate in some form of post-compulsory education – in the majority of cases this was to embark on university education. Geographic location was found to be a strong factor in the educational development trajectory for non-metropolitan students. Their progression to tertiary education was highly likely to be associated with the broader change of leaving home and assuming more independence than was necessary for urban students who go on to pursue tertiary education.

Analysis of the influence of the social address factor of socio-economic status is another of the social address perspectives that features in reports from PISA. Results across all countries participating in PISA confirm the well-documented pattern of students from more advantaged socio-economic backgrounds gaining significantly higher scores on measures of science literacy than students from less advantaged backgrounds (see OECD, 2007: 183). It is of interest here to consider the nature of the PISA index of economic, social and cultural status. The index was constructed by combining information provided by students about their father's and mother's occupations (scaled to reflect status) and level of education, with an index of home possessions including family wealth (e.g. whether students had a room of their own, internet access, etc.), access to educational resources (e.g. a quiet place to study, books to help with their schoolwork, etc.) and cultural possessions. The specific indicators are assumed to represent family environment resources, activities and patterns of interaction that are related to school achievement. Development of the index is referenced to studies of vocabulary development in early childhood, relations between early patterns of school achievement and parental economic and occupational circumstances and levels of involvement in extra activities both in school and out of school (see OECD, 2007: 181).

Other research programmes have investigated how achievement is influenced by students being grouped within schools on the basis of specific ability, referred to in some contexts as 'tracking', 'ability-grouping' or 'streaming'. A wealth of studies demonstrate what Marsh (1987) terms the 'big-fish-little-pond effect', wherein an average student placed in a high-ability class will have a poorer self-concept, and lower self-confidence, than an average student placed in a class with students of varying ability (see Marsh *et al.*, 2008). The greater diversity offered to students in classes with mixed abilities can have other implications for academic development, for instance, in terms of the types of peer interactions that are encouraged.

The social address perspective may take the form of identifying various forms of peer networks and then considering how membership of these networks impacts on educational experiences and outcomes. Over the last decade there have been considerable advances in techniques for investigating and analysing peer relationships. In this stimulating new research, the influence of students' social address is examined by focusing on their position in peer networks. A range of different networks can be investigated and take into account the role of different interactions that operate both through formal school contexts as well as informal school contexts. Rather than referring to a global influence of peers, contemporary social network techniques allow the identification of students' positions in multiple networks, such as friendships and help-seeking. Networks are examined by asking students questions like 'Who are your friends at school?' and 'Who do you go to if you need help with your schoolwork?'

The structure of these networks can be described in terms of their patterns and density. For example, some networks consist of lots of 'dyads' (two-person relations), while others might be more clustered or operate via numerous interconnected 'triads' (three-person relations). Different structures have different implications for the types of cultures operating in the classroom/school. This approach has recently been applied in a research investigation into peer network influences on mathematical anxiety (Buckley, 2009). Buckley examined the structure of help-seeking networks in mathematics classes and found that inter-actions were more likely to be dyadic, rather than clustered, at a school that employed ability grouping for mathematics classes. This means that in the classes where students had been grouped by ability, help-seeking interactions tended to occur between two persons. In contrast, for another school where students were placed in classes of mixed ability, help-seeking tended to be more clustered and structurally similar to the types of interactions characteristic of typical social relationships (i.e. friendships). Thus, the increased homogeneity in classrooms grouped on ability level may have had unintended implications for the informal peer culture related to academic help-seeking.

The process-context model

The second perspective described by Bronfenbrenner (1986) is the process-context model. Here emphasis is placed on processes that are aligned with social group membership that, in turn, account for the relation between social address and the educational outcome of interest. There is a growing body of research, especially in the educational psychology literature, exploring the processes that intervene between factors readily identified as contextual (social address) factors and edu-cational outcomes. A couple of examples from LSAY are described to illustrate this pattern.

One of the important schooling processes evaluated as part of the LSAY research is student engagement, which is defined in terms of students' participation in the life of the school (Fullarton, 2002). Fullarton argues that students' sense of belonging and identification with their school could be indexed through their participation in the range of extra-curricular activities their school offers. Social address and process come together in many of the findings reported (for example, the highest levels of engagement with school were found in students from higher socio-economic backgrounds).

Students who were selected into the LSAY samples as 15-year-olds in 1995 and 1998 were followed up after two years (in 1997 and 2000 respectively) to identify groups of early school leavers. Social address variables such as geographic location were included in the set of predictor variables. While there were significant regional differences in the proportion of students who did not complete their secondary schooling, the important finding was that when prior school attainment – in this case Year 9 literacy and numeracy achievement levels – was entered into the analysis, the predictive effects of the regional location variable was reduced (Jones, 2002). Literacy and numeracy processes, associated with students' geographical location, mediated the effects of geographic location on early school leaving. Students with lower attainment levels were more likely to leave school before completing their secondary education.

Another example of these socio-cultural effects is shown by Buckley (2009) who finds that close friendships may impact on students' anxiety and value towards mathematics. Furthermore, this research demonstrates that peer influence may vary depending on the type of peer relationship considered. In other words, different peer networks can affect different academic attributes. For instance, close friendships might be important for the formation of value attitudes (i.e. how much a student values their time at school). In contrast, help-seeking interactions might be more important for establishing students' confidence to take on new challenges in the classroom and keep any anxiety at bay.

Context is represented in the work of Volet, Summers and Thurman (2009) by the structure of interactive processes within a learning setting. In their investigations of collaborative learning settings, Volet *et al.* identify a number of social regulation processes which highlight the interactive and interdependent qualities of the active learning that occurred. Four key factors are associated with high-level co-regulation or socially scaffolded learning in the collaborative learning groups: question asking; tentativeness; background knowledge; and shared positive emotions. These findings indicate that the context – in this case collaborative learning groups – shape the learning process for the individual and can impact on the quality of the learning experience.

The person-process-context model

The third perspective is the person-process-context model. The addition of the 'person' component highlights the fact that many of the processes observed in varying educational contexts, as well as in social developmental contexts, may operate differently for different types of people. The most commonly researched person variable is gender. Many research questions ask whether the underlying processes connecting context and educational outcome vary according to students' gender. For example, in the LSAY investigation of early school leavers referred to above (Jones, 2002), when gender was included in the analysis the predictive power of geographic location was reduced. Boys were more likely to leave before completing their secondary education than girls.

A wide range of person variables occur in educational research and include variables such as temperament, personality, motivational orientations and attitudes. Much of the discussion of person factors in educational research is looking at identifying qualities, traits and dispositions and identifying how they relate to a range of educational outcomes. Underpinning this approach is a strong assumption that the scores on measures of person variables can be generalised to represent an individual's behaviour and that scores are predictive of future behaviour.

Within a group of early adolescent students, Buckley (2009) found that being a girl was a stronger predictor of higher mathematics anxiety than students' previous mathematics achievement. This anxiety operated like a personality trait or a general attitude that students felt towards the subject. Buckley's research also showed that students who had more of this negative attitude tended to report more anxiety while they were completing a mathematics problem-solving task on the computer. Girls also reported the highest ratings on this 'on-task' anxiety.

These findings demonstrate the predictive capacity of two person-variables (i.e. gender and trait mathematics anxiety) on students' situational academic experience in the classroom (i.e. on-task anxiety).

From this brief discussion it is clear that the general structure described by Bronfenbrenner (1986) allows for a myriad of possibilities in terms of the specific questions researchers choose to address. It also has the simultaneous advantage of providing an organising framework for synthesis across disparate research programmes. The underlying structure of the approach taken in this chapter is to show how research projects typically focus on parts of this system of relations and how specific analytic tools can be used for questions addressing different relations within the multilayered system representing students' educational development.

Contemporary approaches to identifying relations between person, process and context

Gaining increasing prominence in the educational literature is a distinction that underpins the way in which specific research questions are approached. They are separated into variable-centred approaches and person-centred approaches. While this separation exists, it is also necessary to point out that these two approaches are complementary. The appropriateness of each for a particular research programme will depend on the specific research questions being asked.

Variable-centred approaches are those that follow the traditional, experimental design of research. In these cases, the focus is a particular variable and, typically, the causal relations between this variable and other phenomena (Bergman and Trost, 2006). Many of the example studies previously cited in this chapter have adopted the variable-centred approach. For instance, in the PISA studies discussed (see OECD, 2007), the variable of interest was socio-economic background and its effect on achievement. In the Crockenberg (1981) study described, the impact of social support on mother–infant attachment was investigated.

The variable-centred approach is often contrasted with the less well-known person-centred approach. This perspective was developed in line with holistic, interactionist views that emphasise the complexity of the individual as a whole, functioning with interdependent parts (Bergman and Magnusson, 1997). As a consequence, it is necessary to explore variables in combination with one another. Often the way this is accomplished is by searching for patterns or profiles that describe subgroups within a population. The person-centred approach is used in a variety of fields. It is commonly used in medicine, nursing, psychiatry and psychology to combat the complexity associated with diagnosis, psychopathology and patient care (Connell et al., 2006; Crockett et al., 2006; Hui et al., 2006; Landers and McCarthy, 2007; Mezzich and Salloum, 2008). In addition, the person-centred approach has been suggested for workplace conflict management (Du Plessis, 2008), and in educational settings to characterise profiles of beginning teachers (Chine and Young, 2007) and students' help-seeking behaviours (Karabenick, 2003).

To illustrate both the differences and the complementary features of variable-centred and person-centred approaches, details of an early research paper (Ainley, 1993) by the first author of this chapter using both approaches is described. The central research question underpinning Ainley's research concerned the relative effects of different approaches to learning or styles of engagement with learning on, first, the strategies students reported using when preparing for examinations and, second, on school achievement. The influence of general person characteristics (i.e. approaches to learning) were examined in relation to the strategic study processes students employed when preparing for examinations and in relation to their performance on a number of examinations, including their final school achievement grades.

A specific context was defined for students to reflect on their approaches to learning: preparing for an examination. Students were to think back to examinations that had taken place in the previous two weeks. They were asked to report on the specific study processes, more specifically the types of strategies they used when preparing for examinations in their self-nominated strongest and weakest subjects. Achievement was measured by a number of school assessments: Year 11 examinations; Year 12 examinations; and the students' overall grading awarded in the final year of secondary schooling on the basis of a state-wide examination. Approaches to learning were conceptualised as students' general orientation towards their learning and were measured using Biggs' 'Learning Process Questionnaire' (LPQ) (Biggs, 1987). The LPQ identifies three general approaches: a deep approach (aiming and working to master and understand); an achieving approach (aiming and working to achieve high standards); and a surface approach (aiming to balance avoiding failure by doing only the minimum). According to Biggs and his co-workers (Biggs, 1991; Biggs and Rihn, 1984; Ramsden et al., 1989; Watkins and Hattie, 1990), each approach represents purpose and strategy as complementary components of students' general ways of engaging with or approaching learning tasks. The approaches to learning variables – measured using the LPQ – are in many ways analogous to the achievement goal variables that feature in a wide range of studies of students' achievement goal orientations (see Pintrich, 2000; Linnenbrink and Pintrich, 2002; Grant and Dweck, 2003).

The first major question to be answered concerned the relative importance of the learning approach variables (person variables) as predictors of examination preparation strategies (process variables) and school achievement with the subsidiary question of whether students employed different approaches according to whether the subject was perceived as their weakest subject or their strongest subject (context variable). Framing the question in this way represents a variable-centered approach. The question is looking to find an answer that applies across the general group and that can be generalised beyond the immediate sample. The variable-centered approach will provide answers in terms of the overall contribution of specific variables to the outcome measures. But taking the step of generalising beyond the research participants also requires clear specification of the character of the participant group. In this case, participants were all female students 'from a large Australian city girls' secondary college catering to students from mainly professional and middle-class to upper-class families' (Ainley, 1993: 397). Clearly there are some limits on the range of generalisation that can be made from these analyses.

Analytic procedures: a variable-centred approach

A general form of research questions, when the researcher is adopting a variable-centered approach, is to ask whether there is a significant predictive relation between a set of variables (predictors) and a specific outcome or criterion variable. Essentially this is asking about the effect, influence or contribution of each single variable on outcomes such as achievement when all other variables are equal (i.e. when the effect of all other factors is taken into account).

Some of the most common quantitative analytic techniques used in variable-centered approaches include correlation, multiple regression, path analysis and, most recently, structural equation modelling (SEM). These techniques are described in multivariate statistics texts. A good place to start is with a text such as Hair *et al.*, (1998). Analysis starts with the zero-order or basic correlation matrix showing the level of association between each pair of variables in the investigation and then uses multiple regression techniques to assess the independent contribution of specific variables for the level of the outcome of interest to the researcher.

Multiple regression involves techniques whereby research data are in the form of a criterion variable (e.g. achievement) and a set of predictors (e.g. learning approaches). Sometimes these are referred to as dependent (the criterion variable) and independent (the predictors) variables. Multiple regression provides an index of the contribution of the set of predictor variables to the level of the criterion variable. It also provides an index of the independent contribution of each predictor: the level of association between each separate predictor and the criterion after allowing for the association of each of the other predictors with the criterion. In this way the association between specific variables and achievement, for example, can be assessed. SEM, like regression, is also based on the correlation matrix from the variables in the research design and also provides a very powerful means of assessing both the contribution of the set of predictors and each individual predictor variable for the outcome variable.

The Ainley (1993) investigation described above used multiple regression to assess the contribution of general ability scores and deep, achieving and surface approaches to scores on measures of the types of strategies students reported using when preparing for their recent examinations. Examination strategies were described as reproductive (e.g. learning off-by-heart) or transformational (e.g. understanding important ideas and principles). Reproductive and transformational strategies were analysed separately. Within each of these categories there were two regression analyses: one for students' strongest subject and another for students' weakest subject.

On the one hand, when the reproductive strategies were considered in relation to students' strongest subject, it was found that general ability was a negative predictor (i.e. students with higher general ability generally reported lower levels of reproductive strategy use). On the other hand, surface approach, which is the minimal effort strategy, was a positive predictor for using reproductive strategies when preparing for an examination. There were no significant predictors of level of reproductive strategy use for students' weakest subject.

When transformational strategies were considered, general ability was not a significant predictor for either the strongest or the weakest subject. Learning approaches did make a significant contribution, but these varied according to whether the strongest or the weakest subject was being considered. For students' strongest subject, the deep approach (wanting to understand and master) made a significant positive contribution to level of transformational strategy use, while for the weakest subject, achieving approach (concern over achieving good grades) was a positive predictor and surface approach (minimal effort) was negatively related to use of transformational strategies.

The same type of regression analysis was used to determine the contribution of general ability and the three learning approaches to Year 11 and Year 12 examination results and to students' final school achievement grade. The latter was an assessment more than 12 months after they had reported on preparation strategies for their Year 11 mid-year examinations. General ability (measured when students were in their tenth grade) was a significant predictor for all of the achievement outcome measures. Surface approach scores made a significant contribution in a number of these regression analyses and the direction of the relation was always negative. Achieving approach made a small positive contribution to a number of the predictions including the aggregate end of secondary school grading. The deep approach variable did not significantly add to any of the achievement predictions.

These findings allow us to draw conclusions about the relative contribution of each of the approach (person) variables for examination preparation strategies (process variables). At the same time as we can compare the relative importance of deep, achieving and surface approaches for school achievement, we have to acknowledge that the specific answer for each type of approach assumes that all others are controlled. However, awareness of the complex organisations of attitudes, interests and values represented in any group of students suggests cautious interpretation. While an answer based on all other things being equal provides important insights into the dynamics of educational achievement at a theoretical perspective, it ignores some of the complexities associated with different combinations or patterning of these variables in different students.

Analytic procedures: a person-centred approach

A number of researchers over the last two decades have suggested that the traditional variable-centred approaches are effective for indicating the amount of variance in a particular outcome variable that can be attributed to individual predictor variables, but are less effective in accounting for the combined effects of multiple variables, especially when there is co-variation between the predictor variables (see Magnusson, 1988; Magnusson, 1998; von Eye and Schuster, 2000; Wachs, 1996). This has been taken up by a number of researchers who have argued for a person-centred approach using techniques such as cluster analysis, profile analysis and pattern analysis (von Eye and Bogat, 2006).

There are a number of underlying assumptions and questions that distinguish a person-centred approach. The researcher starts with the assumption that there are a number of variables contributing to the outcome of interest, that these variables combine in different ways in different groups of students and that it is the combination rather than the independent contribution of each variable that will identify how the set of variables is related to outcomes.

The research question investigated in the Ainley (1993) paper concerned the relative effects of different approaches to learning, first, on the strategies students reported using when preparing for examinations and, second, on school achievement. When we measure a number of dimensions, such as approaches to learning, each student gains a score on each variable.

Analytic techniques used for identifying the contribution of any one predictor variable for the outcome variable are in effect treating each participant as having the mean score on all other variables. Clearly this is not the case and the person-centred approach in developmental and educational analysis is an attempt to take into account the patterning across a set of variables. For example, students will show different profiles of scores across the three learning approaches. Identifying groups of students who are similar in their score profile and different to the score profiles of other groups of students locates each student on a factor that can then be used to test relations with the important outcome variables. This analytic strategy, which uses statistical procedures such as cluster analysis or profile analysis, provides a complementary perspective to the variable approach that can enrich understanding of the complexity of relations between person, process and context in educational research.

The paper (Ainley, 1993) that has been detailed in this chapter was one of the first studies in the educational psychology area to adopt a person-centred approach. Cluster analysis was used to identify groups of students with different profiles across the set of person variables, including general ability and the three learning approach measures. A six-cluster solution was selected as the most appropriate solution to describe the patterns of relations between the general ability and learning approach scores. Each cluster of students was described and a label generated to identify the special features of their separate profiles. It was argued in the paper that these six groups identified different styles of engagement students had with their learning.

The specific cluster analysis procedure used in Ainley's study involved standardising all of the scores on all of the clustering variables. Thus the descriptions of each group's scores on the variables are relative to the overall group average. The styles were:

1   *Detached*: High-ability students with average deep approach scores and lower than average scores on achieving and surface approaches, suggesting 'an overall low level of involvement, but when engaged the students' focus is most likely to be on mastery'.

2   *Committed*: High-ability students with higher than average scores on deep and achieving approaches and lower than average surface approach scores, suggesting 'they are focused toward both understanding and performance goals . . . they are highly engaged by learning activities'.

3   *Hopeful*: Students with lower than average on general ability, deep and achieving approach scores just below average, while surface approach scores are slightly above average, suggesting 'they do not show a strong commitment to mastery goals, and their approach appears to be predominantly focused on the minimal task requirements'.

4   *Engaged*: Students with a similar profile of achieving and surface approach scores to Cluster 2 (committed) combined with above average deep approach scores and slightly lower than average general ability scores, suggesting 'a student engaged with his or her learning in order to achieve and understand'.

5   *Disengaged*: Students with average general ability scores and higher than average surface approach scores combined with well below average deep and achieving approach scores, suggesting 'minimal involvement with their learning tasks'.

6   *Keen to do well*: Students with average general ability scores and deep approach scores coupled with above average achieving approach and high surface approach scores, suggesting a 'try everything' orientation.

(See Ainley (1993: 399–401) for a full description and graphic displaying the profiles).

Inspection of these profiles reveals important contrasts in the way students approach or engage with their learning (styles of engagement) and, as was argued in the paper, these distinctive combinations of approaches should signal differences in learning.

The first test of this proposition was to look at the patterns of strategy use (reproductive and transformational) that students adopted when preparing for examinations. Generating groups of students distinguished by different styles of engagement meant that strategy data could be used in a factorial design. The style of engagement was the grouping variable with six distinct groups to be compared on scores for two dependent variables: reproductive and transformational strategies. This allowed a $6 \times 2 \times 2$ repeated measures analysis of variance (ANOVA): style of engagement was a six groups between-subjects factor while school subject (strongest and weakest) and strategy (reproductive and transformational) were two within-subjects factors. This produced a number of statistically significant effects:

•   an overall style of engagement effect;
•   a within-group effect of strongest vs weakest subject;

- an interaction between subject (strongest vs weakest) and strategy (reproductive vs transformational) with a larger difference between the level of strategies (transformational > reproductive) on the strongest subject than on the weakest subject;
- an interaction between style of engagement and strategy (reproductive vs transformational).

The significant interaction between style of engagement and strategy is of particular interest for showing the potential of the person-centred approach. The shape of the interaction is displayed in a figure in the paper by Ainley (1993: 402). This interaction between style of engagement and strategy use took the form of a difference in the relative level of reported use of the two types of strategy. The more engaged style groups (i.e. groups with higher scores on the deep approach or higher scores on both deep and achieving approaches combined with low surface approach scores – detached, committed and engaged) – reported higher transformational strategy use than reproductive strategy use. The three groups with high surface approach scores (hopeful, disengaged and keen to do well) reported higher reproductive strategy scores than transformational strategy scores. Hence, student's personal profile of general ability and approaches to learning was associated with different patterns of strategy use when preparing for examinations. This finding was complementary to the significant predictive associations identified for each of the variables separately when a variable-centred approach was applied.

The second analysis (ANOVA) included styles of engagement as the grouping variable and used Year 11 and 12 examination results and final school achievement grading (Year 11 English, strongest subject, weakest subject, Year 12 English, mathematics and aggregate final school grading) as the dependent variables. Again there was significant style of engagement effects on achievement. Across all of the achievement variables, the order of the groups was the same: committed (highest scores), detached, engaged, keen to do well, disengaged and hopeful (lowest scores).

From the one data set, both variable-centred and person-centred approaches have been used to highlight the relationships first, between individual variables and learning and, second, ways that these same variables combine to define distinctive student profiles that also have significant relationships with learning. Clearly these different analytic approaches are complementary and the insights they yield provide a more complete picture of both person and process as they underpin student learning.

Independently, another research group was adopting a similar approach which was published in the following issue of the *Journal of Educational Psychology* (Meece and Holt, 1993). Working with fifth and sixth grade students (both boys and girls), Meece and Holt measured three achievement goal orientations described as 'Task-Mastery' (want to learn as much as possible), 'Ego-Social' (want others to think I'm smart) and 'Work-Avoidant' (want to do as little as possible), which are not unlike the learning approach measures from the LPQ.

Three clusters described the profiles of the fifth and sixth grade students who participated in the study. One of the clusters was defined by high task-mastery goals with low scores on the ego-social and work goal avoidant measures. A second cluster had high scores on both the task-mastery and ego-social measures combined with low work avoidant scores. A third cluster had a flat profile with scores on all three goal measures close to the mid point of the scale. When these profile groups were compared on achievement scores, those students with the high task-mastery profile had the strongest achievement scores. The students who scored high on both task-mastery and ego-social goals did not score as well as the task-mastery group on the achievement measures while the group with the flat profile across all three goals had the lowest scores on achievement measures (Meece and Holt, 1993).

A number of important applications of a person-centred approach are found in longitudinal studies concerned with identifying trajectories of scores on a variable over time. A special issue of *Merrill-Palmer Quarterly* in 2006 published a number of research papers using person-centred approaches to include the trajectories of a specific variable or set of variables over time. Identification of different trajectories defines groups of participants and then differences between the groups on the outcome variable(s) of interest can be assessed. A person-centred approach allows the researcher to look at combinations of variables which may be patterns of scores across a set of variables measured at the same time or combinations may involve the same variable measured a number of occasions over time.

Since the study of styles of engagement (Ainley, 1993), we have made extensive use of software designed to monitor a number of processes indicative of students' on-task engagement (i.e. ways they engage with a specific learning task) (see Ainley and Hidi, 2002). A number of these studies have used variable-centred approaches to look at the predictive relations between successive processes contributing to performance at the end of the task (e.g. Ainley *et al.*, 2002; Ainley and Patrick, 2006; Ainley *et al.*, 2008).

Different ways of using person-centred approaches are employed with data recorded as students work through challenging problem tasks using our software ('Between the Lines' (BTL)). Within the context of any particular task, our model suggests that what the student brings to their learning in the form of person variables (e.g. traits, individual interests, interest in specific school subject domains and achievement goals) along with the specific features of the task combine to influence on-task engagement processes and learning outcomes. Hence the person-centred approach can be used to identify profiles representing the combinations of important variables students bring with them to a task.

A study by Buckley, Hasen and Ainley (2004) explored Year 11 students' responses to reading passages of text concerned with contemporary political and social issues. Person variables including measures of curiosity and students' individual interest in a variety of domains, including political issues, popular music, science, social issues and sport, were used to define student interest profiles. Three profiles were identified representing different patterns of interests. These groups were referred to as 'popular culture', 'anti-popular culture' and 'enthusiast' groups. This way of using a person-centred approach is analogous to the way it was used in the Ainley (1993) research; groups of students with similar profiles across a range of personal interest and/or trait variables were identified.

Most recently we have been using the person-centred approach to define groups of students who show similar patterns of on-task processes, in other words, to identify different trajectories of reactivity across the course of a problem task. In most of our problem tasks we have students report how interested they are in what they are doing at three critical points: immediately after the task has been explained and prior to commencement; midway through the task; and after submitting their answer. This provides three successive measures from which to generate interest profiles or trajectories across the task. In a setting where the same students have undertaken similar tasks on a number of occasions, it is then possible to make comparisons across tasks, identifying where processing patterns are stable and where they might be task specific. For example, on two occasions the same group of students completed problems to do with ecological issues as part of an open learning programme. A question was posed to them and information resources were also available as part of the software used for the problem task. Trajectories of interest in the task were identified for both tasks. Two groups emerged from the interest responses to each task: one with very low interest, which did not change across the course of the task; and one who started out with a moderate level of interest, which was sustained across the task. When the membership of these groups was compared, many of the students were consistent in their responses to both tasks. However, this procedure also identified a group of students who were in the low group for one task and the moderate group for the other task. For these particular students, the context of the problem task they were required to do in the two settings was a stronger factor in their responses than it was for many of the other students. These findings are still being explored, but they do indicate that using person-centred analytic tools in a variety of ways can provide new insights into the ways person, process and task combine in students' learning.

Conclusion

In this chapter we have illustrated a number of models and analytic approaches that can be applied to investigate specific issues that are part of the complex mix of person, process and context in education. The answers to our questions are not absolutes, allowing us to predict exactly what is going to happen for any individual student; there is a delicate dance between the predictive patterns that describe the way specific variables (all other things being equal) influence educational outcomes and the ways that individual students/learners respond to, and shape, the continuing stream of events that make up their educational experience.

are chosen carefully and are trained in data collection and recording. However, the influence of the presence of three observers on the group dynamics has to be considered. Observational analysis can be done after video recording the behaviour/interaction/intervention to avoid this problem. However, it leads to the need for further robust systems to be in place for data protection.

When observation is conducted in a qualitative context (e.g. participant observation), the analysis is based on an open and flexible approach, using an unstructured and not standardised design (Cohen, Manion, and Morrison, 2000; Robson, 2002; Sarantakos, 2005). As mentioned earlier, everything that has been observed is written down before the researcher looks for trends and patterns. One way is to consider the notes and underline behaviours and events that took place. The researcher can look for categories and then revisit their notes to reclassify behaviours and events under these categories.

In the quantitative context, the researcher identifies categories (see Table 2.1) even before they start their observation. These categories are then used as checklists (see Table 2.2) and either the duration or the frequency of the occurrence of what is being observed (e.g. behaviour, interaction patterns during meetings, etc.) is recorded. After completing this for the entire duration of the observation, frequencies and durations are added up to establish patterns and trends.

Case studies

A case study is usually undertaken to study the characteristics of a single individual unit (recognising its individuality and uniqueness), namely, a child, a group, an organisation, etc. The purpose of a case study is to get in-depth information regarding what is happening, why it is happening and what the effects are of what is happening. Case study has been defined as a 'way of investigating an empirical topic by following a set of pre-specified procedures' (Yin, 2003: 15).

Case studies are employed indiscriminately in both qualitative and quantitative research, although to a different extent and for different reasons. However, they are more popular and assigned more value in qualitative research than in quantitative research. Case studies can be used for: exploration; to gain more information about the structure, process and complexity of the research object; to facilitate conceptualisation of the research problem and formulation of hypotheses; to expand the quantitative findings and for further in-depth understanding of those findings; and as a pilot for a larger study. Case studies are used in quantitative research as a prelude to the 'real' research, as a form of pre-test, and/or as a post-research explanation of the 'main' study (Robson, 2002; Sarantakos, 2005). Case studies are often used as a supplement to other strategies. For example, some researchers have used case study as a follow-up to the survey method (i.e. after identifying some cases through survey method, they have then undertaken in-depth case studies). In contrast, in qualitative research, case studies are a research enterprise of their own and are used as methods for the main research.

The data collected in a case study are mainly qualitative and are related to various aspects of an individual's life (e.g. family and work). Various techniques are used to collect the data, which can be both direct and indirect. The researcher needs to be experienced in the use of a number of data-gathering techniques and the related data analysis strategies. One of the main techniques used in case studies is observation, which is the context for this chapter.

The case studies can use single case and multiple case designs. Yin (2003) presents a 2×2 matrix, where the first pair consists of the single and multiple case designs and the second pair can occur in combination with the first pair and is based on whether the unit(s) of analysis are holistic and/or embedded. In this chapter, we discuss two examples of how the authors conducted observational analysis within single case and multiple case designs.

Single case design

There are several reasons for using a single case design. For example, a critical case could be considered to test a well-formulated theory, an extreme/unique case, a representative/typical case, a revelatory case, and a longitudinal case (Cohen, Manion, and Morrison, 2000; Yin, 2003). In this chapter we present a particular type of single case design that was undertaken to look at the effectiveness of an intervention. This type of design is an experimental research design. Inferences about the effectiveness of an intervention are made by comparing the participant's performance or behaviour during different intervention conditions presented to him/her (Kazdin, 2001). The participant is observed on several occasions prior to the intervention to establish a baseline of his/her performance or behaviour and then further to ascertain the effectiveness of an intervention. We accept that it is difficult for researchers to control all variables when working with human beings and it is difficult to have a large pool of participants to study for particular intervention gains. To overcome these challenges, single case designs have been used.

Kazdin (2001) details three major single case experimental designs, namely ABAB (or reversal designs), multiple baseline designs, and changing-criterion designs. In this chapter we focus in particular on ABAB and multiple baseline designs.

In the ABAB design (Kazdin, 1982, 2001) sufficient baseline data are collected to reliably predict the direction this measure would take in the absence of intervention. To ensure that factors other than the experimental intervention are not affecting the behaviour being measured, a reversal intervention or ABAB design is used. This involves a reversal of intervention back to baseline conditions ('A' or pre-intervention) after a period of intervention ('B'). If the trend towards improvement stops or reverses at the same time as this change occurs (from intervention 'B' back to baseline 'A'), it supports the idea that it was the intervention and not some other factor that caused the change. Adding additional reversals makes this argument even stronger.

There are other variations on this type of analysis. For example, Hallahan, Lloyd, Kneedler, and Marshall (1982) used an alternating interventions design of ABACDEF, where A was baseline, B was self-assessment and teacher assessment, C was self-assessment only, D was cue-fading, E was sheet-fading, and F was a one-month follow up. Storey and Gaylord-Ross (1987) conducted three studies to increase positive social interactions of twelve adolescents with a mix of learning disabilities, mental retardation and visual impairment, in the age group of fourteen to nineteen years. In all the three studies, an alternating treatments design was undertaken. They used a multi-component treatment package, where A was baseline, B was model and role play, C was graphic feedback, D was self-monitoring, E was contingent reinforcement, and F was non-contingent reinforcement. In the first study, an A-BCDE-A-BCDE-DE-F design was followed. In the second study, systematic withdrawal of treatment components was done and an A-BCDE-BD-E-DE-F-DE-D-DE-A design was followed. In the third study, an A-BCDE-DE-D-A-D-DE design was undertaken.

However, this type of intervention does raise some ethical and practical implications. For example, it is unethical to use this when the reversal would jeopardise somebody's health. Or it might not be practical to use this design when something cannot be unlearnt (e.g. learning to read). In this event a second design strategy is available. This is the use of single case multiple baseline design.

Multiple baseline designs

Multiple baseline designs involve collecting baseline data across either different settings, across different behaviours of the same individual, and/or across different participants being trained at the same time. The intervention is applied to one setting/behaviour/participant while the others continue in baseline. Finally, the intervention is applied to the other settings/behaviours/participants with a lag of time between them. The graphs that are compiled on the basis of observational data are examined to see if each graph reflects improvement only when the intervention is started in those particular settings/participants/behaviours while other settings/participants/behaviours remain stable until the intervention is used there as well. Comparison across graphs on the same time scale is made visually. This pattern of data supports the proposal that it was the intervention itself and not some other factor that caused the post-intervention data to improve. In order to support the effectiveness of intervention and rule out other causes of improvement, a single subject design must have an extended baseline and the use of multiple baselines across settings/behaviours/participants.

Multiple baseline designs have been used in a range of contexts and with different age groups (e.g. Jindal-Snape, Kato, and Maekawa, 1998; Jindal-Snape, 2004, 2005a, 2005b; Gross, Miltenberger, Knudson, Bosch, and Breitwieser, 2007; Layer, Hanley, Heal, and Tiger, 2008; Mayfield and Vollmer, 2007; Reeve, Reeve, Townsend, and Poulson, 2007).

Phaneuf and McIntyre (2007) used a multiple baseline design across four mother–child dyads to evaluate the effects of adding individualised video feedback to a group-based parent training programme for parents of pre-schoolers with developmental disabilities. Gross *et al.* (2007) evaluated the success of parent training on their children's safety skills in a multiple baseline across participants design. Reeve *et al.* (2007) used a multiple baseline across participants design to assess whether four five- and six-year-old children with autism could learn a generalised repertoire of helping adults with different tasks through the use of a multi-component teaching package. Jindal-Snape used a multiple baseline design across participants, settings and/or behaviours to assess the impact of self-management and other strategies for enhancing social interaction between children with visual impairment in primary school and their sighted peers in the age group of eight to eleven years. In this chapter we use one of those studies to explain how observational data is analysed within a multiple baseline design.

Example of a multiple baseline design

In this section we provide an example of using observational data to investigate the impact of intervention on one child's behaviour (for details see Jindal, 1997; Jindal-Snape, 2003). The specific interventions included reinforcement and self-evaluation. Within self-evaluation, it was considered important to conduct two phases of intervention: self-evaluation with prior verbalisation; and self-evaluation without prior verbalisation. This was done to investigate whether verbalisation plays any part in the impact of self-evaluation on social skills as some researchers have attributed the effectiveness of self-evaluation to verbalisation prior to self-evaluation (Sainato, Goldstein, and Strain, 1992). Some other researchers also tried to investigate the effect of prior verbalisation on the target behaviour, but no clear relationship was found (Baer, Detrich, and Weninger, 1988; Deacon and Konarski, 1987; Matthews, Shimoff, and Catania, 1987). The present study investigated whether self-evaluation was effective in generalisation and maintenance of social skills and whether the verbalisation prior to self-evaluation played any role.

On the basis of interviews with teachers and parents and direct observation by the researcher, the target behaviours of Yvonne were identified. They were conversation and positive play. Initiation was observed as non-target behaviour to see the generalisation across behaviours (see Table 2.1). A multiple baseline design across behaviours was used to see generalisation across behaviours and settings. Training was undertaken in three phases of external reinforcement, self-evaluation with prior verbalisation, and self-evaluation without prior verbalisation. Each session had a duration of twenty minutes.

The generalisation of social skills was assessed across settings and behaviours. After the different phases of the intervention, generalisation probes were conducted to observe generalisation of social skills in non-trained settings and across non-trained behaviour (initiation). Follow up was undertaken eight months after the training was completed to observe behaviour gains. To ensure reliability and validity of observational analysis and intervention gains, the researcher defined the behaviours as specifically as possible (see Table 2.1). The behavioural components were based on previous research literature.

Data were collected through video recording in the different settings. Total duration was measured for reciprocal conversation and positive play. Total duration is the summation of the duration throughout the observed session. The duration was seen as the best measure as it was important to see how long that child could sustain any of the positive behaviours and how the length of negative behaviour could decrease as a result of the intervention. Initiation was measured in frequency as in this case it was important to see how many times the child initiated an interaction with another child.

As mentioned earlier, all the sessions were videotaped. With the help of a video timer, minutes and seconds were also recorded. They were later observed independently by the researcher and two graduates working in the same area as the researcher. Five minutes of every twenty-minute duration were observed. In session one the first five minutes were observed, in session two the next five minutes (i.e. from minute five to minute ten of session two) were observed, and so on, with again the first five minutes of session five being observed. This was done not only to ensure that observer fatigue was minimised by observing five minutes only, but that the behaviour was observed at different stages of the sessions to ensure any changes related to the start, middle, or end of a session were fully observed.

Table 2.1 Definition of target and non-target behaviours of Yvonne

Behaviour		Description
Conversation (Target behaviour)	i)	Self-initiated questions: a. Original b. Copied
	ii)	Prompted questions
	iii)	Self-initiated answers: a. Original b. Copied
	iv)	Prompted answers
	v)	Leading conversation (i.e. doing most of the talking)
	vi)	Helping in smooth flow of conversation (e.g. making appropriate remarks)
	vii)	Listening to conversation
	viii)	Positive answers
Positive play (Target behaviour)	i)	Self-initiated organising and suggesting games: a. Original b. Copied
	ii)	Prompted organising: a. Original b. Copied
	iii)	Playing with peers in a positive way
Initiation (Non-target behaviour)	i)	Approaching a peer: a. Familiar peer b. Unfamiliar peer c. Sighted peer d. Peer with visual impairment
	ii)	Drawing attention towards oneself in a positive way
	iii)	Persistence in initiation or drawing attention
	iv)	Responding positively to initiation by peers: a. Familiar peer b. Unfamiliar peer c. Sighted peer d. Peer with visual impairment

The maximum possible duration for a behaviour to occur in a session was 300 seconds. Table 2.2 shows the checklist for one of those behaviours where the behaviour was analysed in terms of duration. As can be seen, the checklist was divided into a five-minute session with ten second segments. The codes for conversation were assigned as follows: Self-initiated Questions Original (SIQO), Self-initiated Questions Copied (SIQC), Prompted Questions (PQ), Self-initiated Answers Original (SIAO), Self-initiated Answers Copied (SIAC), Prompted Answers (PA), Leading Conversation (LC), Helping Conversation (HC), Listening to Conversation (LTC), and Positive Answers (PoA).

Videotaped observations were undertaken to enhance the reliability of the observations as they allowed the observers the opportunity to review any aspect of the session and they could stop/start at any time, which also helped with the accuracy of their recording. Further, by using videotaped observations, it was possible to enhance the reliability of the analysis without having any impact on the group dynamics that might have occurred due to the presence of multiple observers during the intervention, generalisation and maintenance probes.

Inter-observer reliability was calculated using the formula of number agreements divided by number agreements plus disagreements, multiplied by hundred. In our study it was 84 per cent for the baseline phase and 86 per cent, 88 per cent, and 89 per cent during the three intervention phases, respectively. It had an average value of 85 per cent during generalisation probes. According to Kazdin (1977),

Table 2.2   Checklist for child's conversation

| Behaviour | Session number: | | | | |
	0–1 min.	1–2 min.	2–3 min.	3–4 min.	4–5 min.
SIQO					
SIQC					
PQ					
SIAO					
SIAC					
PA					
LC					
HC					
LTC					
PoA					

per cent agreement that reaches 70 per cent or 80 per cent is regarded as satisfactory. The multiple baseline graph, based on the observational analysis, can be seen in Figure 2.1.

This design can be described as an ABECEDEF design across targeted and non-targeted behaviours, as well as across and intervention and non-intervention settings. Conducting an observational analysis based on this single case multiple baseline design allowed for the participant to receive the intervention programme without the need to revert to the baseline. For further examples of multiple baseline designs across behaviours/settings/participants, see Jindal (1997), Jindal-Snape *et al.* (1998), and Jindal-Snape (2004, 2005a, 2005b).

As can be seen from Figure 2.1, during the baseline, the duration of conversation with active participation on the part of Yvonne was twenty-five seconds of a maximum possible 300 seconds. During the reinforcement phase, conversation increased gradually and went to an average of 168 seconds. However, during the generalisation probe, conversation went down to an average of fifty-eight seconds. In the self-evaluation with prior verbalisation phase, it went to an average of 264 seconds. It was again at an average of 270 seconds during the generalisation probe. Yvonne's conversation behaviour maintained at an average of 286 seconds during the self-evaluation without prior verbalisation phase and was at an average of 276 seconds during the generalisation probe. The multiple baseline approach to the analysis of observational data demonstrated that the behaviour changed with the introduction of intervention.

Duration of positive play with peers was found to be zero during the baseline phase. After the introduction of reinforcement, positive play went to an average of 216 seconds out of a possible 300 seconds. During the generalisation probe it went to 300 seconds at first and then was 154 seconds. After the introduction of self-evaluation with prior verbalisation phase, it stayed throughout at the maximum possible duration of 300 seconds. During the generalisation probe, positive play was observed to be 300 seconds at first. It then decreased to 260 seconds, but this was still above the reinforcement phase. In the self-evaluation without prior verbalisation phase, it again generated an average value of 300 seconds. At probe it was maintained at 300 seconds for three sessions, but it then decreased and was maintained at 240 seconds. Through the use of a multiple baseline approach to observational analysis, we could again demonstrate that the change in behaviour occurred after specific intervention. Again, as mentioned earlier, as the second target behaviour did not change during baseline despite intervention with the first behaviour, it can be said that the change was due to the intervention rather than other factors. Also, it demonstrates that, in this case, self-evaluation was more effective than reinforcement.

Both initiation by Yvonne and response to the initiation by the peers were observed as non-target behaviour. For ease of observation, it was divided into four categories: approaching peer(s); drawing attention towards self (in positive or negative ways); responding positively to peer-initiation; and responding negatively or ignoring peer-initiation.

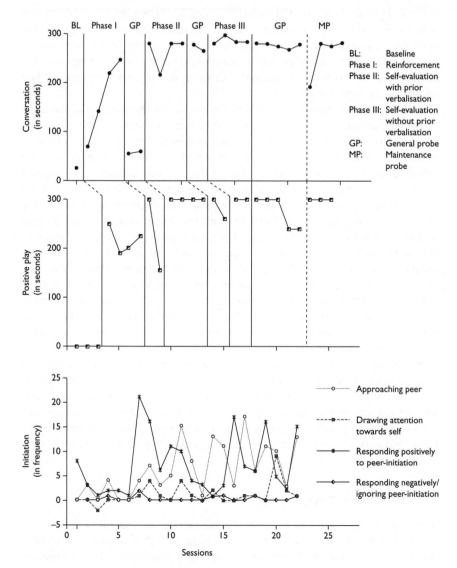

Figure 2.1 Example of a multiple baseline design across behaviours and settings (for Yvonne)

In the beginning, Yvonne was observed staying on her own and waiting for peers to come to her. However, with the introduction of training she started approaching peers. In the beginning, she confined herself to blind peers or familiar sighted peers (i.e. those who sat next to her in the classroom or were participating in the training) only. Later she started going up to unfamiliar sighted peers. In the first seven sessions after the introduction of reinforcement – both the target behaviours were in the reinforcement phase – initiation behaviour was at an average of two and a half times per observed duration of the session. In the next sessions (i.e. self-evaluation with prior verbalisation phase) it was at an average of eight times. By the end (i.e. self-evaluation without prior verbalisation phase), it had reached an average of nine times.

Yvonne not only started approaching the peers, but she was also observed to draw their attention if there was no response from them. Usually the peers responded immediately but there were a few occasions when she had to persist in gaining their attention. Such instances were recorded. In the beginning there were two instances (in the same session) of her trying to draw attention in a negative way (i.e. not waiting for the peer to finish her conversation with another child and interrupting the game). However, later on she drew attention in a positive way only (i.e. waiting till the peer had finished the conversation before drawing attention to herself). Yvonne was usually found to respond positively to peer-initiation, but there were two instances in which she ignored a peer and six instances in which she initially responded negatively but then started to play with that peer. These were all plotted and trends observed on multiple baseline designs.

Follow up was undertaken eight months later. Exceedingly good maintenance was visible with the average duration of active conversation by Yvonne being 257 seconds. Play behaviour was maintained at an average of 300 seconds. The teacher was interviewed for confirmation of results.

As can be seen, multiple baseline design approaches can demonstrate the effectiveness of interventions without returning to baseline and losing intervention gains. However, the impact might not be clear if certain other behaviours change without any intervention being applied to them (Kazdin, 2001). This, however, can also be an important way of looking at impact of intervention on not only target, but also concurrent behaviours, as can be seen from the example presented in this chapter.

Multiple case design

Randomised controlled trials are unusual in education, although they are becoming less so. In this section of the chapter we consider a study that focused on a two-year randomised controlled trial of peer tutoring in reading (i.e. Paired Reading) in over eighty schools in one school district. Peer tutoring involves one-on-one tuition of one child by another child, often following some form of explicit training of the tutor. The literature is large and studies tend to show benefits both for the tutors – perhaps due to their need to reflect and communicate concepts and procedures – and for the tutees. Observational analysis of implementation integrity for this peer tutor reading trial was undertaken mid-project in each year.

The study reported in this section investigated a generically applicable reading tutoring technique: Paired Reading. This was a structured procedure but designed to be applicable to any reading material available in the school. Tutoring procedures are most effective when thoroughly scaffolded (Sharpley and Sharpley, 1981; Cohen *et al.*, 1982; Topping and Ehly, 1998; Topping, 2001). Untrained tutoring behaviours tend to be primitive (e.g. Person and Graesser, 1999), characterised by infrequent correction of errors and inappropriate giving of positive feedback. Roscoe and Chi (2007) suggested that analyses of tutors' actual behaviours are important in enhancing the effectiveness of tutoring. Explaining and questioning are important in reflective knowledge-building, but tutors also tend to persist with simple knowledge-telling. However, the tutoring technique in the current study largely eliminated knowledge-telling. The current project set out to train teachers in a particular method to deliver their assigned condition of tutoring. However, this training was not intensive since the sustainability of the project was important and releasing hundreds of teachers for extensive training not practical. Consequently, implementation integrity was likely to be critical in any ensuing impact.

The tutoring technique

Teachers instructed participating students in the Paired Reading tutoring technique. In cross-age tutoring between two classes of different ages, students in each class were ranked by reading ability. The most able student tutor in one class matched with the most able student tutee in the other class and so on. In same-age tutoring, one class was ranked by reading ability, divided into tutors above and tutees below, and the most able tutor matched with the most able tutee and so on. This meant that in same-age classes the weakest tutee was helped by an average tutor, while in cross-age classes the weakest tutee was helped by the weakest older tutor. Small matching adjustments were made on grounds of social compatibility. Parents were informed of the project and few difficulties arose. Absence of students for any session left teachers needing to rematch un-partnered individuals. Tutors and tutees were trained together. They were told about the structure of the technique and given a demonstration of how to do it. (This was done in Year 1 by role-playing adults, but by Year 2 a training video was available). Pairs then immediately tried out the technique with a book of appropriate difficulty while teachers circulated to monitor and coach. Teachers continued this monitoring and support during the subsequent reading periods; a teacher checklist for observation was made available. Pairs kept a brief written record of their reading. After fifteen weeks children were gathered together and asked if and how they wished to continue.

Paired Reading is a type of supported or assisted reading (Topping, 2001). Pairs choose books (or other reading materials) that are of high interest to them. However, these must be above the independent readability level of the tutee and, of course, not above that of the tutor. Both members of the pair should be able to see the book with equal ease and sit in as quiet and comfortable a place as can be found. Pairs are encouraged to talk about the book, to develop shared enthusiasm, and to ensure the tutee really understands the content. Correction is deliberately very simple; when the tutee says a word wrong, (1) the tutor tells the tutee the correct way to say the word, (2) the tutor has the tutee repeat it correctly, and (3) the pair carries on. However, tutors do not jump in and say the word right straight away – they pause and allow four seconds for tutee self-correction. Praise is important, especially for good reading of hard words, getting all the words in a sentence right, and putting wrong words right (self-correction) before the tutor does. Tutors support tutees through difficult text by reading together. Reading together happens when both members of the pair read all the words out loud together, the tutor modulates their speed to match that of the tutee, and the tutor gives a good model of competent reading. The pair agrees on a sign for the tutor to stop reading together – this could be a tap, knock or squeeze by the tutee. When an easier section of text is encountered, the tutee signals and the tutor stops reading out loud and praises the tutee for being confident. Sooner or later, while reading alone, the tutee makes an error that they cannot self-correct within four seconds. The tutor then applies the usual correction procedure and joins back in reading together. The pair switches from reading together to reading alone many times during a session.

Methodology

Sampling

The multiple case design used for the study reported in this section did not include baseline recordings. It did include two sets of intervention recordings in two successive years with different random samples of students. In the second year, the students had progressed a year and most of them were with new teachers and in new classes. The same eighty schools operated reading tutoring in both years. A few schools dropped out and some changed condition and were excluded, but this did not greatly affect data gathering. In each year observations were scheduled for 50 per cent of the total participant schools, which were randomly selected. In each school three participants were observed in each class. In Year 2 this included schools where reading attainment testing was also completed. In both Year 1 and Year 2, the choice of control schools for attainment testing was very limited as most of the schools were participating in the intervention and many of those that were not had major staffing or building issues. This approach reflects Yin's (2003: 40) Multiple-Case Embedded Design for case study research with two separate embedded units of analysis.

Measures and procedure

In both years, observation of implementation fidelity was undertaken in a randomly selected 50 per cent of participating intervention classes. As these were randomly chosen in each year, limited overlap between schools across the two years could be expected. A researcher made one visit to each class in the middle of the intervention period and, during the Paired Reading sessions, observed three target students. The teacher divided the pairs into top, middle and bottom levels of ability; the researcher randomly chose one pair from each third to observe. The researcher observed each pair for two minutes on three occasions – at the beginning, middle, and end of their reading session – recording on a structured observation schedule.

Aspects of observed behaviour included: both show interest in the book; both talk about the content; talk during reading together and alone; mistakes made; tutor mis-corrects; pause for four or five seconds then correct; tutor repeats words correctly; tutee repeats words correctly; reading together exactly; tutor praises; tutee signals for reading alone; tutor goes quiet straight away; tutor praises for going alone; tutor praises during reading alone; and tutor reads together again after an uncorrected error (see Table 2.3). These factors related directly to aspects of the technique, and as such had surface validity.

Inter-rater reliability was checked before and after the period of observation and found to be satisfactory. The same researcher conducted all observations. In Years 1 and 2, reliability trials were conducted at the start, in the middle, and at the end of the observation periods. The same videotape of eight two-minute windows of pupil behaviour was watched by the researcher, who used the standard sheet to record observed behaviour. Trials took place on the same day of the week at the same time of day. Alpha values for the observation variables ranged from 0.73 to 0.95 (with an average of 0.82).

Results

Year 1 observation

Table 2.3 ranks items in order of frequency. The first four behaviours concern technical aspects of correction and the number of recordings per pair varies from four to three. Clearly, these behaviours were frequently observed. Of the next four behaviours, three concern interest in the book and talking. These behaviours ranged from two to one per pair; they were somewhat frequent. Reading together exactly was frequent, at a frequency of almost two per pair. However, tutor praising was relatively rarely seen, being on average about a half of an observation per pupil. 'Tutor goes quiet straight away' was also infrequent. These are both major aspects of the Paired Reading technique. Tutor mis-correction was very low, which is good. We may conclude that implementation was somewhat variable, with correction, talking, and showing interest in the book being frequent, while tutor praising and the tutor going quiet straight away were infrequent. The low frequency of praise might at first sight seem problematic, but see below.

Other correlations tended to fall into two separate groups. One group concerned the quality of technique regarding the correction of mistakes.

Table 2.3 Year I: aggregated frequencies of behaviours observed per pair

Behaviour	Minimum	Maximum	Mean per pair	Standard deviation
Total mistakes made	.00	22.00	4.3163	4.10330
Total tutor repeats words correctly	.00	22.00	3.6939	3.79476
Total pause 4/5 seconds exact, then correct	.00	22.00	3.6939	3.80290
Total tutee repeats words correctly	.00	22.00	3.6735	3.83359
Total both show interest in the book	1.00	3.00	2.6939	.59911
Total reading together exactly	.00	17.00	1.7959	2.64754
Total tutee signals for reading alone	.00	12.00	1.5510	1.76520
Total both talk about the content	.00	6.00	.9082	1.21915
Total tutor goes quiet straight away	.00	12.00	.8571	1.63089
Total tutor praises for going alone	.00	16.00	.7143	1.80492
Total tutor praises	.00	14.00	.6939	1.75516
Total talk in reading together and alone	.00	4.00	.3878	.84503
Total tutor praise during reading alone	.00	5.00	.1735	.68902
Total tutor mis-corrects	.00	4.00	.0714	.43672
Total tutor reads together again after an uncorrected error	.00	3.00	.0306	.30305

Year 2 observation

Table 2.4 ranks items in order of frequency. The mean per school should be divided by three to indicate the frequency of behaviour per pair. The aggregation here to the level of the school was necessary in order to relate the findings to the reading attainment data, which was also aggregated to the level of the school. The first four behaviours concern technical aspects of correction and the number of recordings per pair varies from over five to just under three. Clearly, these behaviours were frequently observed. Of the next four behaviours, three concern interest in the book and talking. These behaviours ranged from just under three to one and a half per pair; they were somewhat frequent. However, reading together exactly, tutor praising, and tutee signalling were all relatively rarely seen, being on average about a half of an observation per pair. Tutor mis-correction was very low, which is good. We may conclude that implementation was somewhat variable, with correction, talking, and showing interest in the book being frequent, while reading together exactly, tutor praising and tutee signalling were infrequent. However, enjoyment of the book might only be obviously present early in the session and be less evident at the middle and end of the session. The low frequency of praise might at first sight seem problematic.

The variables in the observational data aggregated into schools were then correlated with all others. However, most of the observed factors did not significantly correlate with reading test attainment. One that did was 'total tutor praise' ($r = -0.583$, $p = 0.029$ with standardised score), but this was a negative

Table 2.4 Year 2: aggregated frequencies of behaviours observed per school

Behaviour	Minimum	Maximum	Mean	
			per school	Standard deviation
Total mistakes made	4.00	32.00	15.6176	7.97169
Total tutor repeats words correctly	2.00	34.00	13.6765	8.18333
Total pause 4/5 seconds exact, then correct	2.00	32.00	13.5588	7.90546
Total tutor goes quiet straight away	.00	23.00	8.7353	9.15512
Total show interest in book	5.00	10.00	8.3529	1.27187
Total talk about the content	.00	56.00	7.1765	12.84638
Total tutee repeats words correctly	.00	32.00	7.1471	9.42365
Total talk in reading together and alone	.00	15.00	4.2941	3.47787
Total reading together exactly	.00	11.00	1.9118	3.41977
Total tutor praises	.00	20.00	1.8235	4.86358
Total tutee signals for reading alone	.00	7.00	1.2941	2.31205
Total tutor praise during reading alone	.00	7.00	.5294	1.69991
Total tutor mis-corrects	.00	2.00	.2353	.56230
Total tutor praises for going alone	.00	1.00	.1765	.39295

correlation. Likewise, 'tutor praise during reading alone' was significant but negative ($r = -0.570$, $p = 0.033$ with standardised score).

Other correlations seemed to fall into two separate groups. One group concerned the quality of technique (i.e. pausing and the correction of mistakes). The other group was talk, where items were again positively inter-correlated. However, neither of these two groups (technique or talk) significantly correlated with attainment.

Comparison of Years 1 and 2

The observations from Years 1 and 2 show very considerable similarities, despite being undertaken, in many cases, in different classes with different teachers (albeit with the same observer, who showed good reliability over the two years). In the tables, the first three items and the fifth item are in exactly the same place. Of the remainder, three moved by only one place in the ranking. An improvement is evident in 'total tutor goes quiet straight away' (up five places), 'total talk about the content' (up two places) and 'total talk in reading together and alone' (up four places). A decline is evident in 'total tutee repeats words correctly' (down three places), 'total reading together exactly' (down three places), 'total tutee signals for reading alone' (down four places) and 'total tutor praises for going alone' (down four places). Thus the changes from Year 1 to Year 2 are relatively small. They suggest that in Year 2 there was less concern with the technicalities of correction and more concern with discussing the book. This is reinforced by comparison of the inter-correlations for Years 1 and 2. The same pattern of clustered variables relating to correction and to talk is evident in both years, but in Year 1 the correlations are smaller and the significant correlations fewer in both areas. However, this is particularly relevant to the talk cluster variable. The modest shift from correction to talk is interesting. This could not be just because students were becoming familiar with the observer because the students were largely not the same in Years 1 and 2. Presumably, it was because the pupils were adapting their technique (although it still showed quite a high degree of adherence to the prescription). Figure 2.2 shows Year 1 and Year 2 mean observations, with Year 2 corrected to be per pair rather than per school, and the data standardised on Year 1 (which is why Year 2 looks more erratic).

Discussion

In Year 1, implementation was variable but still showed a relatively high degree of consistency for an intervention that was deliberately introduced on the basis of limited continuing professional development. Two groups of behaviours were identified, each inter-correlated and focused on technical aspects of correction and talking and interest. That these two aspects of the tutoring technique were evident is interesting, suggesting that teachers had been largely successful in training their

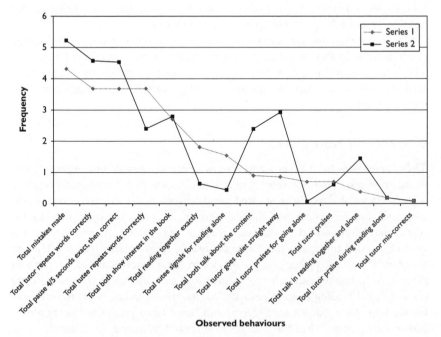

Figure 2.2 Year 1 and Year 2: observed behaviours

classes. In Year 2, talking and interest in the book showed greater prominence in the observation data, but correction remained a substantial element of implementation, so there was no indication that students had reverted to merely listening each other read without appropriately intervening. Separate attainment test results indicated that participating students gained in reading skill more than control students. That this was achieved with somewhat equivocal implementation was even more encouraging; this suggests that the intervention has some effect even without an intensive program of external monitoring. However, there was a puzzling lack of relationship between specific implementation variables and outcomes, as well as a negative correlation between achievement and the use of praise that was particularly puzzling.

Implications for multiple case study designs

In this section we have seen embedded multiple case designs with multiple units of analysis at work. Multiple case designs have advantages and disadvantages in comparison to single case designs. Multiple case designs are sometimes considered more compelling and robust. However, the rationale for single case study designs cannot be satisfied by multiple cases. Nonetheless, the design follows a replication logic that is similar to that for multiple experiments, but with the strategic altering of one certain condition in a systematic manner.

Conclusion

In this chapter, we discussed two case study designs that are commonly used for collecting and analysing observational data. The single case design focused on the behaviour of one child and used multiple baseline design to observe any intervention gains during different intervention phases, generalisation of behaviour across non-target behaviour, in non-trained settings, and with non-intervention peers, and a follow up to observe maintenance gains. The reliability of the data analysis was ascertained using inter-observer reliability measures. As can be seen from the example, it is important to conduct observation more than once and in more than one setting/context to enhance the reliability of the data. The data provided in the single case study example were also collected at different times of the day and in a natural setting for that child.

The multiple case design focused on a two-year randomised controlled trial of peer tutoring in over eighty schools in one school district. It included two sets of intervention recordings in two successive years. Longitudinal data were recorded and compared to ascertain intervention gains.

As can be seen, within case study designs, depending on the purpose of research and sample size, observation can be undertaken using single case and/or multiple case designs. Through observational analysis, both designs were able to effectively demonstrate the nature of intervention gains. They could also indicate aspect(s) of the intervention that appeared to be less effective.

Although data in the above examples were analysed manually, computer programmes such as 'ObserverPro', 'NVivo' and 'INTERACT' can also be used to analyse observation data. It is worth remembering that the software would help in quantifying the observation data. For qualitative aspects, manual analysis might still be more appropriate.

References

Baer, R. A., Detrich, R., and Weninger, J. M. (1988) 'On the functional role of the verbalization in correspondence training procedures', *Journal of Applied Behavior Analysis*, 21(4): 345–356.

Cohen, P. A., Kulik, J. A., and Kulik, C-L. C. (1982) 'Educational outcomes of tutoring: a meta-analysis of findings', *American Educational Research Journal*, 19(2): 237–248.

Cohen, L., Manion, L., and Morrison, K. (2000) *Research Methods in Education*, London: Routledge Falmer Press.

Deacon, J. R., and Konarski, E. A. (1987) 'Correspondence training: an example of rule-governed behavior?', *Journal of Applied Behavior Analysis*, 20(4): 391–400.

Gross, A., Miltenberger, R., Knudson, P., Bosch, A., and Breitwieser, C. B. (2007) 'Preliminary evaluation of a parent training program to prevent gun play', *Journal of Applied Behavior Analysis*, 40: 691–695.

Hallahan, D. P., Lloyd, J. W., Kneedler, R. D., and Marshall, K. J. (1982) 'A comparison of effects of self- versus teacher-assessment of on-task behavior', *Behavior Therapy*, 13: 715–723.

Jindal, D. (1997) 'Generalisation and maintenance of social skills of children with visual impairment: effectiveness of self-management procedures'. Unpublished PhD Thesis, University of Tsukuba, Japan.

Jindal-Snape, D., Kato, M., and Maekawa, H. (1998) 'Using self-evaluation procedures to maintain social skills in a child who is blind', *Journal of Visual Impairment and Blindness*, 92(5): 362–366.

Jindal-Snape, D. (2003) 'Generalisation and maintenance of social skills of a girl with visual impairment using self-evaluation procedures', *Journal of Human Ergology*, 32: 57–68.

Jindal-Snape, D. (2004) 'Generalization and maintenance of social skills of children with visual impairment: self-evaluation and role of feedback', *Journal of Visual Impairment and Blindness*, 98(8): 470–483.

Jindal-Snape, D. (2005a) 'Use of feedback from sighted peers in promoting social interaction skills', *Journal of Visual Impairment and Blindness*, 99(7): 403–412.

Jindal-Snape, D. (2005b) 'Self-evaluation and recruitment of feedback for enhanced social interaction by a student with visual impairment', *Journal of Visual Impairment and Blindness*, 99(8): 486–498.

Kazdin, A. E. (1977) 'Artifact, bias, and complexity of assessment: the ABCs of reliability', *Journal of Applied Behavior Analysis*, 10: 141–150.

Kazdin, A. E. (1982) *Single Case Research Designs: Methods for Clinical and Applied Settings*, New York: Oxford University Press.

Kazdin, A. E. (2001) *Behavior Modification in Applied Settings*, Belmont, CA: Wadsworth/Thomas Learning.

Layer, S. A., Hanley, G. P., Heal, N. A., and Tiger, J. H. (2008) 'Determining individual preschoolers' preferences in a group arrangement', *Journal of Applied Behavior Analysis*, 41: 25–37.

Matthews, B. A., Shimoff, E., and Catania, A. C. (1987) 'Saying and doing: a contingency-space analysis', *Journal of Applied Behavior Analysis*, 20(1): 69–74.

Mayfield, K. H. and Vollmer, T. R. (2007) 'Teaching math skills to at-risk students using home-based peer tutoring', *Journal of Applied Behavior Analysis*, 40: 223–237.

Person, N. K. and Graesser, A. G. (1999) 'Evolution of discourse during cross-age tutoring', in O'Donnell, A. M. and King, A. (eds) *Cognitive Perspectives on Peer Learning*, Mahwah, NJ: Lawrence Erlbaum.

Phaneuf, L. and McIntyre, L. L. (2007) 'Effects of individualised video feedback combined with group parent training on inappropriate maternal behaviour', *Journal of Applied Behavior Analysis*, 40: 737–741.

Reeve, S. A., Reeve, K. F., Townsend, D. B., and Poulson, C. L. (2007) 'Establishing a generalized repertoire of helping behavior in children with autism', *Journal of Applied Behavior Analysis*, 40: 123–136.

Robson, C. (2002) *Real World Research: A Resource For Social Scientists And Practitioner-Researchers*, Second edition, Oxford: Blackwell.

Roscoe, R. D. and Chi, M. T. H. (2007) 'Understanding tutor learning: knowledge-building and knowledge-telling in peer tutors' explanations and questions', *Review of Educational Research*, 77(4): 534–574.

Sainato, D. M., Goldstein, H., and Strain, P. S. (1992) 'Effects of self-evaluation on preschool children's use of social interaction strategies with their classmates with autism', *Journal of Applied Behavior Analysis*, 25(1): 127–141.

Sarantakos, S. (2005) *Social Research*, Hampshire: Palgrave Macmillan.

Sharpley, A. M., and Sharpley, C. F. (1981) 'Peer tutoring: a review of the literature', *Collected Original Resources in Education*, 5(3): C-11.

Storey, K. and Gaylord-Ross, R. (1987) 'Increasing positive social interactions by handicapped individuals during a recreational activity using a multicomponent treatment package', *Research in Developmental Disabilities*, 8: 627–649.

Topping, K. J. (2001) *Thinking Reading Writing: A Practical Guide to Paired Learning with Peers, Parents and Volunteers*, London and New York: Continuum.

Topping, K. J. and Ehly, S. (Eds.) (1998) *Peer-assisted Learning*, Mahwah NJ and London: Lawrence Erlbaum.

Yin, R. K. (2003) *Case Study Research: Design and Methods*, Third edition, London: Sage.

Chapter 3

Tracking student learning over time using construct-centred design

Namsoo Shin, Shawn Y. Stevens and Joseph Krajcik

Introduction

Rather than investigating learning and context as disconnected entities, learning research should investigate how learning and context work together to understand and predict how people learn (Barab and Squire, 2004). In such research, learning scientists address theoretical questions about the nature of learning in context, developing approaches to the study of learning phenomena in real contexts to produce evidence-based claims for their theoretical questions (Collins, Joseph, and Bielaczyc, 2004). For valid evidence-based claims, researchers should consider students' learning over an extended period of time in various contexts because learning challenging content may take years to develop and is influenced by many factors, such as classroom contexts, instructional materials, and students' prior knowledge and experiences (Smith *et al.*, 2006; Duschl, Schweingruber, and Shouse, 2007). Such research involves the development of products (e.g. learning theory, instructional materials and technology tools) and explores the relevance of the products on learning rather than simply examining isolated variables within laboratory contexts (Brown, 1992; Barab and Squire, 2004). Thus, the research programme should be iterative, be process-oriented, and involve design products that work in real contexts. Such programmes of research also need appropriate methodologies. Based on our previous work, we propose using construct-centred design (CCD) as an appropriate methodology (Krajcik, Shin, Stevens, and Short, 2009; Pellegrino *et al.*, 2008).

Because CCD focuses on the construct that students are expected to learn as well as the construct that researchers and teachers want to measure, the CCD methodology provides a flexible and systematic approach for guiding product development, monitoring the development process, and examining the effects on learning outcomes. The aim of this chapter is to illustrate how the CCD process provides a systematic research methodology for learning research using the development of learning progressions (LPs), a new and complex research field in science education, as an example. LPs illustrate students' conceptual growth across time and guide the alignment of instructional materials, instruction, and assessment in a principled way (see for example Smith *et al.*, 2006; Duschl, Schweingruber, and Shouse, 2007). Although we focus on science learning, the

CCD methodology and its form of analysis are applicable to design research for exploring the long-term development of ideas in other disciplines.

Before turning to the specifics of the CCD methodology, we describe the main idea and key characteristics of LPs. Next, we describe the CCD methodology and its relation to other design approaches. Finally, we provide an example to illustrate how CCD can guide the development and refinement of LPs for monitoring students' understanding across time. We conclude by discussing the strengths and weaknesses of the methodology.

Learning progressions

Learning scientists consider LPs to be a valuable framework for designing instructional materials, instruction, and assessment to support meaningful learning because they organize content to provide a potential path for students to develop understanding of a core idea over time (Duschl, Schweingruber, and Shouse, 2007; NRC, 2006 and 2007; National Assessment Governing Board, 2006a and 2006b). Learning progressions are research-based descriptions of how students build their knowledge and gain more expertise within and across a core idea over a broad span of time (Duschl, Schweingruber, and Shouse, 2007; Smith *et al.*, 2006). Core ideas help explain the major concepts in a domain or may offer insight into the development of the field. Thus, they provide a foundation for future learning. They illuminate how learners can develop and connect concepts within and across disciplines as they progress towards a more sophisticated understanding of the key concepts and skills necessary for developing core ideas. As such, they can provide a guide for tracking student learning over time.

There are three key factors to an LP: a lower and an upper anchor to define the range of content within a core idea and defined levels of understanding (Smith *et al.*, 2006; Stevens, Delgado, and Krajcik, 2009). Based upon learning and cognitive research, the lower anchor explicitly defines the knowledge that students must have before they can begin to develop understanding of concepts contained in the learning progression. The upper anchor describes the knowledge and skills that students are ultimately expected to hold at the end of formal instruction corresponding to the LP.

Because meaningful learning can be defined as the ability to connect related ideas and apply knowledge to new situations (Bransford, Brown, and Cocking, 1999), it is important for LPs to specify not only the order in which students develop understanding of the important concepts, but also how they connect and use related ideas. An LP does not describe a linear, one-dimensional path towards greater understanding that historically has often been assumed. Instead, the levels of an LP specify the connections between related ideas that students should be able to make, and identify and characterize not only the ways in which students can develop understanding of the important concepts under the umbrella of the core idea, but also how they should interconnect and reason with the important concepts between related ideas. Thus, a multi-dimensional model of LPs, in which an LP contains a progression of sets of ideas within and among topics that describe how students can develop more expert knowledge, may be more useful. In this way, LPs provide a strategic sequence of ideas that describe how concepts branch off one another and how students should select and combine ideas and apply them to new problems.

Smith and colleagues proposed a research approach that is grounded in students' progressive understanding of a core concept and can inform the development of LPs for all disciplines. In this approach, a coherent set of core ideas was defined, clarified, and elaborated based on the research on students' understanding of associated concepts. Next, they combined the key concepts related to each core idea with scientific practices (e.g. modelling and scientific explanations) to develop 'learning performances' (Krajcik, McNeill, and Reiser, 2008: 9), which are referred to as the articulation of the cognitive tasks that describe how students should be able to make use of the knowledge. From these efforts, they defined levels for each grade range that are suitable for the experiences, knowledge, and cognitive ability of students at that level in order to describe how students can develop understanding of the core idea over time. Finally, the concepts from each level were used to develop an LP and generate assessment items that link to the learning performances. The assessments focus on measuring complex learning skills in a progressive way to place students along the LP. This approach offers promise for improving large-scale and classroom assessment by focusing on students' conceptual growth to monitor their understanding of a core idea across time instead of a one-time measurement using low-level tasks (e.g. description and recall).

The key aspect of LPs and the approach used by Smith and colleagues is the grounding in research and empirical evidence on student learning and understanding of core ideas. Empirical learning research should guide the selection and description of the lower and upper anchors, and the levels of the LP. However, although much progress has been made in the field, numerous unanswered questions still exist in the research literature related to the design and empirical testing of LPs and how they can guide student learning across time. Developing well-grounded LPs requires thorough, longitudinal studies related to how student learning of core ideas develops in a diverse set of contexts. A principled research methodology such as CCD (Pellegrino *et al.*, 2008) is necessary to guide the complex, iterative process of developing and refining an LP and assessments based upon the LP. In the section that follows, we describe the foundation of CCD and present how the CCD methodology can apply to the development of LPs.

Foundation of construct-centred design

A research methodology to guide learning research and the development of products should be flexible enough for (1) mapping out the constructs associated with core ideas and (2) developing assessments and instructional materials that support and measure how students' understanding develops over time. By modifying and adapting the learning-goal-driven (LGD) design process for developing curriculum materials (Krajcik, McNeill, and Reiser, 2008) and the evidence-centred design (ECD) model for developing assessments (Mislevy and Riconscente, 2005), the CCD process (Pellegrino *et al.*, 2008) provides such a model.

Learning-goal-driven design

The LGD design model builds upon and extends the backward design approach presented by Wiggins and McTighe (1998) and current instructional design frameworks (Gagné, Wager, Golas, and Keller, 2005) to provide an approach for the development of coherent instructional materials (Krajcik, McNeill, and Reiser, 2008). This process begins by defining the focus of the instructional materials based on national, state, or local standards. The next step is the unpacking process, which involves explicitly specifying the content contained in the standard of interest and identifying necessary prior knowledge, potential student difficulties and alternative conceptions, and strategies for representing content to engage students in a meaningful way. Learning performances that describe what students should be able to do with the knowledge are then developed based on the concepts identified during the unpacking process and the results of learning research related to student learning of the relevant content. The development of learning performances is a critical step that defines the cognitive tasks for students to accomplish. The learning performances then guide development of learning and assessment activities.

Evidence-centred design

ECD is a powerful and flexible framework for organizing content and developing assessments grounded in the principles of evidentiary reasoning (Mislevy and Riconscente, 2005). A key to this approach is the focus on defining evidence, which describes 'what behaviours or performances should reveal' whether students have the desired knowledge (Messick, 1994: 16). In light of this perspective, the ECD approach answers three questions: (1) Exactly what knowledge is critical and should be assessed? (2) What does it mean to understand that knowledge, and how should students be able to use the knowledge to demonstrate their understanding? and (3) What particular tasks, questions or situations will bring about the appropriate type of response? Within the context of the ECD approach, the content of a domain must be clearly and completely defined. An important part of the ECD process involves specifying what students should be able to do with their knowledge and the practices in which they should engage with that knowledge, which is called a 'claim'. The evidence defines the features that student work is expected to exhibit in a given situation to provide support that the student has met the claim. The evidence provides a detailed description of the precise, level-appropriate knowledge and skills that students should exhibit to illustrate their understanding. The process also defines what tasks or situations should elicit evidence of student understanding of the claim or part of a claim.

Construct-centred design process

Similar to the LGD and ECD processes, the CCD process begins with specifically defining the focus of the construct. We define the construct as the core ideas that students are expected to learn and that researchers and teachers want to measure (Messick, 1994; Wilson, 2005). Because the foundation of the process focuses on the definition and explicit specification of content that lies within constructs, the process is termed a 'construct-centred design'. In describing the process, we do not mean to imply that this is a linear process. In practice, the process is interactive and highly recursive, with information specified at one stage clarifying, and often modifying, what was specified earlier. Figure 3.1 illustrates the CCD process and the relationship between CCD and the development of LPs. A detailed description of each step follows.

Step 1: Select the construct

The first step in CCD is to choose the construct and define the target learners (see Figure 3.1, step 1). The construct is essential as it identifies the set of ideas for which learners will study and be held accountable for understanding. Because students in different grade ranges have different knowledge and experiences that

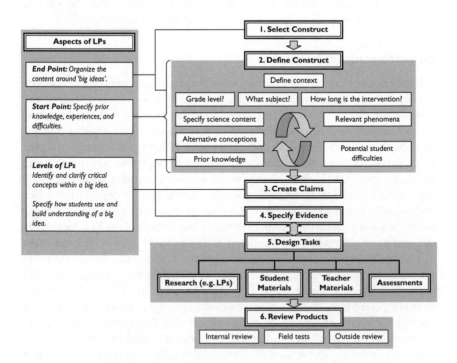

Figure 3.1 Relationship between the LP and the iterative CCD process

influence their learning, defining the target students helps define the construct appropriately and also guides preparation of level-appropriate instructional materials, instruction, and assessment.

Step 2: Define the construct

The next step is to define the construct based on expert knowledge of the discipline and related learning research (see Figure 3.1, step 2). This process, called 'unpacking', involves defining the ideas contained within the construct. By 'unpacking', we mean breaking up the construct into smaller components to explicitly specify the concepts that are crucial for developing an understanding of the construct. Being related to the construct is not enough; the concept must be necessary for building understanding of the construct. The depth of understanding that is expected from students is also clearly defined in this step. As a step towards defining how students should know the content, the prior knowledge that is required both within and from other constructs is also specified. The unpacking process also includes: identifying potential difficulties students might have learning the content; providing possible instructional strategies that may help student learning; and identifying strategies for effectively representing the concepts based on previous learning research to engage students in a meaningful way.

Step 3: Create claim(s)

A set of claims is generated based upon the unpacked construct. Claims specify the nature of knowledge and understanding regarding a particular concept that is expected of students (see Figure 3.1, step 3). In constructing a claim, vague terms like 'to know' and 'to understand' should be avoided. Rather, claims should specifically define what students would be able to do with their knowledge using terms that describe the cognitive behaviours you want students to engage in (e.g. Bloom's taxonomy; Bloom, 1956). For example, students should be able to provide examples of phenomena, use models to explain patterns in data, construct explanations, or develop and test hypotheses. An important part of student learning involves the ability to connect related ideas and apply knowledge to new situations (Bransford, Brown, and Cocking, 1999). Therefore, it is important that the claims specify how students should be able to connect ideas both within individual topics and among related topics in order to describe how students build integrated understanding of the construct.

Step 4: Specify the evidence

The evidence specifies the aspects of student work (e.g. behaviours and performances) that would be indicative of a student who has the desired knowledge to support a specific claim or set of claims (see Figure 3.1, step 4). In particular, this step helps to explicitly define the expected level and depth of understanding that the target learners should demonstrate. Based upon the unpacked construct and a set of claims, evidence for the relevant content for a construct is specified. The understanding defined by the evidence provides a guide for the definition of levels in the LP.

Step 5: Design learning or assessment tasks

The tasks, which are generated based on the claims and evidence, provide a response that offers appropriate evidence to support the relevant claim (see Figure 3.1, step 5). The tasks can be either learning products that will help learners develop the knowledge in the claim or assessment products that measure whether learners have the knowledge stated in the claim. The assessment or learning tasks are designed to elicit or generate students' performances to allow for a judgment to be made about whether sufficient evidence exists to support the learning claim. A single assessment task or situation may provide evidence for more than one claim; multiple tasks may be necessary to assess a single claim. A single task or set of tasks can be associated with a claim or a set of claims assigned to multiple levels on the LP. An individual claim, its evidence, and its corresponding task may link to a single level on the progression.

Step 6: Review products

For each step within this iterative process, the products must be reviewed internally and, when appropriate, externally (see Figure 3.1, step 6). The internal review focuses on critique and revision of the products to ensure that they align with the claims and evidence. External review can include feedback from teachers of the target students or from content or assessment experts. Conducting pilot tests and field trials with target students is an essential component that provides invaluable information of the products. In sum, the CCD process provides a systematic and principled way to iteratively develop and revise all aspects of an LP, and ultimately to design associated research, instructional materials, instruction, and assessments for monitoring student understanding of a core idea over a long time period.

Application of construct-centred design

In this section, we describe the process of developing an LP that focuses on the development of grade 7–14 students' understanding of a core idea (i.e. the nature of matter) to illustrate how the CCD methodology can generally inform the development and refinement of LPs. Since the goal of this chapter is to show how the CCD approach provides a principled and systematic methodology for developing LPs, we limit the discussion of the science content, however more detail can be found elsewhere (Stevens, Delgado, and Krajcik, 2009).

Select and define the construct

The nature of matter is a broad topic that includes the structure, properties, and behaviour of matter. The portion of the LP discussed here focuses on how grade 7–14 students develop understanding of two constructs: the atomic model (structure) and the electrical forces that govern interactions between atoms and molecules. To help define the range of content that needed to be unpacked, the lower and upper anchors for the LP were defined. In this case, the lower anchor was defined using the learning progression for atomic molecular theory for grades K–8 (Smith *et al.*, 2006) and additional empirical research. The upper anchor of the LP was defined based upon national standards documents (AAAS, 1993; NRC, 1996), ideas required as a foundation for nanoscale science and engineering learning for grade 7–12 students (Stevens, Sutherland, and Krajcik, in press) and current learning research related to those expected understandings.

The concepts within the two constructs were then unpacked to define what it means to understand them at levels appropriate for grade 7–14 students. In this example, we unpacked the constructs of atomic structure and electrical forces to identify and describe the concepts crucial for developing an understanding of the constructs. The depth of understanding that is expected from students at the upper anchor is also clearly defined in this step. Table 3.1 illustrates the science content related to atomic structure incorporated into the LP. The unpacking process also includes identifying potential difficulties that students may have learning the content, providing possible instructional strategies, specifying the prior knowledge needed to build understanding of the content, and identifying phenomena to help effectively represent the content based on previous learning research.

Create claims, specify evidence, and design tasks

A set of claims, and the related evidence and tasks, were developed for the relevant content for the two constructs. The development of the claims and evidence were informed by the national standards documents (AAAS, 1993; NRC, 1996) and the learning research literature. Table 3.2 provides an example of a claim and its corresponding evidence and tasks. Based upon the claims and evidence, we developed an LP.

Develop a learning progression

The claims and evidence specify how students should be able to connect ideas both within individual topics and among related topics in order to describe how students build integrated understanding of the constructs. The claims and evidence can be used to refine the levels according to learning research and the logic of the discipline. Figure 3.2 illustrates part of the LP for the nature of matter. The levels in the LP represent sets of ideas that describe a path towards developing a more complex understanding of the constructs. The sets of ideas within a level connect

Table 3.1 Unpacked science content lying between the upper and lower anchors for the learning progression for atomic structure

---

Atomic structure

Atoms consist of electrons, neutrons, and protons.

Protons have a positive charge, electrons a negative charge, and neutrons are neutral.

The number of protons defines the type of element, and represents the atomic number on the Periodic Table.

Neutral atoms of an element have the same number of protons and electrons, but not necessarily the same number of neutrons.

Different numbers of neutrons for a given number of protons create different isotopes of the same element.

Protons and neutrons have similar mass, but electrons have a much smaller mass.

The nucleus takes up only a very small percentage of the volume of an atom, but makes up the vast majority of the atomic mass.

The electrons are distributed in 'shells' that surround the nucleus. These shells represent energy levels (n).

The inner shells plus the nucleus make up the atomic core.

The outer shell of electrons is different from the inner shells of electrons.

The configuration of the outermost electrons determines how an atom can interact with other atoms.

There are a certain number of orbitals in each shell or level (e.g. *1*- 1s; 2- 2s, $2p_x$, $2p_y$, $2p_z$) of an atom.

The Pauli Principle predicts that only two electrons can be in a single orbital. Each electron has a different spin (i.e. $\pm \frac{1}{2}$).

The solar system model does not describe electron distribution within an atom well; the electron cloud model, which describes the electron probability density, provides a better model.

Electrons exhibit both particulate and wavelike behavior.

The Heisenberg Uncertainty Principle states that the position and momentum of an electron cannot be determined simultaneously.

Only energy changes in certain (quantized) amounts are observed in isolated atoms, molecules, or other confined systems.

Different energy levels are associated with different configurations of atoms (and molecules).

Source: Adapted from Stevens, Delgado and Krajcik, accepted

Table 3.2 Examples of the claims, evidence, and tasks for the atomic structure construct

Claim	Evidence	Task
Students should be able to draw and explain a functional model of the atom. (What is functional depends on their level and the level-appropriate phenomena they need to explain.)	*Level 1: The student model of an atom should include:* • atoms (no components) *Level 2: The student model of an atom should include:* • Atoms are made of electrons, neutrons and protons. • Electrons are negatively charged, protons are positively charged, and neutrons are neutral. • Neutrons and protons are of similar mass, mass of electrons is much smaller. *Level 3a: The student model of an atom should include:* • Level 2 evidence + • Electrons are in constant motion, limited to shell (3D)/orbit (2D). • Only a certain number of electrons allowed per shell. *Level 3b: The student model of an atom should include:* • Level 2 evidence + • Electrons are in constant motion, but unlike macroscopic objects, they do not have a trajectory. • The Heisenberg Uncertainty Principle indicates that it is impossible to predict where an electron will be based upon where it has been. • The electron probability density describes the electron distribution. • In the 'electron cloud' model where the 'cloud' describes the probability density of an electron provides a simplified way of visualizing the quantum mechanical behavior of an electron. • Only a certain number of electrons allowed per shell. *Level 4: The student model of an atom should include:* • Level 3b evidence + • The shells in the atomic models represent energy levels.	• Draw a picture of what you think an atom would look like (your model of an atom) and explain it. • (If appropriate) Tell me about the protons, neutrons, and electrons in your model. How do they compare to each other? • Clarify their ideas of electron motion. For example, ask, 'Do the electrons orbit around like planets?' (or whatever is appropriate from their drawing).

Table 3.2 continued

Claim	Evidence	Task
	• Only certain amounts (quanta) of energy will move electrons to another level. • Electrons are distributed in orbitals that surround the nucleus. Only a certain number of electrons (two) are allowed within each orbital (Pauli Principle). • A certain number of orbitals is contained in each level (shell).	

Source: Adapted from Stevens, Delgado, and Krajcik, 2009

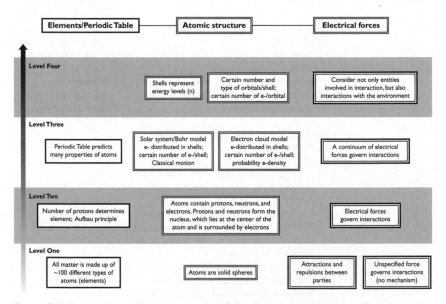

Figure 3.2 Illustration of three strands of the learning progression for the nature of matter

Source: Adapted from Stevens, Delgado, and Krajcik, 2009

in various ways to explain a range of phenomena; higher levels describe the phenomena with greater scientific accuracy. In this way, the levels of the LP describe increasing levels of sophistication of a model that describes the structure and behaviour of matter. Further research is required to address whether the order in which students learn concepts within a single level is important.

Data collection: characterizing how students develop understanding of the nature of matter

To help fill gaps in the learning research related to the two constructs, an interview protocol was developed based on the CCD claim and evidence phases to characterize how ideas related to the nature of matter developed as grade 7–14 students passed through the current curriculum (see, for an example of an interview protocol, Stevens, Delgado, and Krajcik, 2009). Assessing students across the grade range of the LP with the same instrument provides insight into the points of the LP on which instruction should focus, informs the type of instructional strategies that might help students to develop understanding, and supports the development of assessments that can be developed to locate students' positions on the LP on a larger scale.

Participants and procedure

A cross-sectional sample of students representing the range of grades covered by the LP was interviewed. In this case, grade 7 students and high school students (one set had not taken a chemistry course and another set had) from the same district or school system were individually interviewed. At each level, the students who were interviewed were chosen to provide a mix of gender and to represent a range of achievement levels. A 20–30-minute semi-structured interview was performed with individual students to characterize student understanding of all of the topics contained in atomic structure. The interview questions required students to apply their knowledge to explain real-world phenomena. The interviews were conducted in several phases. After each phase, student responses were evaluated and the protocol was revised to better characterize student understanding of the constructs.

Coding scheme

The data collected from the interview was coded following a coding scheme based on Minstrell's (1992) 'FACETS' approach. Each concept from the unpacked construct was unpacked further into small, independent 'facets'. This approach helps prevent predisposition towards predefined models and ensures that all student models can be accommodated. A code of 'Y' was used to signify that the facet was included in the student response while a code of 'N' indicated that the idea was not communicated by the student (see Figure 3.3 for a coding example). Student ideas not included in the coding scheme were coded 'other'. The responses in the other category provide further information on alternative ideas and difficulties students may have learning the content. As such, they inform the instructional strategies that may help students move along the LP. If a question was inadvertently omitted or the interviewer strayed too far from the interview protocol, the code was 'NA'. To achieve inter-rater reliability, one researcher coded

Atomic composition and structure	
Facet	Code
atoms are spherical	Y
atoms are made up of components	Y
atoms contain protons (p⁺)	Y
atoms contain electrons (e⁻)	Y
atoms contain neutrons (n⁰)	Y
p⁺ are positively charged	Y
e⁻ are negatively charged	Y
n⁰ are neutral	Y
nucleus lies at the center of the atom	Y
p⁺ and n⁰ at the center (nucleus)	Y
e⁻ in outer portion of atom	Y
nucleus takes up small percentage of atomic volume	N
electrons in shells	N
certain number of e- allowed in each shell	N

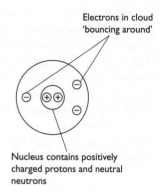

Electrons in cloud 'bouncing around'

Nucleus contains positively charged protons and neutral neutrons

Figure 3.3 Coding example

Source: Adapted from Stevens, Delgado, and Krajcik, 2009

100 per cent of the data. A second independent rater coded 10 per cent of the data that was selected at random. We achieved a correlation greater than 95 per cent between the two raters.

Data analysis and results

We performed a Guttman analysis (Guttman, 1944) to characterize how students typically develop ideas related to the construct. First, we grouped the individual facets into the original unpacking of the construct and then we sorted the coded data using a Guttman scale. As shown in Figure 3.4, a progression consists of six progressive levels of facets including ABCDEF. The scale illustrates that a student who understands D also understands ideas A, B, and C, but not necessarily E nor F. The scale structure can be used to describe the progression of how students' understanding develops.

For testing the significance of each level along the Guttman scale, we used the McNemar test of 2×2 tables using the MH Programme (Uebersax, 2006). The McNemar technique provides a simple way to test marginal homogeneity, which implies that row totals are equal to the corresponding column totals. In this study, a statistically significant difference indicates an ordered connection. In Figure 3.4b, 17 students understand B and C, one student discussed C but not B, nine students discussed B but not C, and eight students discussed neither. The McNemar test showed a significant difference for the step from B to C at $p = 0.0114$, suggesting that this is an ordered connection. In contrast, the step between D to E did not show a statistically significant difference, which indicates that the step is not an ordered connection (see Figure 3.4).

StudentID	S1	S2	S3	S4	S5	S6	S7	S8	S9	S10	S11	S12	S13	S14	S15	S16	S17	S18	S19	S20	S21	S22	S23	S24	S25	S26	S27	S28	S29	S30
Facet F	Y	Y	Y	Y	N	N	N	N	N	N	N	N	N	N	N	N	N	N	N	N	N	N	N	N	N	N	N	N	N	N
Facet E	Y	Y	Y	Y	Y	Y	N	N	N	N	N	N	N	N	Y	Y	Y	N	N	N	N	N	N	N	N	N	N	N	N	N
Facet D	Y	Y	Y	Y	Y	Y	Y	Y	Y	Y	Y	Y	Y	N	N	N	N	N	N	N	N	N	N	N	N	N	N	N	N	N
Facet C	Y	Y	Y	Y	Y	Y	Y	Y	Y	Y	Y	Y	Y	Y	Y	Y	Y	Y	N	N	N	N	N	N	N	N	Y	N	N	N
Facet B	Y	Y	Y	Y	Y	Y	Y	Y	Y	Y	Y	Y	Y	Y	Y	Y	Y	Y	Y	Y	Y	Y	Y	Y	Y	N	N	N	N	N
Facet A	Y	Y	Y	Y	Y	Y	Y	Y	Y	Y	Y	Y	Y	Y	Y	Y	Y	Y	Y	Y	Y	Y	Y	Y	Y	Y	Y	Y	Y	Y

a

	C(Y)	C(N)
B(Y)	17	9
B(N)	1	8

b

chi-squared = 6.4
p-value = 0.0114

	E(Y)	E(N)
D(Y)	6	7
D(N)	3	19

c

chi-squared = 1.6
p-value = 0.2059

Figure 3.4 Guttman scale analysis (a) and McNemar test of 2 × 2 (b and c)

Source: Adapted from Stevens, Delgado, and Krajcik, 2009

The resulting scales provide information about how students develop understanding of the constructs. For instance, Table 3.3 illustrates how students do not move directly (and cleanly) from Level One to Level Two of the LP for the atomic structure construct. Instead, they often have incomplete knowledge of the composition and basic structure of an atom.

The development of an empirical progression that describes how students may develop understanding of the assessed concepts is an important part of the empirical testing and revision of a LP. It is important to realize that this first empirical progression describes the state of student learning using current instructional materials. However, it does not tell us what might be possible given better designed materials. In subsequent iterations, when the LP is being empirically tested using instructional materials designed to support the learning described by the LP, the empirical progression will inform the revision of the LP and associated instructional materials.

The empirical progression also provides some insight into instructional strategies that might help students move along the LP by identifying difficulties and alternative ideas students may have regarding the content (for example, see Table 3.4). Understanding students' ideas is critical in the development of instructional materials and in determining when and how it might be appropriate to introduce the concepts to students. In addition, knowledge of student misconceptions aids the development of assessments that measure students' progress in understanding the ideas in the LP.

Table 3.3 Summary of portion of learning progression and empirical progression for atomic structure

Level	Learning progression	Level	Empirical progression
Two	Atoms are composed of protons, neutrons, and electrons Electrons are negatively charged, protons are positively charged and neutrons are neutral.	**IIc**	Location of protons, neutrons, and electrons Electrons are negatively charged, protons are positively charged, and neutrons are neutral.
	Electrons surround the nucleus, which is made up of protons and neutrons.		Electrons surround the nucleus, which is made up of protons and neutrons.
	Neutral atom contains an equal number of electrons and protons.	**IIb**	Atoms are made up of protons, neutrons, and electrons Composition correct, structure perhaps not.
	Nucleus takes up a small fraction of the 'volume' of the atom, but makes up most of the mass.	**IIa**	Atoms consist of some unknown entities Some or all of the sub-atomic particles are unspecified.
One	Particles are atoms Atoms make up all substances.	**Ia**	Particles are atoms Atoms make up all substances.
	Atoms are spheres (no components).		Atoms are spheres (no components).

Source: Adapted from Stevens, Delgado, and Krajcik, 2009

Refining and empirically testing the learning progressions

Following the CCD process, we developed two products, including an LP and an interview protocol. For each of the steps of this iterative process, the products are reviewed internally. The interview protocol and LP are revised to better characterize student understanding of the construct, based upon the iterative review and revision of the claims and evidence and multiple rounds of student interviews. The next step of CCD is to have external review of the LP, followed by the empirical testing. This requires the development of instructional materials based upon the strategies outlined in the LP, followed by field trials, including pilot and classroom tests in order to iteratively refine the LP.

An important characteristic of LPs is that students may follow different possible pathways from one level to the next along the progression rather than a single defined unidirectional route. Since learning is a complex process, many factors affect the path that students may follow as they build understanding,

Table 3.4 Example of potential instructional strategies to help students move along the learning progression

Level	Potential instructional strategies
Four	Link the quantum effects to more familiar phenomena in addition to or in lieu of the historical phenomena (e.g., conductive to insulator transition vs. photoelectric effect).
Three	Both the solar system, or Bohr model and the electron cloud model of the atom should be introduced, but with an emphasis on the fact that each are *models* and that each can or are better for explaining certain phenomena than the other. Students should be able to apply each model of atomic structure to explain phenomena (e.g., properties of many types of materials) and trends of the Periodic Table and justify their choice.
Two	The exploration and characterization of chemical reactions creates a need for students to develop an understanding of elements and the Periodic Table, which in turn drives a need to develop a model of atomic structure that allows them to answer questions such as: • What is different about each element? • Why is it that atoms of certain elements combine and others do not? • Why do elements combine in only certain combinations? The idea that atomic structure is described through *models*, and the nature of models, should be emphasized.
One	Develop students' knowledge and skills about modeling with a focus on connecting the macroscale and atomic scale to explain a range of familiar phenomena (e.g. smells traveling across the room and phase changes). Do *not* introduce the details of atomic structure.

Source: Adapted from Stevens, Delgado, and Krajcik, 2009

including the learning context, instructional materials, instruction, and students' prior knowledge and experiences. In addition, students bring different personal and cultural experiences to the classroom and, as such, they may thrive in different environments. Thus, in order to refine and test LPs, empirical data should be collected from students who have experienced curriculum materials that were developed following LPs. Since the position of students along the progression is significantly influenced by the previous instruction that students received (Cobb and Bowers, 1999), students must have appropriate learning experiences with an exemplary curriculum that help them make connections among the ideas to develop integrated understanding of a topic described by an LP. This helps us to make sure that students' poor understanding is not because of a lack of appropriate learning experiences, but because of the developmentally challenging ideas to the students. Thus, well-developed, coherent curriculum materials based on an LP should be designed, implemented, and tested iteratively throughout the process of empirically testing and refining an LP.

A longitudinal study is the ideal way to empirically test and refine learning paths of an LP. However, a more realistic way of empirically testing an LP is through testing a series of smaller pieces of the LP. The use of relatively large grain-sized LPs, as proposed by Smith and colleagues, helps define and organize the important concepts in a core idea and is therefore a useful first step in the development of a coherent curriculum (see Figure 3.5a). Testing the LPs empirically requires an instructional sequence that describes how to support students in developing understanding of a portion of the LP. One or several learning goals may describe how students can progress between the levels of the LP (see Figure 3.5b). Based upon these learning goals, instructional materials and assessment are developed to follow how students develop understanding of key concepts of the learning goals in the course of instruction.

The instructional sequences should also be developed following the CCD process. A series of learning goals that will help students to develop the desired understanding should be carefully defined. The learning goals are then unpacked to specify the content students are to learn, the difficulties they may have learning the content, and any alternative ideas they may have related to the content. A set of claims and the corresponding evidence is developed based upon the unpacking. In turn, the claims and evidence guide the design of learning tasks and instruction and associated assessment tasks. In order to empirically test the LP, assessment

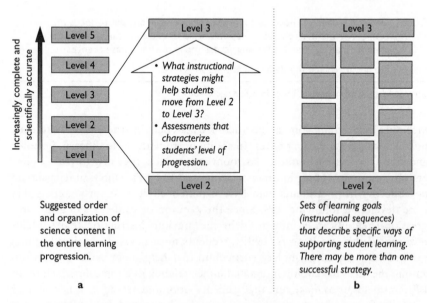

Figure 3.5 Illustration LPs (a) and learning goals based on a small portion of LPs (b)

items that are independent of the instructional materials are developed. The CCD process is also used to develop assessment items that place students along the LP. Thus, the same design model is used for all phases of the development, refinement, and empirical testing of this complex research product: the LP.

Conclusion

A number of learning scientists have discussed the value of a research programme that is iterative, is process-oriented, and involves designing products that work in real contexts that extend our understandings of the nature and condition of learning and development, as well as promote student learning (Barab and Squire, 2004; Brown, 1992; Collins, Joseph, and Bielaczyc, 2004). The typical strategy for this type of learning research employs naturalistic methodologies to investigate how learning occurs and the product development process for building evidence-based claims (Barab and Squire, 2004).

A fundamental challenge for such research is the extensive quantity of qualitative and quantitative data that must be collected and organized in order to provide appropriate evidence to support the research claims (Collins, Joseph, and Bielaczyc, 2004). Based on our previous work, we believe that CCD can become a valuable methodology for learning research that may overcome this challenge. In particular, the CCD approach focuses on clearly defining the construct to focus the research and development strategies. Another critical characteristic of CCD is the explicitly specified evidence based on the unpacking of the construct that links directly to the claims. Specifying the claims and evidence supports the development and alignment of a range of products. Following the systematic process outlined by CCD provides guidance for the collection and organization of data by defining what data are essential for supporting the claims. The CCD process ensures that the design of research and development products is generated in a credible and principled way to meet the needs of learning research and classrooms.

In summary, the CCD approach extracts and expands aspects of the LGD (Krajcik, McNeill, and Reiser, 2008) and ECD (Mislevy and Riconscente, 2005) design frameworks to provide a research methodology for aligning learning research and development. CCD is a flexible process that can support a broad range of complex design research and development products, such as the development, refinement, and empirical testing of LPs, as illustrated in this chapter. As such, CCD provides an important methodology for other researchers interested in developing LPs. Because CCD is a new approach, it can be considered as a component of an iterative development process that is constantly being refined and revised to accommodate the needs of learning researchers. We still have much work to accomplish to make CCD a usable methodology for other researchers. We need to further develop the guidelines and examples for each step of CCD to provide guidance on how researchers can use CCD to accomplish a variety of design-based research goals. To do this, researchers need to apply the CCD process to design various research, instructional materials, learning progressions, and assessments tasks in order to articulate the subcomponents of the various CCD steps more clearly. As we and other researcher use CCD to guide a greater number of research and development products, the process will become better articulated. Design research, along with developing instructional materials, instruction, and assessment, are challenging and time-consuming work. However, if we hope to make progress on promoting the development of meaningful learning, we need to undertake complex research and development.

Acknowledgement

This research is funded by a Developing an Empirically-Tested Learning Progression for the Transformation of Matter to Inform Curriculum, Instruction and Assessment Design grant, number 0822038, and a National Center for Learning and Teaching in Nanoscale Science and Engineering grant, number 0426328, from the National Science Foundation. Any opinions expressed in this work are those of the authors and do not necessarily represent those of the funding agencies.

References

American Association for the Advancement of Science (1993) *Benchmarks for Scientific Literacy*, New York: Oxford University Press.

Barab, S. and Squire, K. (2004) 'Design-based research: putting a stake in the ground', *Journal of the Learning Sciences*, 13(1): 1–14.

Bloom, B. S. (1956) *Taxonomy of Educational Objectives, Handbook I: The Cognitive Domain*, New York: David McKay Co. Inc.

Bransford, J. D., Brown, A. L., and Cocking, R. R. (1999) *How People Learn: Brain, Mind, Experience, and School*, Washington, DC: National Research Council.

Brown, A. L. (1992) 'Design experiments: theoretical and methodological challenges in creating complex interventions', *Journal of the Learning Sciences*, 2: 141–178.

Collins, A., Joseph, D., and Bielaczyc, K. (2004) 'Design research; Theoretical and methodological issues', *Journal of the Learning Sciences*, 13(1): 15–42

Cobb, P. and Bowers, P. (1999) 'Cognitive and situated learning perspectives in theory and practice', *Educational Researcher* 28(2): 4–15.

Delgado, C., Stevens, S. Y., Shin, N., Yunker, M., and Krajcik, J. S. (2007) 'The Development of Students' Conception of Size'. Paper presented at the National Association for Research in Science Teaching conference, New Orleans, LA.

Duschl, R. A., Schweingruber, H. A., and Shouse, A. (eds.) (2007) *Taking Science to School: Learning and Teaching Science in Grades K–8*, Washington, DC: National Academy Press.

Gagné, R. M., Wager, W. W., Golas, K. C., and Keller, J. M. (2005) *Principles of Instructional Design*, Belmont, CA: Wadsworth.

Guttman, L. (1944) 'A basis for scaling qualitative data', *American Sociological Review*, 9(2): 139–150.

Krajcik, J. S., Shin, N., Stevens, Y. S., and Short, H. (2009) 'Using learning progressions to inform the design of coherent science curriculum materials'. Paper presented at the annual meeting of the American Educational Research Association, San Diego, CA.

Krajcik, J. S., McNeill, K. L., and Reiser, B. J. (2008) 'Learning-goals-driven design model: developing curriculum materials that align with national standards and incorporate project-based pedagogy', *Science Education*, 92(1): 1–32, Online. Available HTTP: <http://www.interscience.wiley.com> (accessed 17 November 2007).

McNemar, Q. (1947) 'Not on the sampling error of the difference between correlated proportions or percentages', *Psychometrika*, 12: 153–157.

Messick, S. (1994) 'The interplay of evidence and consequences in the validation of performance assessments', *Educational Researcher*, 23(2): 13–23.

Minstrell, J. (1992) 'Facets of students knowledge and relevant instruction', in R. Duit, F. Goldberg and H. Niedderer (eds.), Proceedings of an International Workshop – Research in Physics Learning: theoretical Issues and Empirical Studies, Kiel, Germany: The Institute for Science Education (IPN) (pp. 110–128).

Mislevy, R. J. and Riconscente, M. (2005) *Evidence-Centered Assessment Design: Layers, Structures, and Terminology*, Menlo Park, CA: SRI International.

National Assessment Governing Board (2006a) 'Science assessment and item specifications for the 2009 National Assessment of Educational Progress' (Prepublication ed.), Online. Available HTTP: <http://www.nagb.org/pubs/naep science specs 2009.doc> (accessed 11 July 2006).

National Assessment Governing Board (2006b) 'Science framework for the 2009 National Assessment of Educational Progress' (Prepublication ed.), Online. Available HTTP: <http://www.nagb.org/pubs/ naep science framework 2009.doc> (accessed 11 July 2006).

National Research Council (1996) *National Science Education Standards*, Washington, DC: National Academy Press.

National Research Council (2001) *Knowing what Students Know: The Science and Design of Educational Assessment*, Washington, DC: The National Academies Press.

National Research Council (2006) *Systems for State Science Assessment*, Washington, DC: The National Academies Press.

National Research Council (2007) *Taking Science to School*, Washington, DC: The National Academies Press.

Pellegrino, J. W., Chudowsky, N., and Glaser, R. (eds.) (2001) *Knowing what Students Know: The Science and Design of Educational Assessment*, Washington, DC: National Academies Press.

Pellegrino, J., Krajcik, J., Stevens, S. Y., Shin, N., Delgado, C., and Geier, S. (2008). 'Using construct-centered design to align curriculum, instruction, and assessment development in emerging science', in G. Kanselaar, V. Jonker, P.A. Kirschner, and F. Prins (eds.), *Proceedings from ICLS '08: International perspectives in the learning sciences: Creating a learning world* (Vol. 3, pp. 314–321), International Society of the Learning Sciences: Utrecht, Netherlands.

Smith, C. L., Wiser, M., Anderson, C. W., and Krajcik, J. (2006) 'Implications of research on children's learning for standards and assessment: a proposed learning progression for matter and the atomic molecular theory', *Measurement: Interdisciplinary Research and Perspectives*, 4 (1): 1–98.

Stevens, S., Shin, N., Delgado, C., Krajcik, J., and Pellegrino, J. (2007) 'Using learning progressions to inform curriculum, instruction and assessment design', Paper presented at the National Association for Research in Science Teaching, New Orleans, LA.

Stevens, S. Y., Delgado, C. and Krajcik, J. S. (2009) 'Developing a hypothetical multidimensional learning progression for the nature of matter', *Journal of Research in*

Science Teaching, Online. Available HTTP: <http://www3.interscience.wiley.com/journal/109083865/issue> (accessed 12 September 2009).

Stevens, S. Y., Sutherland, L. M., and Krajcik, J. S. (in press) *The Big Ideas of Nanoscale Science and Engineering*, Arlington, VA: NSTA Press.

Uebersax, J. S. (2006) MH Program (Version 1.2) [Computer software], Online. Available HTTP: <http://ourworld.compuserve.com/homepages/jsuebersax/mh.htm> (accessed 23 April 2008)

Wiggins, G. P. and McTighe, J. (1998) *Understanding by Design*, Alexandria, VA: Association for Supervision and Curriculum Development.

Wilson, M. (2005) *Constructing Measures: An Item Response Modelling Approach*, Mahwah, NJ: Erlbaum.

Chapter 4

Analysis of interview data using the constant comparative analysis method

Nicos Valanides

The purpose of this chapter is to show how qualitative data can be dissected, conceptualized, and put back together in new ways, using the constant comparative analysis method (CCAM) or grounded theory (GT). The different coding procedure steps, which constitute the heart of the method, will be described and exemplified. In addition, appropriate ways of quantifying the qualitative data for statistical analyses will be also presented. For this purpose, we use interview data generated by primary school children as they investigated the functioning of a device. The interviews adopted the 'think aloud' technique and the interviews were tape-recorded and transcribed later. Using the CCAM scoring, rubrics were developed for identified variables and their constituent parameters.

Constant comparative analysis method

Glaser and Strauss (1967) developed the constant comparative analysis method (CCAM) or grounded theory (GT). It is a methodological approach that follows a cyclical process of induction, deduction, and verification and a set of specific strategies for analyzing qualitative data, such as interviews, that can improve not only the reliability of the data, but also the theoretical depth of analysis. The CCAM involves inductive category coding and comparison of observed behaviours across categories (Goetz and LeCompte, 1981). As a consequence of this categorization, patterns are gradually revealed and constantly refined throughout the data collection and analysis process (Dye, Schatz, Rosenberg, and Coleman, 2000). Glaser and Strauss (1967) describe the constant comparison method as following four distinct stages:

1   comparing incidents applicable to each category;
2   integrating categories and their properties;
3   delimiting the theory;
4   writing the theory.

CCAM (or GT) is not a descriptive method because it attempts to extend beyond any accurate description of a set of data. CCAM attempts to generate concepts that can explain people's actions and thinking in ways that are independent of time and place, while later the descriptive parts of the CCAM are used to illustrate the generated concepts and their organization. CCAM is not exclusively a qualitative method. It is a general method and it can use quantitative or qualitative data (Glaser, 2001). Unlike other research studies where people, patients, or participants in general constitute the unit of analysis, in CCAM/GT the unit of analysis is the incident (Glaser and Strauss, 1967). CCAM analyzes hundreds of incidents that are reported by the study participants. The process attempts not only to identify incidents and code them accordingly, but it also involves organizing them using a never-ending comparison of the different incidents so that similar incidents are put in categories that are related to them in certain ways.

Obviously, the results are not reports of facts and their organization. The results constitute a set of probability statements about the relationship among concepts, while the validity of the process can be judged, for example, by fit. The concept of fit relates to how thoroughly the constant comparison of incidents to concepts is systematically implemented, while the resulting conceptualizations (theory) can be modified when new relevant data are compared to the existing data and their organization.

The central operation in the CCAM relates to the coding process that represents the way by which generalizations or theories are built from data. Coding encompasses the operations that are implemented, and by which the data are broken down, clearly understood, and conceptualized, and finally put back together and organized in new and more informative ways. There are three major types of coding, namely, open coding, axial coding, and selective coding. But, 'the lines between each type of coding are artificial' (Strauss and Corbin, 1990: 28) because the three types of coding do not take place in a sequence or in stages. On the contrary, in a single coding session one can move between one type of coding and another, especially between open and axial coding. Despite the fact that open and axial coding usually take place in the earlier phases of a study and are done in the service of selective coding, these two coding types are often useful even during selective coding because many concepts may remain poorly developed and not integrated.

The coding process starts with open coding that deals with the naming and categorization of phenomena by closely examining existing data. Thus, the data are broken down into discrete parts that are examined in an attempt to identify similarities and differences among them. As the process continues, any new incidents are constantly compared with previous incidents so that similar phenomena are grouped together and labelled to form categories. The labels, descriptions, or conceptual names of these categories are initially provisional or 'in vivo codes' (Glaser, 1978; Strauss, 1987) and may change as the process continues because the properties or characteristics of a category are progressively identified and developed based on data, while different new categories or subcategories may be identified.

There are also different ways of open coding. It is, for example, possible to follow a line-by-line analysis or to code by sentence or paragraph, but this depends on the kind of data and the objectives of the study. It is also usual to write the descriptions of categories or their conceptual names on the interviews, field notes, or other documents, while later the categories and the concepts pertaining to them are used as code notes. This generates a memo that may be useful when writing the final report.

Open coding is also called substantive coding and is considered to be conceptualizing at the first level of abstraction, where everything is coded in order to find patterns within the incidents in the data. These incidents are constantly compared and merged into categories and the researcher goes back and forth while comparing data, constantly modifying and renaming the categories. Open coding is extremely tedious since this is repeated for every new transcribed interview or new field note. In reality, it fractures the data.

Axial coding is undertaken when the researcher puts the data back together in new ways by making connections between categories and attempting to formulate one or more core categories. This is not just an attempt to relate several main categories to form theoretical formulations, but to develop core categories beyond the properties of the existing ones. Thus, several categories are related or organized to generate a core category where some form of relationship exists. The categories are called 'subcategories'. In reality, the data are taken apart in open coding, while in axial coding the data are put back together in a relational form or explanatory framework. This is called a 'paradigm model'. Use of this model can enable the researcher to think systematically about the data and to relate them in different complex ways denoting causal conditions, strategies, and consequences.

Axial coding is a complex process of inductive and deductive thinking involving different steps guided by continuously making comparisons and asking questions. 'In axial coding, the use of these procedures is more focused and geared toward discovering and relating categories in terms of a paradigm model' (Strauss and Corbin, 1990: 114), while the researcher looks continuously for additional properties of each category or new relationships among them. During this process, the researcher can keep track of the outcomes of coding by using logical diagrams or by stating the relationships in a memo, along with examples that support the statement of relationships.

Open coding and axial coding develop the basis for selective coding, which constitutes the final integration or the final leap between creating a list of concepts and producing a theory for explaining a phenomenon. Selective coding depends exclusively on open and axial coding. It is not independent because, even during the selective coding, open and axial coding may be used to fill in categories that need further refinement and development. Obviously, the final integration or selective coding is not very different from axial coding, but it constitutes a higher and more abstract level of analysis. Old field notes or the memos that the researcher produces can facilitate selective coding. Thus, the final integration takes place by weaving the fractured concepts into hypotheses that are put together in an explanatory framework, which emerges during the various steps of the CCAM process.

In the study described in this chapter, open and axial coding were used to develop categories and relationships among them for organizing students' responses in a meaningful way. All the interviews were qualitatively analyzed using the CCAM, while constantly comparing and revising the emerging categories. Finally, selective coding was used for the final integration of the identified categories of data, taking into consideration the purpose of the study. This integration resulted in a theory grounded in data that may explain the student's ability to participate in a simulated investigation during self-directed experimentation.

In the study, the CCAM not only guided the development of core categories and subcategories and the identification of their parameters and their relationships, but it also guided the development of scoring rubrics for the emerging variables of interest. The CCAM was also useful in classifying an answer into an appropriate level of a rubric by constantly comparing an answer with all other answers until the levels of a rubric and its properties were developed. The scoring rubrics were subsequently employed to quantify the data and to enable several statistical analyses.

Introduction to the project

The interview data used to illustrate the constant comparative analysis method (Glaser and Strauss, 1967) concern individual interviews with fourth and sixth grade students as they were investigating the functioning of an improvised device. This approach was based on the Klahr and Dunbar (1988, 2000) model and previous research (see Papageorgiou and Valanides, 2002, 2003; Valanides and Papageorgiou, 2001).

The Klahr and Dunbar (1988, 2000) model is an integrated model that incorporates domain-general strategies with domain-specific knowledge. This model sees scientific reasoning as problem solving that is characterized as a guided search and information-gathering task. The model is known as the scientific discovery as dual search (SDDS) model. According to this model, scientific discovery is accomplished by a dual search process. The search takes place in two related problem spaces: the hypothesis space and the experimental space.

Searching the hypothesis space involves the process of generation of hypotheses based on some knowledge about a content domain either as prior knowledge or as knowledge through experimentation. Searching the experimental space involves the performance of experiments that will yield interpretable results. Search in the two spaces is, however, mediated by a third process: the evidence evaluation process. Evaluation assesses the fit between theory and evidence and guides further research in both the hypothesis and the experimental spaces.

Original descriptions of the SDDS model highlighted the 'dual search', but more recent descriptions acknowledge the co-ordination and integration of all three components (Klahr, 2000; Klahr and Li, 2005). The focus on the evaluation of evidence phase has been influenced by the work of Kuhn (1989; Kuhn and Pearsall, 2000), who argue that the heart of scientific thinking relies on the skills of differentiating and co-ordinating theory (or hypotheses) with evidence. Thus, there has been a move toward research where participants take part in all three phases of scientific activity (Keselman, 2003; Schauble, 1996). These approaches are called 'self-directed experimentation research' (Zimmerman, 2000, 2007). In self-directed experimentation studies, individuals learn about a multi-variable causal system through activities initiated and controlled by the participants.

Within this framework, the project investigated fourth and sixth grade students' ability to conduct scientific investigations in a self-directed experimentation approach. The methodology is described and clarified as an example of sampling procedures and an approach involving collecting appropriate qualitative data using open-ended questions and interview data. The data generated through this project are used to illustrate the constant comparative method in order to show how qualitative data can be also quantified.

Methodology

Population and sample

The study involved two consecutive phases. Initially, ten elementary schools were randomly selected from a geographical district of Cyprus. Among the ten schools, six were from rural areas and four were from from a city. In each school, a fourth grade and a sixth grade class were randomly selected. The total number of students (248 fourth graders and 250 sixth graders) constituted the sample of the first phase. Among the 498 students, 250 were males (119 fourth graders and 131 sixth graders) and 248 were females (129 fourth graders and 119 sixth graders). Fourth grade students had an average age of 9.49 years (SD = 0.29) and sixth grade students had an average age of 11.46 years (SD = 0.27). These students completed a questionnaire that included three problems relating to control of variables and three other problems relating to combinatorial reasoning. Students' performance on the questionnaire had a range of scores (0–18) since a problem answer could score anything from 0 (totally incorrect answer) to 3 (totally correct).

The sample in the second phase consisted of 40 fourth and 40 sixth grade students with equal numbers of boys and girls. This sample was selected from the sample of the first phase, based on students' performance on the questionnaire and following a stratified sampling approach. This sample consisted of two different groups of students. The first group included students who had a score in the range of 4–7 (the low-achieving students) and the second group included those students who had a score in the range of 14–17 (the high-achieving students). These cut-off scores were decided based on the total distribution of students' scores on the questionnaire. The mean score on the questionnaire was 10.48 with a standard deviation of 4.01. Following these guidelines, 97 students were high-achieving and 90 students were low-achieving. Thus, four strata of students for each grade level were formed: high-achieving students (39 boys and 58 girls) and low-achieving students (46 boys and 44 girls). Finally, 20 students were randomly selected from each group of students. An equal number of students from each of the eight subgroups of students was randomly assigned to two experimental conditions. Students in both conditions were instructed to keep records of their experiments and results.

Collection of data

During the second phase, data were collected with individual interviews using two devices that have been developed for the purpose of investigating students' abilities during self-directed experimentation (Valanides and Papageorgiou, 2001). The first device (the simple device) consisted of a small wooden and totally closed box that had on its upper surface a small electric lamp, a switch, and a red push button. The second device (the main experimental device) consisted of a bigger wooden box that had on its upper surface eight small electric lamps in a line, five switches in another line below the lamps, and a red push button below the line of the five switches. The eight small electric lamps were sequentially numbered from 1 to 8 and each one had a different colour so that they could be easily differentiated both by their different number and their different colour as well. In this chapter we will only refer to the lamp by its number.

In both devices, the lamp(s), the switch(es), and the red push button were connected in a hidden circuit inside the box. Each student was in turn instructed to experiment with the simple device first and then with the main device to find out how the lamp of the simple device or the lamps of the main device could light up.

Procedures

When students came to the interview sessions, they were presented with the simple device consisting of one lamp, only one switch, and a red push button so they could become familiar with the environment of the investigation. The interviewer, in a game-like fashion, asked the students to formulate a hypothesis about how the lamp would light up and, through simple experimentation, the students could discover the role of the switch and the red push button that from now on will be called the 'tester'. In reality, the tester was a general switch in the circuit so that only by using the tester one could identify which position of the switch (i.e. up or down) would switch the lamp on. Then, the main device was presented and students were informed that the push button in the main device had the same function as in the simple device. They were then asked to form 'initial hypotheses' about the functioning of the main device and perform experiments in order to find out how the device functioned. The interview was terminated when the students managed to find out how the main device functioned or how the eight electric lamps could light up, or when a student was not able to solve the problem in the predetermined time of 60 minutes. The students were instructed to 'think aloud' prior to and after any experiment using the main device to formulate a hypothesis prior to any experiment and to proceed in a step-by-step fashion, keeping a record of their observations. Each interview was tape-recorded and was then transcribed verbatim for data analysis.

Evaluation of data

The questionnaire

For each of the six questions, students were asked to provide an answer and a brief explanation of their thinking. Each question was given a score of 1 (correct) or 0 (incorrect). Each justification was evaluated with a score of 0, 1, or 2, depending on the degree of its correctness. The levels of correctness were developed using the CCAM. Each of the six questions was initially analyzed within as many levels as possible, and then a scoring rubric consisting of four levels was used to organize students' responses and justifications for each of the six problems. Students assigned to the first level (totally incorrect answer and justification) had a score of 0 and those assigned to the fourth level of the rubric (totally correct answer and full justification) had a score of 3. Students who provided a correct answer but were unable to justify their answer or provided a partially correct explanation of their answer were assigned to the second and third levels and had a score of 1 or 2, respectively.

The interview data

The interview data were first analyzed qualitatively. For the qualitative analysis, protocols were created for each interview. On these protocols, the researcher noted all hypotheses that each student proposed and all experiments that the student performed to test his/her consecutive hypotheses. The hypotheses and the experiments were sequentially numbered for the convenience of the analysis.

For example, a student formulated the initial hypothesis with the statement that 'when all the switches are moved to the down position, then all the lamps will light up simultaneously', and then he performed the corresponding experiment for testing this hypothesis. This hypothesis was coded as H1 (hypothesis 1) and was marked on the protocol. Then on the next column of the protocol, the experiment was noted as EX1 (experiment 1): 11111 = lamp 7, indicating that when all the five switches moved down, then only lamp 7 lit up. (The five numbers correspond to the five switches. Number 1 represents the down position of the switch and number 0 represents the up position of the switch). Then, each interview was analyzed using the CCAM.

Initially, open coding was used to break down the interviews into discrete parts or incidents, such as stating a hypothesis, conducting an experiment, repeating an experiment, etc. These incidents were constantly compared with previous incidents. Based on their similarities or differences, they were grouped together to form separate categories of incidents. These categories of incidents were provisionally labelled, while progressively the labels took their final conceptual names. During axial coding and based on the previous categories of incidents, some core categories were formed based on certain relationships among the existing categories. Finally, during selective coding, six main categories were formed relating to students' investigation ability. In each of these categories, the subcategories were related to each one of the following main categories concerning the identification of the general switch, the identification of the dummy switch, the lighting of the lamps, the ability to control variables, combinatorial reasoning, and the co-ordination between theory and evidence. Finally, six different scoring rubrics were developed, corresponding to one of the six main categories of incidents (dependent variables) that were identified as components of students' investigation ability (IA).

Results

While the project generated many findings, for the purpose of this chapter, we will present only a few of the findings in an attempt to exemplify the CCAM. We show how CCAM was used in the identification of the general switch and we show how it was used when looking at the ability to co-ordinate evidence and theory.

Identification of the general switch (GS) of the main device

Using the CCAM, a rubric was developed to evaluate student performance relating to the GS of the main device. This rubric indicated the way students performed and it consisted of five mutually exclusive levels. The first (lowest) level of the rubric included the students who took into consideration only the positive experiments and excluded from consideration all the negative experiments, that is, those experiments (combination of switches) where the GS was up and thus no lamp could light on. For example, among several experiments, such as, 10000, 01000, 00100, 00010, 00001, only the third combination of switches (i.e. 00100) that could light up a lamp (lamp 2 in the present case) was taken into consideration, while the other experiments were totally ignored. Thus, the students were not able to identify the difference between switch 3 (the GS) and the other four switches. In reality, these students were unable to identify which was the GS, they did not recognize its different role in comparison with the other four switches, and they concluded instead that lighting any lamp was rather accidental.

The second level included the students who unsuccessfully tried to find out why, for certain combinations of the five switches, one of the eight lamps was on, but they did not identify the GS and its role. The students who were included in the other three levels identified the GS, but they exhibited certain differences. The total number of combinations for the five switches (up and down positions) is only 32 (2^5 combinations of switches), while, after understanding that switch 3 should be always in the down position for any lamp to light on, the experimental space is restricted to 16 (2^4 combinations of switches or experiments) experiments only.

Students in the fourth level identified the GS at the very end of their experimentation, but they did this after being prompted to carefully re-examine their recorded data. These students did not exhibit the ability to co-ordinate theory (their hypotheses) with their recorded data (experimental results). The final (fifth) level of the rubric included the students (interviewees) who succeeded in identifying the GS and its role at some point during the investigation, prior to the end of it, and without any help from the interviewer by co-ordinating their hypotheses (theory) with their recorded data (evidence). Table 4.1 presents the scoring rubric that was inductively developed and applied for evaluating students' ability to identify the GS of the main device.

An additional parameter was used to characterize this variable. Evidence for this parameter indicated whether the students who identified the GS gave a correct description of the GS, such as calling it the 'main switch' or the 'general switch' (score 1), or did not do so (score 0). Thus, students' performance on this variable had a range of scores from 0–5.

Table 4.1 Scoring rubric for evaluating students' performance relating to the GS of the main device

Levels of the rubric	Score
Students identified the GS by co-ordinating their hypotheses with their recorded data.	4
Students identified the GS after carefully re-examining their recorded data, while they did not exhibit during the investigation the ability to co-ordinate theory and evidence.	3
Students identified the GS, but they continued to perform experiments having the GS open and to expect to have light.	2
Students tried unsuccessfully to explain why they had positive and negative experiments, but they finally did not identify the GS and its role.	1
Students took into consideration only positive experiments and excluded from consideration all the negative experiments.	0

Ability to co-ordinate evidence and theory

Five different parameters were used for evaluating students' ability to co-ordinate evidence with theory. The first parameter concerned the identification of the GS of the device. Thus, students assigned at the lowest level (score 0) were not able to identify the GS or they identified it without co-ordinating their hypotheses with the collected data (i.e. after they have been prompted to re-examine the collected evidence). Students assigned to the second level (score 1) identified the GS by co-ordinating evidence and theory at some point of their investigation, but they did not take full advantage of the collected data from the beginning of the investigation. Students assigned to the third (highest) level of the rubric were always co-ordinating their evidence and hypotheses and identified the GS very early in their investigation (score 2).

The second parameter of this variable concerned the extent to which the students used information from negative experiments (i.e. experiments where the combinations of switches did not cause any lamp to light on). The rubric that was inductively developed for evaluating the specific parameter consisted of three qualitatively different levels. Students assigned to the lowest level of the rubric (score 0) did not pay any attention to negative experiments (i.e. no light) and did not form any hypothesis based on such information, which was totally ignored. Students assigned to the second level (score 1) did not always ignore information from negative experiments and formulated at least one hypothesis based on evidence from negative experiments. Finally, students assigned to the highest level (score 2) considered both positive and negative experiments as equally informative.

The third parameter concerned students' ability to modify their working hypotheses when the experimental evidence was contradictory. Students assigned to the lowest level of the three-level rubric, which was inductively developed, did not modify their hypotheses based on evidence contradicting them (score 0). On the contrary, students assigned to the second level were somehow able to identify at least one existing contradiction between their hypotheses and experimental evidence (score 1). Students assigned to the highest level of the rubric consistently changed their hypotheses based on contradictory evidence (score 2).

The fourth parameter concerned the extent to which students exhibited verification or confirmation bias. The respective rubric for evaluating this parameter consisted of only two levels (range of scores 0–1). Students assigned at the first level always attempted to perform only experiments confirming their hypotheses (score 0), while students assigned at the second level performed at least one experiment of negative control (score 1).

Finally, the fifth parameter concerned the number of main hypotheses that students proposed during the whole investigation. Students assigned at the lowest level of the three-level rubric, which was also inductively developed, proposed one to three main hypotheses, while students assigned at the second and third level of the rubric proposed four to seven or more than eight main hypotheses, respectively, and thus a range of 0–2 scores was used.

The ability to co-ordinate theory with evidence had a range of scores of 0–9 since it was the sum of the scores from the five different parameters that were used. Finally, students' investigation ability had a range of scores of 0–33 and consisted of the sum of scores of the six different variables that constituted it.

The whole process and the consequent quantification of data is time consuming and it is an extremely tedious task, but the results of this task are, in most cases, very useful and informative. For example, Table 4.2 presents the descriptive

Table 4.2 Descriptive statistics of students' quantified performance on the interviews

	Dependent variables	Range	Low abilities		High abilities		Total	
			Mean	SD	Mean	SD	Mean	SD
Fourth grade	Identification of the GS	0–5	0.55	1.23	1.80	1.74	1.18	1.62
	Co-ordinate theory and evidence	0–9	1.70	1.89	2.55	1.90	2.13	1.92
Sixth grade	Identification of the GS	0–5	0.70	0.92	3.50	1.32	2.10	1.81
	Co-ordinate theory and evidence	0–9	1.60	1.05	4.90	1.41	3.25	2.07
Total	Identification of the GS	0–5	0.62	1.08	2.65	1.75	1.64	1.77
	Co-ordinate theory and evidence	0–9	1.65	1.51	3.72	2.04	2.69	2.07

statistics for the dependent variables that were identified and evaluated during the analysis of the interviews.

Conclusion

The CCAM is a general research approach that provides guidelines for the systematic generation of theory from data regardless of whether it is qualitative or quantitative. Any research claiming to use the CCAM must follow specific grounded theory methodology. For example, an essential characteristic of the approach is the continuous cycle of collecting and analyzing data. Analysis of one set of data is continuously compared with another set, while emerging categories of data are continuously under examination and verification. Thus, the researcher continues to review the categories 'to ensure that data is not being forced into the categories, but rather that the categories represent the data' (Eliott and Lazenbatt, 2005: 50). This approach is followed during the different types of data coding (i.e. open, axial, and selective coding), while the dynamic relationship between data analysis and data collection guarantees that the research findings will more or less accurately represent the phenomena being studied. It is an inductive approach for generating theory that employs a continuous process of checking emerging categories, their parameters, and their properties by analyzing new data.

In summary, the CCAM involves inductive category coding and comparison of observed behaviours across categories (Goetz and LeCompte, 1981). As a consequence of this categorization, patterns are gradually revealed and constantly refined throughout the data collection and analysis process (Dye, Schatz, Rosenberg, and Coleman, 2000). The CCAM can also guide the development of scoring rubrics representing emerging categories or subcategories of data or observed behaviours (variables). Based on these rubrics, qualitative data can be quantified and treated statistically, providing a unique opportunity to integrate qualitative and quantitative research and shed more light on the phenomenon that is being studied.

Acknowledgements

I wish to thank Maria Papageorgiou and Charoula Angeli-Valanides for their assistance with and contributions to this chapter.

References

Dye, J. F., Schatz, I. M., Rosenberg, B. A., and Coleman, S. T. (2000) 'Constant comparison method: a kaleidoscope of data', *The Qualitative Report* [On-line serial], 4(1/2). http://www.nova.edu/ssss/QR/QR3-4/dye.html (accessed 1 May 2009)

Eliott, N. and Lazenbatt, A. (2005) 'How to recognise a "quality" grounded theory research study', *Australian Journal of Advanced Nursing*, 22(3): 48–52.

Glaser, B. G., (1978) *Theoretical Sensitivity*, Mill Valley, CA: Sociology Press.

Glaser, B. G., (2001) *The Grounded Theory Perspective I*, Mill Valley, CA: Sociology Press

Glaser, B. G. and Strauss, A. L. (1967) *The Discovery of Grounded Theory: Strategies for Qualitative Research*. Chicago, IL: Aldine Publications.

Goetz, J. P. and LeCompte, M. D. (1981) 'Ethnographic research and the problem of data reduction', *Anthropology and Education Quarterly*, 12: 51–70.

Keselman, A. (2003) 'Supporting inquiry learning by promoting normative understanding of multivariate causality', *Journal of Research in Science Teaching*, 40: 898–921.

Klahr, D. (2000) *Exploring science: The Cognition and Development of Discovery Processes*, Cambridge, MA: MIT Press.

Klahr, D. and Dunbar, K. (1988) 'Dual space search during scientific reasoning', *Cognitive Science*, 12:1–46.

Klahr, D. and Li, J. (2005) 'Cognitive research and elementary science instruction: from the laboratory, to the classroom, and back', *Journal of Science Education and Technology*, 4: 217–238.

Kuhn, D. (1989) 'Children and adults as intuitive scientists', *Psychological Review*, 96: 674–689.

Kuhn, D. and Pearsall, S. (2000) 'Developmental origins of scientific thinking', *Journal of Cognition and Development*, 1: 113–129.

Papageorgiou, M. and Valanides, N. (2002) 'Sixth-grade students' investigational strategies'. In A. Papastylianou (Ed.), Proceedings of the 2nd International Conference on Science Education (pp. 217–229), Nicosia, Cyprus: ARLO Ltd.

Papageorgiou, M. and Valanides, N. (2003) 'Primary school students' cognitive abilities during the investigation of a simulated problem', in P. Michaelides (ed.) *Proceedings of the 3rd Pan-Hellenic Conference for Science Education and Technology in Education*, Rethymno, Greece.

Schauble, L. (1996) 'The development of scientific reasoning in knowledge-rich contexts', *Developmental Psychology*, 32: 102–119.

Strauss, A. (1987) *Qualitative Analysis for Social Scientist*, Cambridge, UK: Cambridge University Press.

Strauss, A. L. and Corbin, J. (1990) *Basics of Qualitative Research: Grounded Theory Procedures and Techniques*, Newbury Park, CA: Sage.

Valanides, N. and Papageorgiou, M. (2001) 'How do sixth-grade students reason about science', in N. Valanides (Ed.), *Proceedings of the 1st IOSTE Symposium in Southern Europe-Science and technology education: Preparing future citizens.* Vol. II (pp. 400–408). Nicosia, Cyprus: Imprinta Ltd.

Zimmerman, C. (2000) 'The development of scientific reasoning skills', *Developmental Review*, 20: 99–149.

Zimmerman, C. (2007) 'The development of scientific thinking skills in elementary and middle school', *Developmental Review*, 27: 172–223.

Chapter 5

Using metamatrices to analyse learning from multiple data sources

Lindsey N. Conner

This chapter focuses on how research investigating students' learning about social and ethical issues in a final year high school biology class was developed from a research framework and how analytic tools called 'metamatrices' enabled multiple sources of data to be triangulated when analysing students' learning processes.

Introduction: a bioethics learning research context

This was a phenomenographical study that explored students' learning about social and ethical issues in a final year high school biology class. Through phenomenography I could develop an understanding of the relationship between the students' experiences of the teaching and learning with the quality of the learning outcomes. This phenomenographical study was informed by the interpretive epistemology of constructionism. The unit of work used individual and collaborative enquiry activities that were supported by a range of teaching and learning strategies to help twenty-one students identify their prior knowledge and develop knowledge of the biological, social and ethical issues and of learning processes, as required by the New Zealand school curriculum (Ministry of Education, 2007). The teaching and learning strategies included ways to allow students to select (i.e. evaluate) appropriate information and to allow them to become more aware of how they could investigate their topics. I assumed at the outset that, within the single class under investigation, there would be a wide range of individual differences, both in terms of prior knowledge, interpretations of tasks, information and learning approaches and consequent learning outcomes. The aim of this study was to describe how the intervention was perceived in a common sense across the class and how it was interpreted differently by individuals, that is, how members of the class differed from each other in unique ways as far as possible. I used a range of interconnected interpretive methods to try to understand the experiences of the students in this class. These included: classroom observations, questionnaires, pre- and post-unit interviews and a range of artefacts generated as part of the learning process, such as brainstorm sheets, journal entries and essays. These were triangulated with my participant observations of classroom activities and interactions.

I used a case study reporting mode to frame my interpretations of whole class changes and individual characteristics (Conner, 2002). Metamatrices were used to triangulate numerous data sources in order to provide some insight into students' learning processes.

Research framework

Crotty (1998) outlines four elements that need to be considered in developing a research outline: epistemology; theoretical perspective; methodology; and method. Each of these elements informs one another. For example, the epistemology justifies the assumptions we bring to the research. In particular, what kind of knowledge do we believe will be attained by our research? What should observers make of the outcomes? The epistemology is the theory of knowledge embedded in the theoretical perspective, which impacts on the methodology. The theoretical perspective is the philosophical position that informs the methodology. It provides a context for the research process and grounds it in logic and criteria. The methodology is the plan, action or strategy used to design and formulate the choice and use of particular methods. The methods are the techniques or procedures used to get and analyse data related to the research question(s).

For this study I used a constructionist epistemology (Papert and Harel, 1991) and my theoretical perspective was interpretive phenomenology (Bogdan and Bilken, 2007). In designing the research, it was clear that outcomes would not necessarily provide a clear picture of what individuals experienced during the unit of work, especially since I intended to use a naturalistic research paradigm. Further, Denzin and Lincoln state that:

> subjects, or individuals, are seldom able to give full explanations of their actions or intentions; all they can offer are accounts, or stories about what they did and why. No single method can grasp all the subtle variations in ongoing human experience.
>
> (2000: 19)

Consequently, a range of interconnected interpretive methods was used to try to unpack the experiences of the students in the class. I used a case study reporting mode to frame individual characteristics and changes that applied to the whole class.

I have organised this chapter according to the phases in the research process outlined by Denzin and Lincoln (2000: 20). In the first phase, I outline the interpretive epistemology of constructionism. This section gives a summary of the premises that framed and guided my research. Then, I discuss my research strategies, which included the study design, the theoretical perspective of phenomenological studies, how my study was situated in naturalistic enquiry and use of case studies as my methodology.

I explain how the various data sources were analysed and, in particular, how the data sources were combined for each student in metamatrices (Miles and

Huberman, 1984) to allow me to visually compare data sources and students for trends in learning characteristics across the group(s) and to see individual subtleties and peculiarities.

A constructionist epistemology

A constructionist epistemology allowed the building of an understanding of how features of the tasks – whether students utilised ideas given by the teacher or text materials particularly in their essays, students' evaluation of the usefulness of ideas and students' perceptions of their own learning needs – dynamically interact within the classroom. What the participants revealed about their experiences, what they said influenced these experiences and my observations linking these to what students actually did allowed me to interpret what happened and why it may have happened (Conner and Gunstone, 2004; Conner, 2007). The ideas presented here are very much embedded in the context of teaching and learning about bioethics.

The class was used as a case study for describing the overall approach: students' thinking about bioethical issues and students' thinking about learning. Additionally, to delve deeper into the nuances and characteristics of learners, I developed five individual case studies (Conner, 2002).

Phenomenography

The unit of work, in a research sense in this study, was considered the phenomenon and the set of activities and experiences gained by the students were considered elements of this phenomenon. Phenomenography is a research method that is used to map the qualitatively different ways in which people perceive phenomena (Bogdan and Bilken, 2007). It involves investigating reflections on people's experiences and their conceptualisations and understanding of the phenomena. Creswell (1998: 51) states that: 'A phenomenological study describes the meaning of the lived experiences for several individuals about a concept or phenomenon.'

Phenomenography as a research approach grew out of research in the early 1970s that was driven by the need for more in-depth approaches to describing the meaning behind the variation in students' learning. The basic idea of the phenomenographic approach is to describe individual's perceptions as faithfully as possible. The underlying intent of the research is to disclose different ways of seeing, experiencing or understanding. It is the ideas about the phenomena (e.g. the interactions between people and concepts and learning processes) which are important rather than trying to precisely determine a truism or reality.

Phenomenography is very useful in investigating teaching and learning because the intent is to develop an understanding of the relationship between the students' experiences of the teaching and learning with the quality of the learning outcomes. It uses naturalistic enquiry methodologies that focus on discovering meaning for a particular context (Merriam, 1988). Due to the complexity of most educational contexts, collecting and analysing real-life data can be messy and disjointed and may require creative ways to systematically make it trustworthy, compelling and creditable since the outcomes and ambiguities cannot be predicted.

Naturalistic enquiry

A naturalistic enquiry approach meant that the data were gathered in the classroom during the lessons planned for the unit of work on bioethics with twenty-one high school students. This setting provided a rich source for descriptions of the factors that influenced learning. The characteristics of naturalistic enquiry outlined by Lincoln and Guba (1985) have been translated to explain the characteristics of naturalistic enquiry of this project:

- A natural classroom setting was used since the phenomenon was the teaching and learning of the bioethical issues associated with cancer.
- The students and the teacher were the participants for data gathering.
- Qualitative methods were chosen because they were adaptable to dealing with the multiplicity of factors and the unknown elements that we anticipated emerging from the nature of the classroom context.
- I purposefully used a specific class because of my previous teaching relationship with them. I had previously taught 12 of the 16 volunteers in the study.
- The data were analysed inductively to derive categories from the sources so that the multiple interpretations could be documented.
- The guiding substantive theory emerged from the data. No a priori theory could include all the interpretations that would be likely in this particular context.
- What became important, in terms of the design, was determined, to some extent, by what happened, and therefore what needed to be followed up. During the research process, I needed to respond to emerging trends or to check with individuals about how I was interpreting their learning char-acteristics or what I was observing. This involved changing the emphasis on some questions during the post-unit interview, to focus more on learning strategies.
- In some respects, the open nature of the interviews allowed me to negotiate the meanings and clarify them with the informants.
- I used case studies for reporting the characteristics of learners and their learning.
- The data were interpreted ideographically because they were peculiar to this context.
- I did not intend to make broad generalisations, but rather the aim was to derive tentative applications of the findings for learning in enquiry and in socio-scientific contexts.
- The credibility of this research approach was determined by the subtleties it exposed, and the degree to which it was plausible and linked with previous findings.

My own tacit knowledge of the students was important as well as the propositional knowledge gained from data gathering. I was aware of some of their behaviours, strengths and limitations from having previously observed them for three years as a teacher of some of their classes. This alone gave me valuable background knowledge and allowed me to interact with the students and interpret their responses in ways that an outside researcher would not have been able to do.

As a participant observer, I took part in approximately three-quarters of the lessons in this unit of work. Mostly, I sat at the back of the classroom and took notes. Occasionally, I would answer questions from both the teacher and the students. I also asked questions and prompted the students during class work sessions as I wandered around the room while making observations. I recorded my field observations in a notebook that was divided into whole class observations and labelled sections for each of the sixteen participants. The notes included behaviours of the students and the teacher, as well as some comments they made during class sessions. I also recorded some classroom instruction sessions and classroom conversations using a small dictaphone that was placed either on the desk in front of me or in my pocket if I walked around the room. Therefore, it was unobtrusive as far as the students and the teacher were concerned. Mostly, the participants were unaware of when I had it turned on or off. I consider that the presence of the dictaphone had very little impact on the behaviour of the students or the teacher.

As soon as possible after each observation, I transcribed the classroom activities and annotated my notes. I also wrote questions and memos to myself to remind me of aspects I wanted to explore in more depth with individual students in the post-unit interviews. I also wrote comments and questions in students' journals to give them feedback on their journal writing. This was partly because the teacher did not have time to do this after most sessions and partly because I wanted to monitor the use of journals so as to offer guidance and support for students.

The effects of my presence on the outcome of the unit of work are unknown. No doubt there were advantages in having an extra teacher to answer questions. The students were expected to work independently, but they also expected me to respond if they asked me a question.

Case studies

Case studies are examinations of specific situations or phenomenon (Merriam, 1988). Yin states:

> A case study is an empirical inquiry that investigates a contemporary phenomenon within its real-life context, especially when the boundaries between phenomenon and context are not clearly evident.
>
> (1994: 13)

Interpretations of case studies are always couched in the contexts in which they are observed. Of prime importance is what can be learned from the case(s). I used the case study method because I deliberately wanted to uncover contextual factors.

Cases provide examples of what happened and why it happened. In this study, there were several layers to the case study approach; each layer sought to describe the cases in more detail. On the first level, I used the class as one case. The material was condensed in order to observe trends relative to student achievement in their essays. On the second level, to gain a more detailed description, I clustered students into five groups that represented categories related to their essay marks and sought commonalities about the ways in which students approached their learning within these groups. On the third level, for an even more detailed analysis of learning characteristics, I randomly selected one individual from each of the five groups as specific cases to preserve the integrity of the source material and to illustrate how these students were similar and contrasted with the other students (Conner, 2002).

In order to get a more holistic understanding of the case(s), I triangulated multiple sources of data as recommended by Smith and Deemer (2000). Triangulation sanctions the 'criss-crossing' of all the information in multiple directions to allow for convergence of the data sources (Yin, 1994). This allowed me to identify the different ways the phenomenon was seen or interpreted by the students.

Triangulation also helped to establish internal reliability of the findings (Merriam, 1988). What people think they are doing, what they say they are doing, what they appear to others to be doing and what in fact they are doing may be quite different. Therefore, it was important to consider multiple data sources to gain an overview and authenticate the claims about the cases.

Analysis of data

No one method of data analysis would be able to describe this intervention adequately. For this reason, I have employed a multi-method approach that combines microanalysis of tasks and cognitive behaviour and a detailed investigation of students' knowledge and evaluations, as well as the teacher's understandings and my own experience. The overall research question for this study was: How can learning be enhanced in a bioethical context? The specific sub-questions are given in Table 5.1. This table also provided a framework for checking that there would be multiple data sources to triangulate for each research question. It shows the links between the multiple data sources and the research questions and indicates how these were analysed. In the following sections, I elaborate on each data collection method to provide background about them and give more detail about how the sources were analysed.

Table 5.1 Links between the research questions, the data sources and data analysis

Research questions	Research objectives	Data sources	Analysis
1. Can students' views about social and ethical issues be broadened?	To investigate how Year 13 students perceive the 'biological concepts' and 'social, ethical and biological implications' of cancer.	Pre-questionnaires and post-unit	Categorise answers to both pre- and post-questionnaires and compare.
		Brainstorm responses based on classroom activity	Categorise brainstorm answers.
		Journal entries	Record and categorise comments/ conversations during class work sessions.
		Essays	Initiate and monitor records in learning journals.
		Post-unit interviews	Collect and mark essays.
			Categorise post-unit interviews according to types of issues.
2. Which activities influenced student thinking about the social and ethical issues associated with cancer?	To analyse students' and teachers' comments about different types of activities.	Journal entries	Categorise all data sources according to activity.
		Post-unit interviews	
	To use classroom observations for reliability.	Teacher interview	Re-categorise comments and other sources according to emergent themes.
		Observation notes	

Research question	Purpose	Data sources	Analysis
3. What kind of relationship is there between students' prior knowledge of bioethical issues and the content of their essays?	To evaluate students' prior knowledge about social and ethical issues.	Pre-unit questionnaire	Document specific issues written in pre-unit questionnaire in comparison with specific issues mentioned in the essay.
	To evaluate the social and ethical issues mentioned in essays and compare them with the prior knowledge.	Essays	
4. Which activities helped in developing learning?	To analyse students' and teachers' comments about different types of activities.	Journal entries	Categorise all data sources according to activity.
		Post-unit interviews	Re-categorise comments and other sources according to emergent themes.
	To use classroom observations for reliability.	Teacher interview	
		Observation notes	
5. What kind of relationship, if any, is there between students' prior knowledge of learning strategies and their use in researching and essay writing?	To investigate whether students can identify strategies/ approaches that make their learning more effective.	Pre-unit interviews	For each student, categorise learning strategies according to whether students knew or used them.
		Post-unit interviews	
	To identify own learning needs.	Journal entries	Analyse journals for statements and questions that might indicate learning strategies.
	To plan, monitor and evaluate their work.	Observation notes	Analyse essays for planning and text structure and allocate marks.

Table 5.1 continued

Research questions	Research objectives	Data sources	Analysis
6. What evidence is there that the intervention helped the students to be self-monitoring and self-regulating in their learning?	To analyse student performance in planning, researching, note making, self-questioning, summarising, editing and writing.	Post-unit interviews	Analyse journals for questions or planning, monitoring or evaluation evidence.
		Journal entries	
		Observation notes	Categorise planning, monitoring or evaluation and other evidence of self-reflection in post-unit interviews.
		Essays	
			Analyse essays for evidence of planning, researching, self-questioning, summarising, critical analysis.
7. What other factors, regarding the teaching and learning environment in this context, might influence the way in which students learn about social and ethical issues?		Post-unit interviews	Categorise factors and collate comments mentioned by both students and the teacher.
		Teacher interview	
		Observation notes	Add in contextual factors noted in the classroom observations.

Questionnaires

Categories for answers to questions were inductively generated from the students' responses. Each student's answers were allocated to a particular category. These categories were modified and extended as the answers were tabulated. The categories were checked independently to verify their clarity and coverage of the responses. The number of categories given by each student for questions was tabulated for both pre- and post-unit questionnaires. These were compared to indicate changes in thinking about the biological, social and ethical issues and implications by the end of the unit.

The purpose of the post-unit questionnaire was to illicit students' knowledge of the issues and implications at the end of the unit of work. One student did not take the post-unit questionnaire very seriously. She left blank spaces for some of the answers even though she had completed answers for these questions in the pre-unit questionnaire. Therefore, the value of the post-unit questionnaire as a research instrument for this student is questionable. Whether this problem extends to other students is unknown, but it is unlikely since for many students, the number of categories increased compared with the pre-unit questionnaire. This suggests that they did in fact treat it seriously.

Brainstorm sheets

Items written on the A3 pages were coded according to the following categories: types of cancer, causes, biological effects, treatments and social and ethical issues. The number of items in each category was derived from group totals. All of the students who contributed to a particular group for the brainstorm activity were given the totals derived from their group.

Pre-unit interviews

Quotations were selected from the interviews and electronically categorised according to students' perceptions as to what they did regarding various aspects of their learning. The categories were: 'good at' (perception of ability); reason for being 'good at' (perception of control); 'needed help with' (awareness of weaknesses); reason for needing help (perception of control); achievement expectations; planning; ease of essay writing; discrimination of information; evaluation of essays; learning mode preference (individualistic or group); help-seeking characteristics; self-control over learning; and distracters.

These were then compared with other data sources. The learning strategies were not pre-determined. Instead, students' knowledge and use of learning strategies were gauged indirectly by interpreting the students' responses and categorised accordingly.

Post-unit interviews

The post-unit interview answers contributed to many aspects of the overall data analyses. The first phase was a selection procedure carried out within each interview transcript. For research question 1, I searched for quotations to illustrate students' ideas about the biological, social and ethical issues. These were categorised into multiple themes. Answers to the interview question 'Have your ideas about what ethical ideas are, changed?' were used to determine if they perceived there was a change in their thinking.

For research questions 2 and 4, I selected quotations and categorised them by activity. Not all students commented on all activities since they were asked to identify activities from the prompt list that they thought were helpful. The second phase of analysis involved sorting the quotations within the categories for similarities and differences to derive a pool of meanings for each classroom activity. These were then sorted so that those with similar themes were grouped together. Quotations were also categorised in the metamatrices for learning characteristics. This is explained in the section on metamatrices.

Journal entries

Journals were analysed for evidence of thinking about the biological, social and ethical issues. Entries that indicated planning, monitoring or evaluation were also selected and entered into the metamatrices. The number of questions written by students in their journals about content or processes for learning was tabulated.

Essays

Essays were marked according to a marking schedule that had been negotiated with the students. Since producing an essay was the intended product outcome of the unit of work (and would be the form required for their end of year examination), students were grouped into the following categories according to the quality of their essays: 'invisible product', 'satisfactory product' and 'quality product'. Students in the 'invisible product' category did not hand in a final essay. Students in the 'satisfactory product' category produced essays with a range of marks of 13–24/40. Students in the 'quality product' category wrote essays that gained a mark between 26–32/40. Those students who wrote more than one essay, as a practice exercise, in either the 'satisfactory product' or the 'quality product' categories were put into separate sub-categories of 'multiple satisfactory' and 'multiple quality'.

Metamatrices

Metamatrices have been used by a number of researchers to collate and analyse different data sets (Miles and Huberman, 1984). These provide a means for visually collating and displaying key elements from multiple data sources. In this study, a separate metamatrix or master chart was constructed for each of the sixteen students who volunteered to be part of the study (there were twenty-one students in the class). Using metamatrices allowed multiple data sources related to students' learning, to be collated. These sources included quotations from pre- and post-unit interviews, extracts from students' learning journals (in particular, the number of questions students wrote in their learning journals to help drive their enquiries), observational notes and essay results. It enabled me to link individual's learning tendencies to their learning outcomes.

The grid categories for the metamatrices went through several iterative changes because of the need to sort within categories and to cluster some of the original ones. As Miles and Huberman (2002) indicate, iteration is essential because often the analysis involves data reduction and finding ways to display data effectively or in different ways. This requires also being open to new categories as the analysis emerges. It is worth recording the changes as they are made as sometimes original categories are the ones that turn out to be the most useful. Critical friends who can check through your categorisation may see your data differently and be able to make helpful suggestions regarding categorisations or interpretations of the links or ambiguities in the data sources. The final main categories were: ability perception; perception of essay writing; planning; researching; essay writing; seeks help; monitoring of progress; self-questioning; and other evidence of reflection. The metamatrix for Liz, one of the five students used as an individual case, is given in Table 5.2 as an example. Where there was no evidence for a category from a data source, the cell was left blank. Sometimes in this kind of data analysis it is not possible to have a complete data set.

The data represented in the metamatrices allowed me to cross-reference my sources to determine if students knew of learning strategies and whether they used them. This relates to the idea that often participants can tell you what they ought to be doing, but it may be very different from what they actually do as evidenced from their classroom contributions or other outputs. Cross-referencing data in this way adds to the trustworthiness and credibility of the findings. Often, it was also necessary to keep track of more detailed aspects of the data sources. As shown in the metamatrix for Liz (see Table 5.2), the quotations were linked through numbers below each respective set of categories in each table. The lead-in question or comment from the research was also included to provide the context of the answer.

In order to identify specific learning strategies, the metamatrices were analysed and new tables were created for each student for each of the targeted learning strategies. The strategies were divided into three major categories: declarative; procedural; and metacognitive awareness and control. Each of these was further subdivided according to the categories outlined by Derry (1990).

Table 5.2 Metamatrix for Liz showing data source references for learning characteristics

	Ability perception			Perception of essay writing	
	'good at'	'help with'	mark prediction	easy	difficult
Interview I	listening discussions❶ dictation	with the formula for writing essays❷	60		trouble linking stuff and connecting the introduction to the main body of the essay
Interview 2	links mark with effort		motivated by marks❸		
Journal					
Class observation					

Table 5.3 Data for Liz relating to planning and researching

	Planning		Researching		
	Plans use of strategies	Planning structure for essay	Uses key words or questions	Summarises (own words)	Multiple sources of information
Interview I			key points	key sentences❺ aware of T and T❻	
Interview 2		kind of❹	no, it doesn't help		
Journal					
Class observation					
Essay					

❶ Researcher (interview 1): So in terms of thinking about how you learn, what are you good at?

Liz (interview 1): Not essays. I'm probably better at listening and taking stuff in than reading stuff and then regurgitating it. But I am better at regurgitation than thinking for myself.

Liz (interview 1): I work well with discussions because I work well with bouncing ideas off other people. Dictation, that works well because I can take my own notes.

❷ Liz (interview 1): I am not any good at writing essays but I've got better as I have had to write essays in the last few weeks. But I think it is probably because I have never really written essays that you are supposed to. I have just written, not with any formula, I need help with the formula of essays. And I have to unpack the question, which I find hard usually unless I'm told exactly what to unpack.

❸ Liz (interview 2): I've had to get better because I have to get those marks in bursary. Before this year, I hadn't really tried. From 6th to 7th form was a huge jump. Like last year we didn't have to write an essay in 6th form Biology.

❹ Researcher (interview 2): What about planning your essay overall, how did you do that or did you do that?
Liz (interview 2): Kind of. I started to plan it but then I ended up just writing it. I thought it was a lot easier.

❺ Liz (interview 2): I have been doing it for a while. I usually need a bit more than just a few key words. I need key sentences.

Table 5.4 Data for Liz relating to essay writing achievement and seeking help

	Essay writing			Seeks help
	Structure (it flows)	Content coverage	By marks	
Interview 1				Yes, from the teacher and peers.
Interview 2				
Journal				
Class observation				21/10 Seeks clarification of cell structure pictures (linked to journal question 'What do cancer cells look like?').
				27/10 Is willing to take risks to clarify under-standing during class sessions. Contributes to teacher's questions.
				Makes multiple attempts at draft essay with response to feedback from teacher and peers.
Essay	essay 1:10/10 essay 2:7/10	essay 1:22/30 essay 2:15/30	essay 1:32/40 essay 2:22/40	

Table 5.4 continued

Reflective processes			
	Monitoring progress	*Self-questioning*	*Other evidence of reflection*
Interview 1	Choice of using strategy, see summarising		Hypothesises that motivation may be an issue ❼
			Independence: 'I am better at figuring stuff out for myself.'
Interview 2	Linked what needed with question ❸	Checks for relevancy in essay ❾	'It gets easier the more you write.'
	I know when I know it ❿	Thinks about what to include in essay	'I kind of found it hard to write in my own journal. The things I asked weren't really important. I didn't really care about the answers. The prompters weren't useful.'
	Teacher feedback ①	'Nothing specifically, not enlightened on something. When some information came up, it made me think in terms of the essay.'	'I think I'm a bit too reliant on my own brain. I think oh, I'll remember that, so I don't write it down. It would be better for me to write things down.'
			'I've got to organise my time better. If it was part of internal assessment it would be more motivating.'
Journal	4 statements of things learnt	14 questions Answered 2 in journal	'I believe the most effective way to prevent cancers is to educate people especially against smoking. Encourage exercise, use of sunscreen etc. raise awareness especially in young children and make the problem seem more urgent.'
Class observation			No recorded evidence.
Essay			No specific examples.

⑥ Researcher (interview 2): What about the Trash and Treasure activity?
Liz (interview 2): I was kind of already aware of that. Sometimes I blindly copy. Sometimes it's better when people dictate notes but when you have them on an overhead, you tend to copy everything. He's told us during the year not to write down everything, and gives us a choice.

⑦ Researcher (interview 1): But you said you take things in by listening?
Liz (interview 1): Listening as well because I can remember heaps of what Mr S said about bumble bees and stuff, irrelevant stuff. Maybe it is just that it is interesting. And I remember a lot when he tells me stuff, I know it is the same in chemistry I remember it heaps better than if I just have to learn it myself. Maybe it is just lack of motivation. I don't know.

⑧ Liz (interview 1): I just read it and picked out bits that went for one of the headings of the questions.

⑨ Researcher (interview 2): How do you know if you've written a good essay?
Liz (interview 2): I've done it! (*completed it*) . . . it used to be . . . now I check over it.
Researcher: What sort of things (*do you check for*)?
Liz: Just that I keep it relevant, don't go off on a tangent.

⑩ Liz (interview 1): I'm not really a marks orientated person. I know when I know it and that's good enough for me.

① Liz (interview 2): You know what your essay lacked and what to put in next time. I didn't have time to do more than one essay, but I had lots of other things to do at this time of the year. It might've been better at a different time of the year.
Notes: She had never used a journal before. Confident in ability. (co) 21/10, 27/10 Attention seeking. Chips in with examples of friends during class discussions. Sent essay answer from end of year exam to researcher.

Declarative strategies were divided into locating and focusing, schemas and elaboration. Locating and focusing information includes using text structure to identify important points, underlining or highlighting important words or phrases or using key words or key phrases to search information. Schemas include the use of concept mapping or any graphic organisation to structure, order or rank text, the use of mnemonics such as Generalisation, Explanation Example (GEE) and visualisation techniques for memorising. Elaboration includes explaining ideas (e), answering questions and using generative note making strategies (q) and summarising or paraphrasing (s). Procedural strategies were subdivided into generalisation, discrimination and practice/effort. Generalisation strategies are those where summaries or overviews of particular ideas are constructed. Discrimination strategies are those where information is sorted according to relevance or importance. Practice/effort related to whether the students perceived that practice or effort was important in writing a good essay. Metacognitive strategies included planning, monitoring, asking evaluative questions and making decisions about the learning process. Planning included setting goals or making an intention for the enquiry process clear. For some, this involved writing lists of content that needed to be investigated or included in essays, making headings or writing a flow chart for the structure of their essays. Monitoring included self-checking on progress, re-reading material if it was not completely understood and using information from peer-checking or setting priorities. Asking evaluative questions was indicated by journal entries or gauged from self-reports during interviews. Asking questions is also very much a part of planning and monitoring, whereas control aspects of metacognition relate to making decisions about the learning process and acting on these decisions. Control aspects were linked to whether students used the declarative, procedural or metacognitive strategies.

Part of the research was to design and evaluate the activities that were part of the intervention unit of work. It was also important to consider: the teaching process; the students' experiences and how those experiences (or reflections on them) linked to their perceptions; and understandings of both the content and processes of learning. Also, because research into teaching and learning has shown that what students do in the classroom is closely linked to their perceptions of the requirements of the learning task (Biggs and Moore, 1993), it was important to use the students' perspectives as a research tool. Where possible, I also used the teacher's perspectives and my own observations to expand on these inter-pretations.

Summary

This chapter has provided a description of the research process used in a particular study that focused on students' learning processes. I chose to use the students' experiences in a classroom as an ecologically valid way of assessing how activities were perceived and implemented. A constructionist epistemology allowed the building of insight into how features of tasks, authority, evaluation and students' perceptions dynamically interact within the classroom. I used the range of methods and analyses to describe how learning was achieved:

- by groups and individuals as well as enabled by elements of the learning context;
- from the individual students' perspectives, using interviews and classroom observations rather than large-scale approaches;
- by relating processes and products rather than just products to personal characteristics;
- by examining learning processes (i.e. knowledge and use of specific learning strategies) through a range of data sources.

This chapter outlined a framework for describing and interpreting the multiple methods and multiple sources of information that were important for cross-checking and establishing the knowledge and use of learning strategies. The disadvantage of using metamatrices is that they may become cumbersome.

The categories originally chosen may not be applicable to all cases. Therefore, several rounds of iteration may be needed to derive categories that are appropriate. However, the collation of data sources into metamatrices provides a visual method for displaying, linking and cross-checking data sources for particular categories. It could be applied to a range of data sources in a range of educational contexts.

References

Biggs, J. B. and Moore, P. J. (1993) *The Process of Learning*, Third edition, Melbourne: Prentice Hall.

Bogdan, R. and Bilken, S. K. (2007) *Qualitative Research for Education: An Introduction to Theory and Methods*, Fifth edition, Boston: Allyn and Bacon/Pearson.

Conner, L. N. (2002) 'Learning about social and ethical issues in a biology class', unpublished PhD thesis, Monash University, Melbourne, Australia.

Conner, L. N. (2007) 'Cueing metacognition to improve researching and essay writing in a final year high school biology class', *Research in Science Education*, 37 (1): 1–16.

Conner, L. and Gunstone, R. F. (2004) 'Conscious knowledge of learning: accessing learning strategies in a final year high school biology class', *International Journal of Science Education*, 26 (12): 1427–1443.

Creswell, J. W. (1998) *Qualitative Inquiry and Research Design: Choosing Among Five Traditions*, Thousand Oaks: Sage.

Crotty, M. (1998) *The Foundations of Social Research: Meaning and Perspective in the Research Process*, Sydney: Allen and Unwin.

Denzin, N. K. and Lincoln, Y. S. (2000) 'Introduction: the discipline and practice of qualitative research', in N. K. Denzin, and Y. S. Lincoln, (eds) *Handbook of Qualitative Research*, Second edition (pp. 1–28), Thousand Oaks: Sage.

Derry, S. J. (1990) 'Learning strategies for acquiring useful knowledge', in B. F. Jones and L. Idol (eds) *Dimensions of Thinking and Cognitive Instruction* (pp. 347–379), Hillsdale: Lawrence Erlbaum.

Lincoln, Y. S. and Guba, E. G. (1985) *Naturalistic Inquiry*, Beverley Hills, CA: Sage.

Merriam, S. (1988) *Case Study Research In Education*, San Francisco, CA: Jossey-Bass.

Miles, M. B. and Huberman, A. M. (1984) *Qualitative Data Analysis: A Source Book of New Methods*, Beverley Hills, CA: Sage

Miles, M. B. and Huberman, A. M. (2002) 'Reflections and advice', in A. M. Huberman and M. B. Miles (eds) *The Qualitative Researcher's Companion*, Thousand Oaks: Sage.

Ministry of Education (2007) *The New Zealand Curriculum*, Wellington, NZ: Ministry of Education.

Papert, S. and Harel, I. (1991) 'Situating constructionism', in S. Papert and I. Harel (eds) *Constructionism*, Chicago: Ablex. Available HTTP: <http://www.papert.org/works. html> (accessed 23 February 2009).

Smith, J. K. and Deemer, D. K. (2000) 'The problem of criteria in the age of relativism', in N. K. Denzin and Y. S. Lincoln (eds) *Handbook of Qualitative Research*, Second edition (pp. 877–896), Thousand Oaks: Sage.

Yin, R. (1994) *Case Study Research: Design and Methods*, Second edition, Thousand Oaks: Sage.

Chapter 6

Narrative interrogation

Constructing parallel stories

Bev France

The methodology of narrative analysis presumes that personal narratives are organised into implicitly evaluative schemas that help the speaker to construct and understand their life as well as that of others (Linde, 1993). One of the criticisms levelled at the coding of qualitative data is that such coding tends to fragment the data. The strength of narrative analysis is that there is an emphasis on the whole and the narrative is able to encompass all the ramifications of this situation. For example, the narrative should sit not only within the lifespan of the storyteller, but it should also indicate how the episodes making up the story are interconnected (Bryman, 2004). In this chapter I describe the use of connective stories as an outcome of a research activity and illustrate the merit of this research methodology. Narrative enquiry is not simply an account of what happened; the focus of narrative enquiry is on how people make sense of what happened. To show how to carry out an analysis so that such a narrative can be constructed, I use data generated through a project that involved six scientists, who recount their school memories of science, and I provide teachers' responses to such accounts. There are limitations with this mode of enquiry and I identify them and provide advice with regard to how to lessen the negative effects.

Introduction

Last week I reread Janet Frame's short story 'You are now entering the human heart' (Frame, 1983), where the narrator painted a vivid picture of that sad, tired time at the end of a sightseeing day where the magic of science displays are waning and decisions are made by visitors to leave such an experience for another day.

In this story an experience with a well-worn and scruffy model of the human heart was passed over for a visit to the nearby natural history museum. There, a lesson on the conservation of snakes was being taught by a museum attendant to an elementary class and their teacher. As she watched, the museum curator dragooned the elderly teacher into demonstrating that she was not afraid of this snake. She observed the terror on the teacher's face when she was confronted with the challenge of the 'harmless' grass snake being wrapped round her neck. Not only was she expected to endure this torture, but the museum attendant discounted her courage by telling the children that her action was not brave because the snake was harmless. The children watched with fascination as their teacher's terror was cruelly exposed by the museum curator. It was left to the reader to surmise that this aging woman's heart had been broken by this humiliating experience.

The story has haunted me all week. Frame's skill in allowing me to see, without explanation, an aspect of the human condition directly related to my pedagogy. It reminded me of how less is more when telling a story. As Connelly and Clandinin (1990) remind us, the strength of narrative is to provide an opportunity to create further meaning for the reader. They describe this characteristic as the 'restorying' quality of the narrative. Frame's apparently simple description of two episodes occurring at a science and a natural history museum provided this reader with the space to construct her own story and place herself in a similar situation.

My snake experience involved a small boa constrictor that was brought to school by a pupil. My image as a biology teacher fascinated by the animal world was tested as I allowed the animal to coil round my arm. I believe I passed the bravery test when demonstrating my 'relaxed' interest in front of this class of 13-year-olds in this central London school, but I still remember the rise of panic as the boa squeezed my arm while I gingerly held its head. As this story reminded me, the fabric of a teaching persona can be very fragile.

Of course there are lots of pedagogical issues that I could discuss about this incident, but for me the most important is the power of spaces within a narrative. Such spaces can establish strong connections with the reader. For this discussion, I focus on the process of developing a narrative and use a research project that focuses on the stories that scientists recount of their school memories of science, and teachers' responses to such accounts, as a context for this description of the construction of science education narratives. I propose that in common with Frame's short story, the goal of this research is the construction of narrative that can make connections with the reader – in this case, teachers of science.

There are two questions that need to be posed at this stage. Why construct connective stories as an outcome of a research activity? If one becomes convinced of the merit of this research methodology then there is another question to answer: How to carry out an analysis so that such a narrative can be constructed?

Justifying the construction of narratives

What is a narrative? It is certainly not a chronology of events, but instead a narrative can be considered to be a methodological device that can interpret experiences or events that reflect a more general understanding of similar experiences or events (Carter and Doyle, 1996). A characteristic of narratives is that they are underpinned by a larger issue or theoretical perspective, thus enabling the reader to independently make sense of this encounter.

A narrative with connection or carrying power can provide a mechanism for the reader to have a parallel internal conversation with the story and their own parallel situation (Linde, 1993). Although the story may appear simple, as was Frame's story, the strength of narratives is that they are able to accommodate the complexity of the ongoing stories being told and retold during the process of story building and their interaction with the reader. As Connelly and Clandinin explain, the difficulty of writing narrative is

> . . . in finding ways to understand and portray the complexity of the ongoing stories being told and retold in the inquiry. We are, as researchers and teachers, still telling in our practices our ongoing life stories as they are lived, told, relived and retold. We restory earlier experiences as we reflect on later experiences so the stories and their meaning shift and change over time. As we engage in a reflective research process, our stories are often restoried and changed as we, as teachers and/or researchers 'give back' to each other ways of seeing our stories.
>
> (1990: 9)

Consequently I propose that an effective narrative is one that provides opportunities for the reader to connect with the situation being described. A skilful narrator will not bog the reader down with the minutia of content. Instead, the development of a scene and plot will provide the reader with spaces to fill in the gaps about the context from their own experience. Therefore, a narrative with connectivity should be able to indicate the complexity of the whole from which the story has emerged.

Similarly, the endpoint of narrative enquiry is to tell a story. As a consequence, the process of construction (or analysis) towards the narrative endpoint should be transparent in order to demonstrate the efforts that have been made to avoid causality where the narrative has been used to justify rather than explain an outcome (Neuman, 2000). When the processes of narrative construction are made transparent, the resulting narrative should become plausible to the reader so that the account is not a justification but instead a description of an event that has been experienced (Clandinin and Connelly, 2000).

At this point I hope the case is made for the power and relevance of narrative enquiry as a research methodology. It is proposed that narratives can provide an immediacy with the reader by providing stories that are colourful and interesting, as well as having the power to establish a connection with the reader that may provide meaning and resonance. It is hoped that narratives constructed through the process of narrative enquiry have the potential to accommodate the diversity and richness of the routes through educational experiences as well as the variety of individual responses to these encounters.

At this point I have justified the place of narrative in reporting this research methodology, but I have yet to describe how it is achieved. The following account describes how a narrative can be constructed. As indicated, there are limitations with this mode of enquiry and where appropriate they are identified and suggestions are discussed to lessen the negative effects.

The process of narrative construction: developing Mary's story

First, narratives have an underlying issue or event that provides the purpose of the exercise. In this case, the research question provides this underpinning framework: What are the significant educational (formal and informal) episodes you remember in your choice of career?

The research from which this example has been drawn involved six scientists, but this account uses the narrative construction of Mary's story. Even though the focus at this early stage of the research was the co-construction of scientists' science education stories, the larger research issue was to use these stories as a context for teachers to be able to explore their teaching from another perspective. Ultimately, it was hoped that an exposure of multiple stories from scientists about their science education could surface the tensions that emerge at the intersections of the scientists' educational memories and a science teacher's lived experience (Olson and Craig, 2005).

In order to develop a narrative that provides a rich story with an invitation to participate, the following components of narrative construction were paid particular attention when constructing Mary's story. These were:

- the establishment of a collaborative relationship between the researcher and participant that allowed the co-construction of the story (Devault, 1990);
- the fostering of a process that enabled both participants to make sense of the data and developing story (Linde, 1993; Bryman, 2004);
- that the completed narrative reflected the complexity of the underpinning episodes and had a connective power that demonstrated the apparency and verisimilitude of the outcome (Connelly and Clandinin, 1990; Clandinin and Connelly, 2000).

Establishing a collaborative relationship

Data for this research came from telephone interviews with scientists who had been purposively selected because of their profession and the fact that they had been professionally associated with the researcher. The group were informally approached before a formal request was made. This negotiation of entry was given particular attention in order to give a sense of equality between participants. Mary and the researcher were members of the same science-focused committee. This interaction provided them with a sense of equity that was greater than the normal researcher–participant relationship. Nevertheless, attention needed to be paid to the development of a sense of equality and the following actions helped develop this collaborative partnership.

In order to counterbalance the feeling that Mary's narrative was being steered by the researcher in a particular direction that was determined by the research question, Mary was provided with insider information about the overall aims of the research and why these stories would be important for teachers. The overall educational endpoint after this initial research was to find out 'What educational stories are provided by science teachers to support their response to a scientist's recollection of interpreting scientific observations in secondary school?' and 'What pedagogical practices underpin these teachers' responses to this story?' It was hoped that because Mary was aware of this overall research endpoint it would be easier for her to make an 'equal' contribution to this narrative construction.

The interviewer focused Mary to the demands of this stage of the research by providing her with a list of semi-structured interview questions before the recorded and transcribed telephone conversation interview (Bryman, 2004). It is important to note that these questions provided a focus but did not prescribe the direction or pace of the conversation.

Semi-structured interview questions:

- Tell me about your job. Tell me about your journey to this position?
- Tell me about your experience of science at school. What were your impressions?

These open-ended questions provided flexibility within the interview process so that the interviewer could follow the scientist's lead while not losing sight of the overall focus (Casey, 1996). It was important that Mary was given time and space to develop her stories, so the interviewer made notes during this initial interview rather than interrupting her flow of memories with specific questions. It was anticipated that further details could be developed in later discussions.

A transcribed telephone interview was sent to Mary at the first stage of this narrative co-construction. She was asked to record changes (e.g. additions, elaborations and contradictions) using a track change facility. If any differences of opinion or alterations could not be resolved, both versions could be recorded on the completed narrative with footnotes. An example of such an interchange is included in Figure 6.1, where Mary and the interviewer were developing the story about her life on her family farm. The text shows the contributions and changes that Mary added during this collaboration. The text is not an exact replica of the original manuscript because of anonymity issues and the mechanical problem of the track change process converting the script into a clean corrected copy! The example 'Life on the farm' was selected not only because it showed the interactions between Mary and the interviewer, but also because these informal educational experiences have been explained by Mary as examples of her developing observational skills that she considers important in her role as a senior development scientist.

Bold text, script and <u>underlining (and in **bold**)</u> represent the different interchanges during the collaborative development. Marker words and explanatory phrases are shown in **bold** and show that Mary was providing coherence when she reflected on the significance of her actions, as well as a framework of time and place. The written comments linking the dialogue were kept to a minimum as it was important to keep the scientist's voice at the forefront.

Episode 2 Life on the farm

However feelings of inadequacy and subsequent hard work were not the only outcome from living in the country. Familial expectations and conversations about work on the farm provided her with values and interests that she believes have been transferred into her working life. She commented on the qualities that she brought to her science she made the comment that her focus may be a reflection of her upbring-ing on the farm. Mary made a comment about her focus on careful observations.

The fact that I take care about my observations. I write everything down even though it may not seem relevant at the time. Keep good notes, logical.

Q. When did you learn those things?
I don't know. **In some ways** being on the farm actually was part of that. **Because** we were given responsibility quite early on. **And I was the eldest child.** When I was [at secondary school] my parents and siblings went on holiday and left me in **charge of the farm. So I had to** be rational and to make decisions about what you were going to do and to take responsibility for them. **Early on** I always had chores to do on the farm. I had pet rabbits to look after which were totally **my own responsibility. And I never questioned that I had to do these things. I just did it because that is what you did.** <u>These chores became more complex as I grew up. For example fixing fences, gates, water troughs as well as the maintenance and development of the land for example removing weeds, planting trees for shelter.</u> (Her familiarity with machines gave her me an added practical skills) I was able to work with machinery on the farm.

Figure 6.1 An example of collaborative interaction during narrative construction

On reflection Mary noted that **in farming (many of these decisions were based on careful observations)** she needed to make decisions based on her observations. For example:

Observing the weather – is it going to rain, snow, be windy or sunny. The resulting decisions would be stock shifting if there is the potential for snow or flooding, irrigation if no rain. Or when to plant, harvest or start haymaking.

Observing the stock. your observations affect the animal welfare for example when to feed out and provide water, shift stock – observing for disease or sickness in order to treat or cull. Then there is the long term planned observations to provide the stud stock-keeping records of sires, dams and offsprings for example their weaning weights . . . Also there is the on-going monitoring of animals and planning for vaccinations, drenching. These observations require decisions and practical responses for example working with animals in the yard as well as shifting stock with dogs. (Additions made by Mary at a later stage in the narrative development)

Mary considered careful observations and recording of these observations an important part of her job. The following comment provides a link between her attitude to science and the link to her school experiences:

Seeing the results. That still gets me up in the morning. When I go to work. **Have I got results to go and look at? Because** it is really exciting to see what's happened. You have set up an experiment for a reason you are endeavouring to find out something. You are trying to work out a puzzle or to solve a problem. What's the answer going to be? Can you interpret an answer? Is it completely different from what you expected? That sort of thing really gets me going.

Q. Did that happen in school?
I'm not sure that it did because the sort of experiments you did . . . usually lasted a class. Or sometimes they lasted longer I guess, biology type experiments. But they were so prescribed that everything was so curricula that I am not sure it was quite as dynamic **and anything could happen type of situation.** Because everything was supposed to happen in a certain way. And I think that it is the way it is supposed to work at university too but at university they encourage you to look for something different. Or if something doesn't work which can often be the case in a lab. Why it didn't work. That can be more interesting.

Figure 6.1 continued

Making sense of the data and developing story

Initially, this narrative sketch was developed from an evaluative schema that had been imposed by the overall research question. The sketch included a broad description of the plot and the scene. For Mary, the plot was her description of her educational route to her present position, and the scene or setting was her description of her work and her role at work.

Because time is essential to plot – the past conveying significance, the present conveying value and the future conveying intention – and narrative explanation and meaning consists of significance, value and intention, a sequence of educational experiences provided the framework of the narrative sketch. A chronology of sorts was constructed using this framework. The interconnections between the educational episodes were commented on and elaborated by Mary in this initial draft. As well as time, a narrative is set within community, which is described as the 'setting' or 'scene'. Mary was able to set the scene for this narrative by describing her role and work as an industrial scientist.

In the second part of the analysis, open coding was used to identify themes and concepts that underpinned the stories. For example, significant actions were indicated in the initial coding and themes and concepts were identified, which provided a structure on which the educational episodes could be used to provide illustrations. Thus the levels of the story were the episodes (first level) that were combined into a narrative that illustrated a particular theme or concept that gave meaning (second level) (Gudmundsdottir, 1991).

The ideal situation for this analysis process would be for the researcher and Mary to co-construct this initial narrative sketch and the subsequent themes and concepts. However, both participants discussed the time constraints and geographic distances involved, agreeing that this initial coding would be carried out by the researcher/interviewer. Subsequent telephone conversations and email interchanges provided many opportunities for Mary to have input into the developing narrative (see Figure 6.1).

In order for Mary to understand and have a sense of ownership of this initial stage of analysis, notes about the analysis process, as well as the full transcript, were sent to Mary. Therefore, the early stage of the narrative analysis included notes indicating the themes, concepts and examples of Mary's evaluative and explanatory statements that were referenced from the transcript. All of this material is illustrated in Figure 6.2.

It is important to note that in addition to an explanation of this initial analysis, the accompanying notes provided Mary with evidence that her 'lack of grammar' in recorded conversation was not 'ungrammatical' but a perfectly normal way of negotiating a story between the speaker and listener in the process of developing coherence or causality. For example, marker words such as 'because, . . . and so' (Linde, 1993) indicate that the speaker is demonstrating coherence and 'you know' indicates an attempt at shared understanding between the speaker and the listener (Devault, 1990). The addition of phrases to these marker words further emphasise

Narratives are told from a theoretical perspective or from a larger issue (Carter and Doyle, 1996). You may wish to be reminded of the **research question** that provides the underlying meaning for this narrative construction.

- **What are the significant educational (formal and informal) episodes that may have influenced this scientist in their choice of career?**

I hope the **research design** provides you with an opportunity to recollect stories about your school science career as well as provide a framework for you to make sense of these recollections. Remember I sent you a series of questions to start our conversation.

The following ideas underpin the analysis of your telephone conversation. These are that the focus of this analysis is 'to find out how people make sense of what happened and that the story often involves other accounts that relate to these episodes and their interconnections' (Bryman, 2004).

You may notice that there are words that have been coloured **bold** within your quotes. Evaluative and explanatory statements are indicated by marker words e.g. **'because'**, **'and so'** which indicates that you are making sense of your account. Sometimes phrases are added to the marker words to further emphasise that explanations and evaluations were occurring. For example **'so that'**, **' so of course'**, **'so I decided'**, **'so that's kind of'** (Linde, 1993). Other examples of marker phrases include **'you know'** that implies that you aniticipate a shared understanding between you and the reader. There are other phrases that indicate that the speaker had made sense of the experience for example **'and I thought'**, **'and I really realised'**, **'and I think'**, **'and of course'**, and **'you know'** (Devault, 1990).

During narrative analysis researchers identify <u>major themes</u>, patterns, issues and events in the text as well as <u>concepts</u>, ideas and categories. In this analysis the following themes and concepts have been <u>underlined</u> as they have been used to construct this initial narrative sketch.

The <u>major themes</u> that have been identified from your transcript are:

- The importance of careful observation that has developed from a childhood on the farm, during your school and in your professional life.
- The thrill of doing science and seeing the results and solving problems
- The importance of experimentation and careful observations when carrying out scientific activities.

Figure 6.2 Explaining how Mary's interview has been analysed

The <u>major concepts</u> that became apparent when reading your transcript were:

- The importance of careful observations and recording
- The importance of not being influenced by pre-conceptions. Record what you see.
- Science education comes alive with practical work.

At this stage the story can be constructed in levels. For example at the 1st level is a series of episodes while at a 2nd more complex level, the episodes are combined into a narrative which is infused with meaning that has been gained from identified themes and concepts (Gudmundsdottir, 1991).

The educational episodes that have been selected to illustrate the answer to the research question are:

- The country girl in the city school
- Life on the farm
- Practical work making science come alive
- Watching the teacher teach.

These episodes have been used to write this narrative sketch that is composed of a lived biography (summary of worklife and quotes to illustrate these stages and interests). Finally the significant educational episodes have been written up with quotes from the research literature to show you why such statements have been included.

References: Please tell me if you would like to read the full quotes from these references and I will send them on.

Figure 6.2 continued

that such explanations and evaluations were occurring (e.g. 'so that', 'so it's all come back again', 'so of course', 'so I decided', 'so I did that' and 'so I worked away at doing that').

It was also explained that in a conversation there will be discontinuous constituents (e.g. 'not only . . . but also', 'if . . . then' and 'on the one hand . . . on the other hand') (Linde, 1993) that can also indicate that the speaker is examining the routes through this story. These were indicated in the script in bold.

The initial narrative was constructed to include an educational life history (to provide plot and scene), followed by educational episodes that provided some illustrations.

Consequently, Mary was provided with a theoretical explanation for this initial coding. Subsequent conversations provided opportunities for her to shape her narrative containing episodes that illustrated themes and underlying concepts.

A narrative that reflects complexity, apparency and verisimilitude

Because it was important to show the complexity of the stories that were being told and retold, the following writing devices were used: where possible, the scientist's voice was left unedited; indicator words were identified; explanatory comments were included within brackets; and the researcher's voice was kept to a minimum with the occasional question or linking statement that contributed to the story.

In order to establish an invitation to participate – where the reader connects with the narrative by recognising the community from whence the scientist is located – an account of Mary's life story contributes to this narrative's apparency (Connelly and Clandinin, 1990). Though the notion of apparency is difficult to define, it can be considered in terms of how the reader makes sense of the details and the degree of recognition of someone's life. Although this location in place and time is a strength of narrative research, there is always a spectre of causality (Neuman, 2000) caused by this emphasis on self-examination as the story is being told. The focus of narrative enquiry is on how people make sense of what happened rather than just giving an account of what happened. This focus on interpretation makes it very important that the surrounding scene is identified so that the reader can independently understand the decisions that might have been made by the participants and can make their own connections and suppositions as shown in Figure 6.3.

The goal of a connective narrative outcome is that the reading of this narrative would provide a dialogue of comparison and recognition, as well as providing opportunities to remember that could make one's experience a lens of empathy (Carter and Doyle, 1996). Consequently, this narrative is constructed with the presumption that the reader will make links to similar science education experiences.

Providing an opportunity for teachers' interrogation of the narrative

It was proposed that scientist's stories would provide the focus for the next stage of the research. In this account, Mary's story was highlighted as one of five stories that were presented to teachers to comment and tell their own stories that parallel, confront or confirm learning science.

Here I return to Frame's story 'You are now entering the human heart' to reconfirm the connective power of this story and draw lessons for constructing a connective narrative. A feature of narrative research is that narrative interrogation can provide a mechanism for the reader to have an internal conversation with the

Mary is an industrial scientist working for a company that produces valued-added products from animal sources. Her team of two full-time and two part-time scientists carries out biological testing of new products (e.g. the bioactive compounds used as ingredients in food products). Her laboratory provides information about biological activity of these compounds. In her role as a senior development scientist, Mary designs experiments based on the company's needs, plans the experiments that she and her team carry out, analyses results, writes reports and project reviews for management and sometimes reports information to potential customers.

One significant comment that reoccurred in the interview was the importance of observations.

> The fact that I take care about my observations. I write everything down even though it may not seem relevant at the time. Keep good notes . . . logical.

This quality of careful observation was given special attention when she commented on the process of obtaining reproducible results.

> Observing what you get, and observing things that may not seem important at the time. **Because** you can always go back and have a look at it when you get another result that may shed light on the situation. **Possibly** the people that I manage don't appreciate this but I always insist that everything is written up and that you don't just do an experiment and then discard it. Write it up properly so that you can go back to it and refer to it.

> **Because** in industrial research I tend to find that I write up things as reports **because** I am reporting that to my boss . . . or to other people in the group. And that is going to be different style from when you write it up in the lab book, which I find I do myself a lot more informally. So possibly I put a lot more observations in my lab book. I draw diagrams. Whereas in a report there is not sort of thing that you would do.

Significant educational episodes

Because narrative analysis relates not just to biography but also to accounts of episodes and to the interconnections between them (Bryson, 2004) the following comment provides an interesting insight into her attitude to science and the link to her school experiences.

Figure 6.3 Lived biography

Seeing the results. That still gets me up in the morning. When I go to work. Have I got results to go and look at? **Because** it is really exciting to see what's happened.

Q. Did that happen in school?
I'm not sure that it did **because** the sort of experiments you did . . . usually [they] lasted a class. Or sometimes they lasted longer. But they were so prescribed that everything was so curricula **that I am not sure** it was quite as dynamic and anything could happen type of situation. **Because** everything was supposed to happen in a certain way.

Figure 6.3 continued

story and their own parallel situation (Linde, 1993). Consequently, it was hoped that the following research questions would provide such a vehicle for this connectivity with teachers:

- What educational stories are provided by science teachers to support their response to a scientist's recollection of interpreting scientific observations in secondary school?
- What pedagogical practices underpin these teachers' responses to this story?

I hoped that a narrative interrogation of these stories by teachers could provide an opportunity for border crossing as teachers experienced the scientist's gaze on their classroom and they attempted to interpret this snapshot in the light of their pedagogy. This explanation of the difficulties that people encountered and their changing perceptions as they penetrated new communities has been documented by Aikenhead (1996). I propose that a form of border crossing is made apparent when teachers are confronted with a scientist's view of their classroom practice. Furthermore, teachers' interrogation of a scientist's story about the observation and interpretation of data could provide an opportunity for pedagogical comment about how the nature of scientific enquiry is interpreted in their classroom. As Koulaidis and Ogborn (1995) comment, it cannot be assumed that scientists and teachers share a common understanding about the nature of scientific enquiry. It was proposed that this method of enquiry could identify underlying pedagogical principles that these teachers employed to demonstrate the skills and difficulties involved with scientific observation and the interpretation of experiments.

Teachers of secondary and tertiary students were sent a paper (see France and Buntting, 2008) describing the first stage of this research, where scientist's narratives about their science educational experiences were described and analysed.

Mary was aware of the teaching that was happening in her classroom. This interaction with her teacher is significant because it influenced her subsequent actions as a scientist that is her focus on careful observations.

And in chemistry, I don't know what it was about chemistry that fascinated me it was **just maybe** mixing the chemicals, doing stuff in test tubes, **because** there were reactions, there was something happening there was either a gas coming off or there was changing colour or something was going on. **And it was all about the observation of it.** It was crucial that you looked at what was going on.

Trying to understand it, whether it was a solid that formed, was it a gas that formed. Why did it change colour? **Because** that's quite a mystery. Mysterious thing that you could add two colourless solutions and suddenly you would have a really brightly coloured result.

. . . well it was really funny at the time, I remember one of my science teachers always had this pre-programmed thing in her mind about what the colour should be or what the reaction should be. And sometimes it wasn't that at all and it used to drive her nuts. And it was hilarious for the class when she would say look at this bright pink and it wasn't pink at all, it was red or whatever colour it was.

Q. And how would she cope with that?
I think she said well okay its not bright red but it's almost red. Well **you know** it was interesting because instead of waiting to see what would happen she would always precipitate it in terms of what was supposed to happen. **And I suspect** probably the chemicals weren't pure so you weren't to see necessarily the true reaction.

But I think one of the things too is why I always in enjoyed about [the practical work] was the observation. Writing down what you see not making a predetermined guess about what you should see but actually what you observe.

Q. You wrote down quite carefully what you were seeing?
Yes, to be honest, to this day **that it is something that I remember doing.** And even when I am talking with other people now 'what did you see, don't tell me about what you expect to see, what did you actually see'.

Figure 6.4 Watching the teacher teach

Teachers were asked to discuss Mary's narrative 'Watching the teacher teach' and were given the following questions that I hoped would initiate discussion during the interview.

- What features were noteworthy about this narrative?
- What teaching strategies were evident to you?
- Why do you think these strategies were significant?
- Can you remember any similar instances in your teaching career?

The outcome of this narrative analysis was to construct a parallel dialogue (alongside Mary's story) that could provide clues to each teacher's pedagogy. This narrative construction process progressed in the same manner as outlined in the construction of Mary's story (i.e. evaluative schemas were identified through open coding to develop a narrative sketch followed by narrative themes and concepts underpinning the ideas and episodes). The following Figure 6.5 shows this process. The stories were co-constructed with the teacher using track changes as she edited her reflective response with her additions that are underlined. In addition, the researcher's corrections or additions to the quote have been indicated with square

The <u>underlined</u> words are additions to the text that Clare made.

Clare (a tertiary educator) commented about the pedagogy revealed from a primary perspective.

At primary level . . . <u>it appears that</u> teachers [have(d)] been **'doing experiments', you know,** . . . after the curriculum . . . was implemented <u>it seems that</u> that they (we) did[n't] have to know <u>or teach</u> the science concepts. <u>Science was</u> 'doing (we just did the) experiments'.

But what it did focus them on was the importance of kids observing. . . . In my experience they don't teach it explicitly though. They just expect kids to realise that science has an empirical base. . . . and that the observation becomes the <u>learning</u> [end point] . . . If they don't observe the 'right thing' <u>though</u>, **then the experiment is a complete waste of time. So** not only are you not getting any theory or conceptual development, (but) you are not getting (on the) nature of science <u>aspects taught</u> either because the <u>students'</u> observations <u>become the important aspect of the lesson whether they are aligned to current scientific understanding or not . . .</u> (becomes too important).

Figure 6.5 The narrative construction process

Table 6.1 Narrative responses from teachers

Educational stories	Teaching strategies used	Pedagogy revealed
'Analysing problematic data takes time' (Snoops)	Recounting experiences of recent science research	Narratives to model experimental design
'Making pedagogical capital (POE)' (Nadja)	Using POE as a tool to focus students' observations	Predict, observe and explain
'Observations are more than just looking' (Noel)	Drawing pictures. 'Is this what we are expecting? Will this give us sufficient information?'	Data used for prediction and explanation
'Welcoming the unexpected' (Margo)	Encouraging exploration of concepts	A discovery approach
'Problem solving using unexpected data' (Eileen)	Isolating and testing all components	Unexpected data provides a route to understanding
'Observation is theory laden' (Beatrice)	Comparing the model with the reality	The subjective nature of observation

brackets in order to enable the reader to understand her statements. The (. . .) words and phrases were those that the teacher removed. Finally, the words in bold were highlighted by the researcher to show how the teacher was making sense of this recollection.

Teachers were asked to respond to this story with pedagogical stories of their own. Their stories (see Table 6.1) were told in response to Mary's story. As these teachers developed their stories, they identified teaching strategies they used and reflected on the pedagogical principles that underpinned their responses.

These teachers provided some interesting responses to this story. For example, Snoops, a secondary biology teacher, made the candid observation that 'Finding out why it didn't work takes time'. He remembered his own school days and said 'I had a teacher who used to blame mistakes on atmospheric pressure'. He reflected on the realities of the classroom when he commented:

> When it goes wrong I tell kids this is what should have happened because experiments are highlighting a concept and you do want the kids to understand the concept and unfortunately time doesn't allow for you to sit back and see why it didn't work.

This honesty was given deeper meaning when he talked about his own experiences as a scientist and how he was able to tell stories to his students about his difficulties when carrying out practical work. At this point, Snoops told me the story about his year as a scientist. The following story, called 'Analysing problematic data takes time' was in response to my question 'Did you tell them about your research?'

I do and the frustrations. Last year I spent a year at university doing science research. My experiment was to replicate the biological rhythms in a terrestrial isopod called *Scyphax ornatus* that inhabits the inter-tidal zones of North Island beaches. This animal responds to darkness and to the tides. My role was to repeat previous experiments and then to extend that work by finding out if the change of the daily cycle by .5h would lengthen the long period rhythm (not feeding for 6–8 nights) of the animal.

There were problems. The equipment wasn't working, the software was old, animals escaping, finding the animals. **All those were wonderful things because** you would spend time working out what the problem was and then **trying to come up with solutions. The fact that it didn't work meant** that I had to have a good understanding of how the system was supposed to work and then look for ways around the problems. I felt definitely frustrated but at the end when things did start working there was elation and all the hard work was worth it.

When I sit back and when I reflect that I didn't really get to complete the experiments to a stage that I would have been happy with. But I don't see **that as a failure you know because I did sort out** a lot of kinks.

Doing science **is not guaranteed is it? Which is the lesson I guess that kids do need to learn.**

(Snoops)

What was evident from Snoops's reflections of his classroom practice and the story about his own experiences doing science is that he was able to reveal the tension between the role of an experiment to illustrate a concept and the role of empirical data in knowledge building not only to this interviewer, but also to his students.

Snoops made connections with Mary's story when he stated that stories are the best way of communicating ideas about scientific enquiry to his students:

> **Science is not guaranteed is it?** Which **is the lesson I guess** that kids do need to learn. I know that kids do like listening to stories. I tell them stories about my research and the frustrations. You can never sort of know how effective story telling is to someone's learning but when you are marking exam papers and you pick up a little gem. **And you think I only just mentioned** that in passing but it obviously made an impact and they put it back out on an **exam paper. I guess** that is one way that you do get feedback.

It was very apparent that these teachers enjoyed co-constructing and telling parallel stories to Mary's story. During interviews, it was apparent that a layering of the story was occurring as they returned to Mary's story while they were talking about their own situation. In fact, Mary's story allowed them to interrogate their practice. The parallel story titles listed in Table 6.1 show that Snoops and the other teachers made links between Mary's emphasis on the importance of observation and how they nurtured the development of scientific skills.

Like Snoops, Beatrice also acknowledges the power of narratives:

> I think there is enormous power in a story. The story engages you at different levels. You can have a paragraph of text that states the importance of observation that would explain these things. But to have it given to you as a narrative where you enter the world of the person that is telling the story makes it a much more powerful piece of learning for yourself.
>
> (Beatrice)

Certainly, I entered the world of the elderly elementary teacher in Frame's story. In her sparse account, I was able to transfer her situation to my classroom experience and, in particular, my strategy for engendering children's empathy with animals. Mary's story about a misguided teacher's reaction to an experiment did not provoke these teachers into condemnation of her teacher but instead generated an empathetic response about the difficulties of bringing the world of scientific enquiry into the classroom. In a similar manner to Frame's story about the ageing elementary teacher, Mary's story about her schoolgirl science experiences gives power to the quotation 'It is often not the facts and events of a life story that are important for teachers, but the interpretation given to them that is meaningful' (Halai and Hodson, 2004: 205).

Certainly, these teachers provided a range of interpretations with their parallel narratives. This is not the place to discuss them but to instead make the assertion that stories can not only provide an opportunity for the crossing of different viewpoints or borders between educationalists and scientists (Aikenhead, 1996), but they provide an opportunity to see the world from other viewpoints. Thus, a narrative provides an opportunity for the narrator to layer events into a communal practice of lived experience (Wenger, 1998).

The construction of narratives that have the potential to engender connections and allow that restorying process can occur when attention is given to the process that allows the story to speak to the reader within the spaces that the narrator has constructed. A successful narrative will allow the reader to make their own connections by an interpretation with their own story. Unexpectedly, Frame's story provided me with a window to examine how narrative analysis can also provide these potent gaps within a story.

References

Aikenhead, G. S. (1996) 'Science education: border crossing into the subculture of science', *Studies in Science Education*, 27: 1–52.

Bryman, A. (2004) *Social Research Methods*, Oxford: Oxford University Press.

Carter, K. and Doyle, W. (1996) 'Personal narrative and life history in learning to teach', in J. Sikula, T. I. Buttery and E. Guyton, (eds) *Handbook of Research on Teacher Education*, Second edition, London: Prentice Hall International.

Casey, K. (1995–1996) 'The new narrative research in education', *Review of Research in Education*, 21: 211–253.

Clandinin, D. J. and Connelly, F. M. (2000) *Narrative Inquiry: Experience and Story in Qualitative Research*, San Francisco, CA: Jossey Bass.

Connelly, F. M. and Clandinin, D. J. (1990) 'Stories of experience and narrative inquiry', *Educational Researcher*, 19(5): 2–14.

Devault, M. L. (1990) 'Talking and listening from women's standpoint: feminist strategies for interviewing and analysis', *Social Problems*, 37: 96–116.

Doyle, W. and Carter, K. (2003) 'Narrative and learning to teach: implications for teacher-education curriculum', *Journal of Curriculum Studies*, 35(2): 129–137.

Frame, J. (1983) *You Are Now Entering the Human Heart*, Wellington, NZ: Victoria University Press.

France, B. and Buntting, C. (2008) 'Choosing biotechnology: a narrative exploration of significant educational episodes influencing career choices in biotechnology', in M. Hammann, M. Reiss, C. Boulter and S. D. Tunnicliffe (eds.), *Biology in Context: Learning and Teaching for the 21st Century*, London: Institute of Education.

Gudmundsdottir, S. (1991) 'Story-maker, story-teller: narrative structures in curriculum', *Journal of Curriculum Studies*, 23(3): 207–218.

Halai, N. and Hodson, D. (2004) 'Munazza's story: shedding light on a science teacher's conceptions of the nature of science through a life history study', *Canadian Journal of Science, Mathematics and Technology Education*, 4(2): 193–208.

Koulaidis, V. and Ogborn, J. (1995) 'Science teachers' philosophical assumptions: how well do we understand them?', *International Journal of Science Education*, 17(3): 273–283.

Linde, C. (1993) *Life Stories: The Creation of Coherence*, Oxford: Oxford University.

Neuman, W. L. (2000) *Social Research Methods*, Fourth edition, London: Allyn and Bacon.

Olson, M. R. and Craig, C. J. (2005) 'Uncovering cover stories: tensions and entailments in the development of teacher knowledge', *Curriculum Inquiry*, 35(2): 161–182.

Wenger, E. (1998) *Communities of Practice*, New York: Cambridge University Press.

Chapter 7

The potential of using stimulated recall approaches to explore teacher thinking

Paul Denley and Keith Bishop

Our purpose in this chapter is to consider the origins of stimulated recall approaches in qualitative research. After presenting some of the strengths and limitations, we share something of the way we have used video stimulated recall in our own research.

Introduction

Although there may be earlier examples of stimulated recall use, most of what has been written about stimulated recall recognises Benjamin Bloom as one of the first users of the approach. He uses it in his study of students' thinking in different instructional contexts:

> The basic idea underlying the method of stimulated recall is that a subject may be enabled to relive an original situation with vividness and accuracy if he [*sic*] is presented with a large number of cues or stimuli which occurred during the original situation.
>
> (Bloom, 1953: 161)

Bloom's study involved audio recordings of class sessions that were replayed to the students within 48 hours of the event. It is not clear what was going on when the students then were asked to recall their thinking in an interview. Bloom recognised that in this situation recall was only partial and students would select what they determined were significant events to talk about. He also acknowledged that the relationship with the interviewer was a significant factor in the selection process. Despite these reservations, acceptance of Bloom's basic assertion about the value of the technique has led to many other studies in a variety of contexts, including that of teacher thinking and decision making. Most of the studies since the 1970s have used video-recordings as the basis for the stimulated-recall interview (see for example Housner and Griffey, 1985; Butefish, 1990; O'Brien, 1993; Gass and Mackay, 2000; Lyle 2003; Egi, 2008). Due to the increasing ease of the use of camcorders to provide an instant record of classroom events, the use of audio recording has dwindled. In the rest of this chapter, we use the term 'stimulated recall' to refer to the use of a visual stimulus, usually a video recording. There are some open questions that do not seem to have been addressed in the literature about the difference between recall based solely on audio stimuli compared to a video recording, which has both video and audio stimuli. There seems to be an implicit assumption that video recordings will provide a richer source of stimulation for recall but it may be that the visual cues dominate perception and the soundtrack plays a secondary part. No comparative studies seem to have been carried out.

A resurgence of interest in stimulated recall followed a review of the technique (Calderhead, 1981) and its application to research on teacher thinking. Calderhead suggests that three sets of factors may influence the status (and therefore validity) of data collected through stimulated recall:

1   *The extent to which teachers consciously and selectively recall and report their thinking.* Viewing oneself on video can be a stressful and anxious experience and can challenge confidence. The relationship between teacher and researcher can be crucial in encouraging a focus on reconstructing thought patterns rather than explaining or defending actions. Explaining or defending actions (e.g. poor classroom behaviour or even teacher mannerisms) might sometimes be perceived by the teacher to be viewed negatively by the researcher. The importance of building rapport with the teacher in advance of the lesson and familiarising him or her with the conduct and process of the stimulated recall activity can help to 'reduce these influences and result in fuller recall commentaries' (Calderhead, 1981: 213).

2   *The extent to which it is possible for teachers to articulate their thinking.* This is an issue to which we have already alluded. If much knowledge about practice is tacit and, to use Berliner's (2004) term, automatised, can teachers talk about it? As Calderhead says, 'the teacher may have long since forgotten the rationale for behaving in such as manner and the behaviour may be engaged in unthinkingly' (Calderhead, 1981: 213). He goes on to suggest that, in their attempts to present their actions as rational, they may construct an explanation after the event because of the difficulty of being able to actually recall their thinking – retrospection rather than introspection? This is more difficult to deal with in practice. Perhaps, as with the previous issue, the rapport between teacher and researcher would encourage the more honest 'I'm not sure why I did/said that . . .' rather than a post-hoc rationalisation.

3   *The extent to which teachers' commentaries are framed by their understanding of the purpose of the research.* If teachers are aware of the purpose of the research, this may influence the nature of their responses. We have already suggested that the teacher's response is going to be both consciously and subconsciously partial. Some degree of understanding will be inevitable through the process of contacting teachers and negotiating entry to classrooms, so will this influence what they focus on in talking about their thinking? Calderhead suggests that 'the ways in which teachers are prepared

for their commentary and how they are instructed to comment' (Calderhead, 1981: 214) can potentially bias responses. This is another difficult area as ethically it would not be possible to carry out research of this sort without informed consent, and that involves giving some insight into what the researcher wishes to find out. Similarly, it would be wasteful of time and frustrating for the teacher not to be given some guidance about what to focus on in the recall interview. Calderhead leans towards the view that it is preferable that any attempts to categorise types of thinking or decision making should emerge inductively from the recall data rather than being too evident in advance. This has clear implications for the sort of protocols used in preparation for the recall interview and the sort of prompts and interventions that the researcher might consider appropriate during the interview.

Calderhead's conclusion is that the technique can give insights into teacher thinking, but users should be aware of its limitations, particularly that it cannot provide a complete account of thinking and needs to be complemented by other sources of data. A more detailed critique is presented by Yinger (1986), whose focus is on the examination of thought in action and the use of 'stimulated recall as the primary source of data for interactive thought'. Yinger suggests that, based on studies on memory and recall, 'there is good reason to doubt the validity of stimulated recall as means for accurately reporting interactive thinking'. Reviewing previous studies, Yinger asserts:

> Researchers not only make the relatively conservative claim that stimulated recall promotes recall of what was said and done but also a much stronger claim that the technique allows the participant to remember what he or she was thinking at the time.
>
> (1986: 268)

Yinger is perhaps the only researcher who has attempted to examine what is going on in stimulated recall at a neurological level. He addresses the question of what cognitive processing is taking place when a participant views a video recording and how the experience of viewing the event relates to the actual event itself. Using an information-processing conception of memory, Yinger develops a model to show the complexity of response in the stimulated recall interview and the process of interaction between short-term memory (STM) and long-term memory (LTM) from the original event through to the reconstruction of it in the stimulated recall interview. Put briefly, he suggests that, because information is either lost or transferred very quickly to long-term memory, direct recall from STM is impossible. Any recall even a few hours after the event will involve retrieval of information from the partial data set in LTM into STM for verbalisation and then, Yinger suggests, it may not only be information from that event that is retrieved; it may be contaminated by information from other similar events in providing an account. The use of video or audio data to stimulate recall adds a further layer of complexity. The new information coming into STM and hence into LTM from the actual stimulus will influence the selection of information from LTM in a sort of feedback loop. His view is that 'stimulated recall primarily produces a record of a subject's reasoning about the videotape stimulus and only secondarily about thinking related to the original event' (Yinger, 1986: 270). The hypothesis developed is that the observer's position in viewing the video recording is different from the actor's position in the actual event. Even though observer and actor are the same person, the focus in the former case may be on explaining past action, while in the latter case it was on determining the action. In order to at least acknowledge this multi-layered problem, Yinger draws attention to the nature of prompts used in the interviews and the effect these might have on information retrieval.

Yinger's conclusions are that:

> data generated during stimulated recall interviews may be at best only tangentially related to actual thinking during the recorded event and at worst entirely fabricated . . . the teacher, though a participant in the original event, relates to the video stimulus as a different event rather than as a means to remember the original. The task for the teacher then becomes one of making sense of the action viewed on the videotape instead of the original experience.
>
> (1986: 273)

This may seem a damning indictment of the technique, but Yinger sees value in it in terms of reflecting on, rather than in, action. Thus, provided one is not making a claim that the commentary is an accurate reconstruction of the event, it may have value in providing 'access to the ways in which teachers make sense of teaching episodes' (Yinger, 1986: 273) and to elicit implicit theories of teaching and beliefs which are seen as being important in guiding action.

In a more recent review of the use of stimulated recall, Lyle (2003) comments on how stimulated recall is viewed in most studies that have used it as being an unproblematic methodology despite both Calderhead's and Yinger's discussions of its limitations in the 1980s. In terms of research into its teaching, Lyle (2003) cites 17 studies between 1985 and 2002 which used stimulated recall either alone or in combination with other data collection methods to consider aspects of teacher thinking and decision making. He also cites studies in other fields – from counselling and psychiatry to nurse education and sports coaching – where stimulated recall has been used.

In most of these studies there is little discussion of the method itself or how limitations have been addressed beyond a common view that the stimulated recall interview should take place as soon after the actual event as possible. To illustrate this, we consider two examples.

Butefish (1990) attempted to analyse teacher' perceptions of interactive decisions, basing his conclusions on data gathered mainly though stimulated recall interviews of video-taped lessons. The related concepts of pre-, post- and interactive decision making are drawn from Clark and Peterson (1986), who use them as the basis for exploring teacher's thought processes. Butefish's only method-ological reference is to Clark and Peterson (1986), who provided an endorsement for the use of stimulated recall in the investigation of teachers' thought processes. In the post-lesson stimulated recall interview, Butefish (1990: 108) reminded the teachers that the purpose of the session 'was to identify those points in interaction wherein the teacher had to deviate from planned behaviour or routine'. Responses from the interviews were used to categorise decisions made with no further consideration of the validity of the recall data or the influence of the guidance given to the teachers in the interview – the latter point having been recognised as important by both Calderhead and Yinger in influencing the cognitive process during recall.

Housner and Griffey (1985) studied differences in pre-active and interactive decision making with experienced and inexperienced teachers. Stimulated recall was complemented with a 'think-aloud' technique as the teachers planned to teach small groups of children sports skills. As with the previous study, the teachers were instructed to focus on identifying points at which they deviated from their planned activity. Although there is some critical evaluation of the conclusions drawn in this study, there is little to question the validity of the data in terms of the extent to which the teachers were actually reconstructing the teaching activity as it took place at the time rather than responding to the fresh stimulus of the video recording.

Lyle, in his study involving stimulated recall with volleyball coaches to examine interactive decision making, concludes that stimulated recall should be 'acknowl-edged as an indirect method of obtaining evidence of cognitive activity, and like all such methods, findings should be evaluated with an acknowledgement of this constraint' (2003: 872).

Although his research was not into classroom teaching, Lyle considers this to be sufficiently similar to the coaching context. Lyle suggests that a stimulated recall procedure 'has significant advantages for research into teaching, particularly in capturing the complexity and subject specificity of classroom interaction (2003: 874).

For a very detailed consideration of the use of stimulated recall, the monograph by Gass and Mackey (2000) explores its use in the context of second-language research. They locate stimulated recall in the context of introspective research methods and the field of 'verbal reporting'. Their review of studies extends beyond the use of video or audio recordings to provide the stimulus for recall. For example, they consider how the use of diaries and other documents, questionnaires or personal questioning by an interviewer can be used to stimulate recall. Their book provides detailed guidance about the conduct of stimulated recall research, including the recall interview itself and how to deal with the secondary data generated by it. Although the focus is on use with learners as well as teachers in second-language learning, much of this guidance could be more generically applied to other teaching contexts. They even go so far as providing scripts to use in briefing participants and prompts to use in interviews. There is also an extensive discussion on data analysis and coding.

The key issue remains the claims that might be made for an account or commentary generated through a stimulated recall interview: Is it a reconstruction of the event drawing on stored memory relating only to that event or a re-interpretation of the event drawing on a variety of stored memories? Although today, through neuroscience research, the operation and structure of memory are better understood, the original information processing ideas of STM and LTM continue to be the dominant model for memory; no challenge has been made to the neurological basis of Yinger's critique of claims for stimulated recall. It is clear that despite some similarities between the brain and a computer, the brain does not store memories of events in a complete and uncompressed form which can be recalled like a video file from the hard disk and exactly reproduce what was there in the first place. Further, what is important in stimulated recall research is not recall of the event, but an attempt to recall the thinking, reasoning or decision making at the time.

However, recognising the inevitability of having to use 'after-the-event' techniques to study teacher thinking, it seems intuitive that recall will be enhanced by some sort of stimulus (compared to attempting recall without one). The importance of any claim to the accuracy of the account is the key point. If the focus is on the particular event and a reconstruction of the teacher's thinking at the time, the use of stimulated recall becomes problematic. If the focus is on using an event to be in itself the stimulus to reveal more general aspects of teacher thinking, perhaps use of the technique can be justified.

Background to our study involving the use of stimulated recall

We now discuss our use of stimulated recall in a study with a group of experienced secondary school science teachers. Our aim in the research study (Bishop and Denley, 2007) was to generate some case studies of the practice of highly accomplished – as identified by their peers – science teachers. We wanted to examine the way in which these accomplished teachers were able to bring together the different knowledge bases, which underpin their teaching, and how their thinking influenced decisions before, during and after their lessons. We were not only interested in the knowledge base which underpinned their teaching, but also the nature of their thinking in deploying that knowledge. Our assertion was that a key indicator of accomplishment in teaching is not so much to do with the quantity or level of knowledge, but the teacher's capability to transform knowledge into forms that are accessible to learners. That capability is evident in both the pre-active stage of lesson planning and designing engaging learning experiences and in the inter-active stage of classroom teaching.

The use of a stimulated recall approach seemed to be a possible way to access this sort of thinking. Like Meade and McMeniman (1992), we felt that other methods such as conventional post-lesson interviews, direct classroom observation and interaction analysis would not give much insight into thought process and decision making. As Reitano (2006) asserts, stimulated recall diminishes cursory self-presentation when teachers have to address their own actions.

As in Meade and McMeniman's study (which was also with science teachers), the framework we used to categorise the knowledge base was that initially developed by Shulman (1987). It also included the elusive notion of pedagogical content knowledge (PCK), which has been a focus for much science education research (Gess-Newsome and Lederman 1999; Loughran, *et al.* 2006). Shulman presents PCK as an 'amalgam' of subject and pedagogical knowledge, and it is often viewed as being characteristic of accomplished or expert teachers. Our view of PCK is that rather than trying to pin it down in terms of propositional knowledge, it might be evident, and to some extent 'visible', in its application through teachers' pre-active and inter-active thinking. This became an indirect focus for our study: Could stimulated recall provide a way of eliciting PCK in action through the commentaries accomplished teachers can generate in describing and explaining their thinking and decision making?

Our sample and our approach

Our group of fourteen teachers was identified by professionals such as subject advisers as showing high levels of accomplishment in their science teaching. In some cases this had been recognised in their promotion to leadership positions in their schools; in other cases their capabilities had been recognised differently (e.g. through becoming what in England are termed 'Advanced Skills Teachers'). Contact was made with the teachers. We then negotiated with head teachers and principals to gain access to their schools for the purposes of the research that centred on a single lesson for each teacher. Because the intention was to video-record in the classroom, parental permission also had to be sought. Initial discussions with the teachers explained the purpose of the research and how it was to be conducted. The teachers were sent a short briefing sheet indicating the areas to be explored in pre-lesson and post-lesson (stimulated recall) interviews. We recognised the balance here between providing an open and honest picture of the research and (perhaps subconsciously) suggesting we had a particular agenda and pre-determined foci for the lesson analysis: 'What are they [i.e. us, the researchers] looking for?'

Thus, our briefing sheet outlined possible areas for discussion across the two interviews rather than listing specific questions for each interview. As experienced and accomplished teachers, they were all used to being observed. We did not detect anything other than a genuine interest in the research and the opportunity to engage in a professional dialogue about their science teaching.

The pre-lesson interviews mostly took place one or two days before the video-recorded lesson to discuss lesson objectives, content and intentions. There was no intention that the lesson should be special in any sense, just one that might typify the teacher's normal approach to a science lesson. As well as collecting data relating to the lesson itself, the pre-lesson interview also explored the teacher's background and influences of his or her development as a science teacher. This was partly to strengthen our relationship with the teachers and reduce any apprehension about the lesson to be recorded and partly because we wanted to relate their own analysis of influences on practice to what we saw in the lessons.

The actual lessons were recorded using a digital camcorder mounted on a tripod and usually positioned in the back corner of the classroom, facing the teacher but set to record as much of the field of view as possible. The researcher was also present in the classroom, but the researcher tried not to touch the camera or make any attempt to selectively record classroom activity. The aim was to generate a 'fly on the wall' recording, which would not focus attention on particular aspects of teacher or pupil activity, but would require the teacher to decide on which events were significant or important in relation to his or her intentions and plans.

Where possible, the post-lesson interviews took place on the same day as the lesson, but in no case was there an interval longer than one day. The interview started with a reminder of what would happen. We were going to watch the video together, but the teacher would largely be in control of the playback. The interviews were audio-recorded for subsequent transcription, so it was important that the voices and other classroom noise on the video did not interfere with the teacher's stimulated recall commentary. Thus, the teacher was asked to pause the tape or turn down the volume when he or she wished to comment. The teachers were also told that they could fast forward through segments of the lesson if they did not have anything to say about it or rewind if they wished to view segments again.

Researchers in some studies using stimulated recall from classroom video have edited the whole recording to focus on particular phases of the lesson in order to cut down the length of the interview. In our experience, the technique of allowing the teacher to fast forward through less significant portions of the lesson meant that the stimulated recall interviews normally lasted about the same time as the lessons themselves, which were mostly 50–60 minutes in duration.

The question has already been raised about the researcher's contribution to the stimulated recall commentary. It is difficult to resist the temptation to reach out to rewind the recording if the teacher goes past some event which the researcher thinks is significant but the teacher chooses not to comment on. We tried not to intervene too much in the commentary but, when the teacher did pause the recording, we might then refer back to something that had been passed over. As we have explained, our intention was not to hold to a claim that the stimulated recall commentary was an accurate reconstruction of the teacher's thinking in the lesson as he or she was thinking at the time. We wished to have a professional dialogue with the teachers to probe the way in which their knowledge for teaching is operationalised; they are able to articulate their actions to reveal the thinking which guides them. Thus, we did not adopt a totally neutral position in the stimulated recall interviews. Although the teacher was in charge of the replay of the lesson, when the recording was paused, we did engage in some discussion of the comments made.

We also had the data from the pre-lesson interview and so were able to explore the relationship between pre-active and inter-active decision making where the lesson deviated from the planned activities or the teachers had to respond to unanticipated events in the classroom. This seemed to us to be a rich source of data for our study, but at the same time we recognised the dangers of compromising the purity of the recall commentary as a record of the teachers' thinking. For the most part, the questions we asked were for clarification and explanation rather than intervening more specifically (unless the discussion drifted away too far from the context of the lesson itself). We tried to encourage the teachers to examine their own thinking without appearing to be judgemental if we asked a simple question like 'Why did you do that?'. We also tried to manage the conduct of the interview to ensure that within the total time available we had the chance to review the whole lesson.

The nature of discussion in our study

It is difficult to provide a feel for the nature of the discussion which took place in the stimulated recall interviews. The transcriptions themselves do not make a lot of sense without a lot of contextual information and, particularly, without seeing the video recording which stimulated the comment. However, perhaps two differing extracts would give an indication of the sort of discussion which was generated.

This comment was from Isobel's lesson. This was a revision lesson on chemical bonding with a group of 15- and 16-year-old pupils. Unusually for a revision lesson, it took place in a school hall and was a very active lesson, with the pupils acting out different examples of ionic and covalent bonding and using molecular modelling kits:

Researcher: When they've done it before they haven't done it in teams?

Isobel: No, they've done it on desks and having a bit of a play initially, just to get used to the models and stuff and then I'd put some on the board and just told them to see whether they could try making them and whether they thought they were right and we put the colours up on the board as well. So they haven't done it in a competition way. They've done it in a more generalised way having a bit more of a play and trying to do something physical. To finish off what is essentially quite a dry topic, because there aren't a lot of things you could do apart from do it on the board and show them how to draw them out. So this is a different way of doing that.

They're devastated [in response to a group not getting the right answer in making a molecular model]. I love the way they're looking at one another. They're so amazing initially 'Miss, look at this' . . . 'No, no, no, you've got to come to me', which is quite funny.

What's interesting is that this group didn't work very well as a group, whereas all the other ones team-wise did quite well. This one, I don't know whether it was the different levels but they didn't work particularly well as a group.

I think from here they just do a few more of these and then it's trying to make a good use of time with packing up the models . . . because obviously at the end of the lesson it comes to quite hectic timing and getting them into the idea of the fact that they're going to need some paper and start writing down some answers now, which they were absolutely pathetic at, which is really interesting because we did a whole lesson on the 'cross-over rule' [to work out numbers of atoms in particular molecules] and writing out formulae of ionic compounds and they so got it. They were brilliant and I could have asked anyone in the class. We went through these five steps and they were absolutely fantastic and . . . [now] . . . just couldn't do it! Which is fine because the biggie . . . [is] . . . I've now got to go back over that.

This extract contains a mixture of types of comments. It is partly an explanation or rationale for the specific activity creating molecular models, partly observations which the teacher might have made at the time and partly observations which seem clearly to be in response to viewing the recording. Even in this short extract, there is evidence of pre-, inter- and post-active decision making, as well as the deployment of both subject and pedagogical knowledge. It is not disciplined by the researcher or the teacher to concentrate solely on what the teacher was thinking at the time, but it does give a broader picture of the teacher's thinking and the complexity and multi-dimensionality of a lesson where past, present and future are brought together.

In the following extract the teacher is more focused on what is going on in the lesson and the classroom dynamics. Iain is teaching a lesson on in vitro fertilisation with a class of 14- and 15-year-old pupils:

Researcher: What kinds of questions are you asking?

Iain: Well in the first instance, . . . I'm really trying to get them to work as a team. What happens is that Jasmine is sitting over there reading the cards and the boys are sitting there going 'What's going on?' and I want them to work together on it and read it to each other or share in this collective, which ultimately didn't really work with that group because the girls did their thing and Nathan worked with the girls to a certain extent and the boys didn't really do a great deal or contribute a great deal.

There . . . you see . . . I'm trying to get them to be sensible and mature by bringing in something like the gay couple. Yes they're a gay couple, but that's the point. You've got to discuss whether they're any more entitled or less so than the others and what should they do? So Rob made some stupid comment that he thinks is stupid 'I'll go to the sperm bank.' 'Excellent Rob, well done, but why should that affect the decision?' So Rob's sat there thinking he's made some sarky comment and in fact I've used that to go 'OK, brilliant.' And he thinks 'Well that wasn't meant to happen. It was meant to be a sarky comment.' So it didn't work with Rob, he didn't get more engaged.

I give Jasmine a bit of responsibility there. I'd spent too much time there and it was kind of obvious that I'd said everything I needed to about working as a group and discussing it and I needed to go and speak to some other groups and check they were OK, so as I walked away and I kind of did it on purpose, I looked at Jasmine and Sam and said 'Jasmine, you're going to need to take control here and get these guys working with you' and so she immediately felt it was a bit of praise and responsibility.

I started to panic mildly because I heard Katia shout across to Jasmine 'When do you work on a Thursday?' and at that moment I thought 'Wait a minute. That's got nothing to do with what we're doing and it means Katia isn't engaged and she's trying to get Jasmine not engaged as well so I thought I'd better sort it out ASAP.' I think I went across to Jasmine, got her back on task, encouraged her a little more and then came straight over here and sorted this group out because I knew they weren't doing what they were meant to be doing.

It might be assumed that Iain is reconstructing his thinking at the time by his use of the present tense. However, Yinger (1986: 271) suggests that this could also indicate a reconstruction in the present, built around the viewing of the video. Despite this possibility, the way in which Iain is able to comment on the event (whether this comment relates to as it was in the past or is as seen in the present) reveals a depth of thinking which shows the sensitive way in which he handles some potentially difficult discussion, employing his knowledge of his pupils, as well as holding on to his learning objectives and keeping the pupils engaged.

Analysing the data generated in our study

In our research study we transcribed the dialogue in the lessons themselves as well as the pre-lesson and stimulated recall interviews. These data were then imported into a qualitative data analysis software package, NVivo (QSR 2009). This software not only provides an easy-to-use data management tool, but it also allows different levels of analysis. Our use involved applying a coding system to the transcript data, built around a number of themes which emerged from the interviews. The software could then search for and aggregate codings to produce documents containing all instances of a particular code across the entire data set or sub-sets of it.

We also identified instances of particular knowledge categories and the way these are brought through the teachers' action and evidenced through their decision making. These were then used in generating accounts about the practice of each teacher, which attempted to show the quality of thinking that underpinned his or her planning and classroom teaching.

In the accounts we generated for our research, we were able to integrate our own commentary on the lesson, the transcript of the lesson and the transcripts of the pre-lesson and stimulated recall interviews. Each of the accounts we constructed were fed back to the teachers to offer their views on the validity of our interpretations and to give them the opportunity to further clarify anything they had said to us.

We found that the stimulated recall transcripts provided a rich source of data to form the central thread of the accounts around which the contextual data could be woven. The extent to which the teachers in our study were *recalling* their thinking at the time or *reconstructing* what their thinking was is a matter open to question. In reality, they may well have been doing both and perhaps other things, such as relating experiences from the lesson under study to other lessons. For our purposes, this was less significant than the potential in gaining insights into the teachers' minds and their ability to explain their actions. These insights might be hard to expose in general discussion with accomplished teachers, like those with whom we were working; the stimulus of a real lesson enabled them to talk about their teaching and what has informed their practice and influenced their professional development in ways which we believe will be accessible to other teachers.

So what do we know?

We would like to summarise some key questions emerging from previous studies (including our own), using stimulated recall to explore teacher thinking and professional knowledge, and then suggest ways in which the method might be used in other fields.

Perhaps the most important question to be addressed relates to the purpose for the use of stimulated recall. If it is to investigate teacher thinking where stimulated recall is being used as a proxy for the sort of commentary that a teacher at the time of a lesson might give if he or she was not caught up in the actual act of teaching, then the issues about the authenticity of the account and the nature of the primary source of data for recall become important.

It is worth noting that those providing the most detailed critical appraisals of the technique (Yinger, 1986; Lyle, 2003) do not dismiss its use out of hand and support its use for exploring tacit knowledge and implicit theories of teaching. The point is an epistemological one relating to the knowledge claims one might wish to make from the recall data. It is possible to use stimulated recall to investigate teacher thinking provided that one recognises its limitations.

Other questions relate to procedural aspects in using stimulated recall. These are presented in no particular order and are clearly inter-related in developing a research design.

How long after the event should the recall interview take place?

The general guidance suggests 'as soon as possible', but practicalities often impose a delay before the teacher is available and not under pressure to undertake the interview. It would seem a common-sense perspective to believe that the longer it is between the event itself and the discussion of it, the more chance that thinking will be constructed or reconstructed rather than recalled. However, claims have been made that recall is possible as much as 48 hours after the event. This would seem to be a maximum time interval.

The risk of 'recall decay' needs to be balanced with the time available for the recall interview and the conditions under which it takes place. For example, it might be better to wait for a few more hours after a lesson to conduct the interview at the end of a working day rather than immediately after a morning lesson with pressure of teaching other classes in the afternoon. It is important that the teacher is relaxed and that the interview takes place somewhere without outside disturbance, where he or she can concentrate on the viewing.

What length of time should the recall interview take?

Too long and the participant may become fatigued; too short and recall may not be as full as possible. There are few recommendations here, but the point stressed is that it should be decided in advance and communicated to participants.

Issues such as facility with language and capability of participants to articulate their thinking might influence decisions made. An intuitive rule of thumb might be that the interview should not exceed the total length of the event/lesson. Assuming the ability to fastforward through some segments, this would be possible but may require some steering of the interview by the researcher.

What is the nature of the stimulus material?

Although video recording is commonly used to provide source material to encourage recall, consideration should be given to whether other material/media could perhaps provide an appropriate stimulus. Several examples are given by Gass and Mackey (2000), including use of written outcomes from classroom activities.

If using a video recording, how much of the recording should be used?

In its pure form, the participant should perhaps have the recording of the whole event to view in the recall session, but there might be arguments for the researcher pre-selecting segments to view, particularly if the event was very long and there were long periods of a single activity (e.g. writing an extended prose response or watching a video). The question here is clearly what criteria the researcher might apply in selecting segments. This could be on the basis of capturing different classroom activities or in relation to some theoretical framework underpinning the research. It seems to go against the principle of allowing the teacher to be in control of the recall interview for the researcher to pre-select what is viewed, but there may be circumstances in which this is necessary. The time taken to identify segments and perhaps edit the recording may have an influence on how soon after the event the recall interview can take place.

What guidance should be given to the interviewee?

A variety of approaches has been used here. Beyond the technical guidance about how to control the viewing of the recording, the main issue is the extent to which the researcher might give guidance to the teachers about what they should be looking for and commenting on. There seems to be an inductivist–deductivist spectrum in methodological terms. Should the researcher try to be neutral and allow the teacher to identify significance without any intervention from the researcher? Or is the use of some non-directive questioning or prompting acceptable? Or should the researcher steer the viewing towards points which may give insights within a pre-determined framework? This is a difficult balance for the researcher to achieve in keeping the interview moving (particularly if it is taking place within an inflexible timeframe) and directing the teacher towards events which are significant to the researcher but perhaps not to the teacher.

In our study, we were somewhere between the two ends of the spectrum. We did not have a standardised set of questions for the interview, but we did comment on particular aspects while viewing the recording. The teacher was in control but, as described earlier, we did engage them in a professional dialogue about what was taking place in the lesson. In terms of the stimulated recall interview itself, the balance seems to be towards the non-directive approach with any imposition of theoretical frameworks coming through the data analysis.

Where could a stimulate recall approach be used?

As Gass and Mackey (2000) suggest in their extensive review of stimulated recall, there are many ways in which it might be used. Our focus has been on its use in the exploration of teacher knowledge, thinking and decision making, but this is not the only field. It might be used to study learning more directly by, for example, a teacher talking to pupils about their learning using the stimulus of the video recording of them in the lesson. In the field of second language learning, there is a wide variety of potential uses, which might be applicable in other subject areas.

One other field, which has been explored where stimulated recall approaches seem to have potential, is that of teacher development, both in initial teacher training and continuing professional development contexts. Reitano and Sim (2004) used stimulated recall in a longitudinal study with beginning teachers, arguing that professional development should take into account the 'social situatedness' of teachers' work (Clarke and Hollingsworth, 2002) and claiming that stimulated recall could have an important part to play in professional development as well as educational research. Because teachers are actively involved in the stimulated recall interview and because the focus of there is on their practice in its social context, they will have the opportunity to reflect on their practice and come to understand it more clearly. This would then form the core of an approach to their professional development, working with other teachers or outside agents. With current interest in a more school-focused approach and use of coaching in professional development, there may be potential for this approach. In England, the National College for School Leadership has drawn on work in Australia by McMeniman *et al.* (2000) to promote the use of stimulated recall as a way of evidencing the impact of educational research on practice. There could be particular value in using stimulated recall as a way of novice and expert teachers working together, or as Ethel and McMeniman (2000) put it, 'unlocking the knowledge in action' of expert practitioners.

In our study we did not collect systematic data about the impact of the teachers' involvement on their own professional development, but anecdotal comments suggested they found it a useful experience in giving them the opportunity to talk about and learn from their practice in this way. We hope that, with awareness of the limitations of the technique, others will use it in research on teaching and with teachers.

References

Berliner, D. C. (2004) 'Describing the behaviour and documenting the accomplishments of expert teachers', *Bulletin of Science, Technology and Society*, 24 (3): 200–212.

Bishop, K. N. and Denley, P. (2007) *Learning Science Teaching*, Maidenhead: Open University Press.

Bloom, B. S. (1953) 'Thought processes in lectures and discussions', *Journal of General Education*, 7: 160–169.

Butefish, W. L. (1990) 'Science teachers' perceptions of their interactive decisions', *Journal of Educational Research*, 84: 107–114.

Calderhead, J. (1981) 'Stimulated recall: a method for research on teaching', *British Journal of Educational Psychology*, 51: 211–217.

Clark, C. M. and Peterson, P. L. (1986) 'Teachers' thought processes', in M.C. Wittrock (ed.) *Handbook of Research on Teaching*, Third edition, New York: Macmillan.

Clarke, D. and Hollingsworth, H. (2002) 'Elaborating a model of teacher professional growth', *Teaching and Teacher Education*, 18(8): 947–967.

Egi, T. (2008) 'Investigating stimulated recall as a cognitive measure: reactivity and verbal reports in SLA research methodology', *Language Awareness*, 17(3): 212–228.

Ethel, R. G. and McMeniman, M. M. (2000) 'Unlocking the knowledge in action of an expert practitioner', *Journal of Teacher Education*, 51(2): 87–101.

Gass, S. M. and Mackey, A. (2000) *Stimulated Recall Methodology in Second Language Research*, Mahwah, NJ: Lawrence Erlbaum Associates.

Gess-Newsome, J. and Lederman, N. G. (eds) (1999) *Examining Pedagogical Content Knowledge: The Construct and its Implications for Science Education*, New York: Kluwer.

Housner, L. D. and Griffey, D. C. (1985) 'Teacher cognition: differences in planning and interactive decision-making between experienced and inexperienced teachers', *Research Quarterly for Exercise and Sport*, 56(1): 45–53.

Loughran, J., Berry, A. and Mulhall, P. (2006) *Understanding and Developing Science Teachers' Pedagogical Content Knowledge*, Rotterdam: Sense Publishers.

Lyle, J. (2003) 'Stimulated recall: a report on its use in naturalistic research', *British Educational Research Journal*, 29(6): 861–878.

McMeniman, M., Cumming, J., Wilson, J., Stevenson, J. and Sim, C. (2000) 'Teacher knowledge in action', in Department of Education, Training and Youth Affairs (DETYA), *The Impact of Educational Research*, Canberra, Australia: DETYA.

Meade, P. and McMeniman, M. (1992) 'Stimulated recall – an effective methodology for examining successful teaching in science', *Australian Educational Researcher*, 19(3): 1–18.

Qualitative Solutions and Research (QSR) (2009) 'NVivo software for analysis and insight', Online. Available HTTP: <http://www.qsrinternational.com/products_nvivo.aspx> (accessed 10 April 2009).

O'Brien, J. (1993) 'Action research through stimulated recall', *Research in Science Education*, 23(1): 214–221.

Reitano, P. (2006) 'The value of video stimulated recall in reflective teaching practices', paper presented at the Australian Consortium for Social and Political Research, Social Science Methodology Conference, Sydney, NSW, Australia, December.

Reitano, P. and Sim, C. (2004) 'Providing a space for professional growth through research', paper presented at the Australian Teacher Education Association Conference, Bathurst, NSW, Australia, July.

Shulman, L. S. (1987) 'Knowledge and teaching: foundations of the new reform', *Harvard Education Review*, 57(1): 1–22.

Yinger, R. J. (1986) 'Examining thought in action: a theoretical and methodological critique of research on interactive teaching', *Teaching and Teacher Education*, 2(3): 263–282.

Chapter 8

A developing narrative

Analysing teachers in training/tutor conferences

Charles Anderson and Pauline Sangster

A common challenge faced by researchers employing qualitative methods is that general approaches to research and analysis do not come 'oven-ready'. There is a need to form a defensible personal interpretation of the nature of a particular research approach and to think through carefully how this understanding can then be translated into action. Another challenge is posed by the range of approaches that is now available to a qualitative researcher, for example, grounded theory, discourse analysis, critical discourse analysis, narrative enquiry and ethnographies. Each of the approaches in the preceding list also can be seen to have distinct variants and to be marked by internal debate rather than representing a homogenous set of epistemological and ontological assumptions and agreed research procedures. How does one make a choice that is well principled? These two challenges are likely to be particularly acute when one explores a less-established field of study where there are no well-trodden paths of analysis to follow. This chapter sets out how, in a current study, we have wrestled with these challenges to find approaches that were fit for our immediate research purposes and well-tailored to capture the patterns and forms of meaning that became visible in our body of data. The study examined the discussions between an experienced tutor, Pauline Sangster, and ten students training to be teachers of English that took place after these students had given a lesson (at different points during their training year). It involved close analysis of transcripts of the talk in these individual sessions by Pauline Sangster and Charles Anderson.

Introduction

The chapter focuses on the work of analysis in this study and the reasoning that informed this analytical work, but it also considers other central methodological matters, including the issues raised by one of the researchers' 'insider' role and her responsibilities as a tutor as well as an observer, and the differing but converging positions of the two researchers. Before we give an account of the approaches that we adopted to analyse our data, we felt it was necessary to reflect on: our role as analysts; what we were individually and jointly bringing to the process; and the advantages and limitations of our individual positions in relation to the study.

Our focus in this chapter is not to engage in a critique of the conceptual basis of different varieties of reflexivity, but to give a concrete sense of what for us were key foci of concern in reflecting on our roles as researchers and on the ideas that we were bringing to the work of analysis. We describe how we reflected on and attempted to take account of the effects of: our researcher roles; our positioning in relation to research participants; and our values and ideas. The analysis itself involved three main phases: an initial phase of interactive reading; a phase that centered on thematic analysis of the transcripts; and a final phase that examined the transcripts through the lens of narrative.

The research questions that gave a focus to the study are listed under the section on our aims. In this chapter we set out to give a sense of exactly how they featured in our analysis. Looked at as a set, they reveal our interest in attempting to establish *what* exactly happened and *how* particular activities were achieved. In the second phase of the analysis our attention focused more on *what* happened. In the third (narrative) phase of the analysis our attention focused more on the *how*, but throughout there was a concern to be alert to the relationship between form and substance. Wanting to give due weight to the whats and the hows drove the deployment of both thematic and narrative approaches to analysis. This phase of the analysis focused on examining: narrative structure; narrative perspective; story and emplotment; characterisation; setting; tone; themes; and discourses. Before we set out to explore these methodological decisions and concerns, it is first necessary to sketch in the broad contours of the study itself.

Outline of the study

While there is a very substantial body of research and theory on the initial professional development of teachers and the encouragement of reflective practice (e.g. Forde *et al.*, 2006; Pollard *et al.*, 2008), the one-to-one sessions in which an academic tutor and a student discuss and reflect on episodes of teaching have been relatively unexplored (Alger, 2006; Ottesen, 2007; Stevens and Lowing, 2008). Such discussions have the potential to be an important resource for the development of students' classroom practice and an influence on the formation of their professional identity and values. Examining these sessions enabled us to pursue our intrinsic interest in an unexplored area that intrigued us and to contribute to the understanding of a central facet of teacher education. It was also driven by Pauline's desire to gain a more nuanced and analytical awareness of her own practice as a tutor in such sessions.

The following section details the research questions that emerged from these general drivers of the study. First, it is important, as a reflexive move, to give a general sense of how we frame the nature of teachers' professional formation. Our general understanding of, and key concerns related to, reflexivity are discussed in a following section. Rather than confining attention to the acquisition of a set of discrete skills and outcomes, we see student teachers as grappling with the intermeshed challenges of gaining new forms of 'knowing, acting and being'

(Barnett and Coate, 2005: 59–65). This wide view of teacher *formation* as involving not only the acquisition of theoretical, embedded and embodied knowledge, but also the performance of specific professional ways of acting and being has implicitly and explicitly informed all phases and aspects of our study.

Aims

Our research questions centered on delineating the activities and purposes pursued within these sessions, and the nature and the form of the interaction. In other words, there was a focus both on what happened and how it happened. Specifically, there was a concern to:

- examine the nature and form of the interactions between each student and Pauline, including possible changes over time;
- analyse the nature of the accounts provided by students of their teaching, how they positioned themselves within these accounts, what they attended to and what they did not notice, what discourses they employed and possible changes in all of these features over time;
- explore how the tutor acted to focus students' attention, scaffold reflections on their planning and teaching and encourage analytical engagement and position the student within debriefing sessions and in relation to his or her own developing practice, the school students and the teaching profession;
- analyse variation in Pauline's interactions with 'struggling' versus more competent students.

The students' placement experience

Setting this study in context, the student participants were undertaking a one year Professional Graduate Diploma in Education (Secondary) (PGDE(S)) during the 2007–08 academic session. This professional qualification course entails three school placement experiences, which are evenly spaced over the year. A central driver of placement choice is to ensure that over the course of the year student teachers work in schools that serve contrasting socio-economic communities. In each placement they are expected to plan and implement lessons for different ages and stages of school students. The normal pattern of interaction with university tutors during these school placements is that students are visited and have their lessons observed on four occasions during the academic year, twice in the first term and once in each of the second and third terms. (However, should problems arise, more frequent visits are made.) Throughout each of the placements students are required to maintain an extensive Professional Development Portfolio (PDP), which details their planning, teaching, assessment activities and self-evaluation and reflection. Before observing a lesson within the sequence of the student's planned programme of teaching, the university tutor will have read the student's PDP and have available a detailed plan for this particular lesson. During the academic session

2007–08, both visits in term one were formatively assessed and each of the visits in terms two and three were summatively assessed. We will return shortly to discuss matters that arise for the study in relation to the tutor's assessment role.

The study design/data creation

Recording the sessions

The study centred on the recording of the discussions that took place between Pauline, in her role as a university tutor, and the students after she had observed their lessons. Ten students out of a year cohort of 69 students volunteered to take part in the study. The group comprised nine women and one man, a gender ratio that closely mirrored that of the whole cohort (9:1). In all, 42 student/tutor sessions were tape-recorded (four with each of nine students recorded over the three terms and six with one student who was experiencing difficulties and received additional visits). The shortest of these sessions lasted 47 minutes and the longest one hour and 27 minutes. There was thus a substantial corpus of talk to analyse. The decision to record sessions in each of the three terms was an important element of the study's design. Given the focus on teacher formation, it was important to be able to track any changes in students' accounts and in the nature of student/ tutor interaction over the course of the year.

Transcriptions

Transcription, we were aware, involves a process of construction rather than simple reproduction. While the study did not take a conversation analysis approach to the analysis of data and therefore did not need to follow the very fine-grained procedures of transcription associated with such an approach, we were very alert to issues surrounding transcription that feature in the methods literature (e.g. Atkinson, 1992; Riesmann, 1993) and, more specifically, to the need in a study of talk to scrutinise transcription decisions closely, returning, where necessary, to the recordings themselves to ground our interpretations.

Observation notes

In addition to the recording of the sessions themselves, we had available to us the student's plan for each lesson, the detailed notes that the tutor had made while observing the lesson that was being discussed and the tutor's subsequent report. These were consulted when analysing individual transcripts.

Student interviews

While not the primary focus of data creation in the study, it seemed both necessary and useful to gain the students' views on how they had found these sessions and how they represented their development over the course of their training year. Accordingly, at the very end of the year, once all evaluations of their performance were complete, Charles conducted a semi-structured interview with each of the ten students in conditions of anonymity that allowed them to offer frank responses. Charles had never met the students prior to these interviews and the students were asked not to identify themselves to him by name. While the conditions under which the interviews took place meant that individual interviews could not be matched with particular sets of transcripts, these interviews did inform our general analysis of the transcripts.

Key ethical considerations

Close attention also clearly needed to be given to questions concerning anonymity and confidentiality at the stages of analysis and reporting, with care being necessary to ensure that individuals could not be identified from quotations that we employed from the transcripts. While the students had volunteered to take part in the study, this was not at all viewed as sufficiently dealing with the question of consent. In this context, consent required particular attention given the unequal nature of relations between students and academic staff and the fact that students were being assessed on their teaching performance. Additionally, consent given at the beginning of a year could not be informed by the students' actual experience of teaching and these post-lesson discussion sessions. Accordingly, students were regularly assured that they could leave the study at any time and, if they wished, that they could transfer to another tutor. Consent to tape-record was sought on each occasion and it was made clear that taping could stop at any time – in one instance a student did ask the recording to stop for a while and resume it later.

While it was necessary to address these central ethical matters in the study, to confine our attention to actions in relation to anonymity, confidentiality and consent would, in our view, have imposed a limiting perspective on the moral positioning and responsibilities of a researcher. One danger of such a narrow focus of attention is that it can lead one to take an overly instrumental approach to moral questions. In Schwandt's words:

> ethical-moral relations can be defined as a kind of 'problem' that must be solved by adopting the right kind of research ethics for 'gazing', or by using the right kind of textual form, or by employing the right kind of methodology . . . [reducing] the dilemmas of human existence to objective problems in need of solutions.
>
> (2003: 319)

He goes on to note how an alternative approach to 'the question of relations and representation . . . understands the situation of "How shall I be towards these people I am studying?" as one that demands a particular kind of understanding . . . as practical-moral knowledge' (ibid.).

Our own approach to conceptualisation and action in relation to research ethics resonates with the position of writers who can be characterised as neo-Aristotelian, for example MacIntyre (1981), Macfarlane (2004, 2008) and especially Nussbaum, who exhibits a 'general mistrust of the moral/non-moral distinction' (1986: 28). On our reading, one main thrust of these writers' emphasis on practical-moral knowledge is to move attention away from the idea of research ethics as a neatly delineated sphere of issues and concerns to foreground the relationships between researchers and participants and the qualities that the researcher can be expected to exhibit in such relationships. For Nussbaum in particular (1990; and see Schwandt, 2003: 317), central importance is given to close attentiveness and responsiveness to others and to 'the refined perception of the contingencies of a particular situation' (1986: 318).

The need for close attentiveness to others' needs and experiences was especially salient in this study, given that in these post-lesson discussions the students needed to be respected as research participants but were primarily required to be engaged with appropriately as *student teachers* where it was central, instrumentally and morally, to establish a relationship of trust in which vulnerabilities could be revealed and respected. For this to be achieved, Pauline had to be fully in her role as tutor in these sessions with the role of researcher falling into the background.

Analysis

Our positionings as researchers/aspects of reflexivity

A very different balance of roles clearly had to be achieved when we moved to the stage of analysing transcripts, although the need to display appropriate qualities as researchers remained (Macfarlane, 2008). Before we discuss the approaches that we adopted, we look first at ourselves as researchers. In discussing our roles we recognise that reflexivity is now a contested concept and that there are multiple versions within the methods literature of what reflexivity may entail. For a very clear, trenchant review of the array of versions of reflexivity, see Lynch (2000). As Langdridge (2007: 60) notes, discussion of reflexivity can concentrate on 'the *personal* (the effect of the individual) and *functional* (the influence of one's role as a researcher)'. He also points to the type of reflexivity discussed by Wilkinson (1988) that 'she terms *disciplinary reflexivity* and entails a critical stance towards the research in the context of debates about theory and method'; and a form of reflexivity that 'involves a critical stance towards academic discourse itself (ibid.)'.

As we noted earlier, our focus in this chapter is not to examine the conceptual foundations of different varieties of reflexivity, but to give a concrete sense of what were our key foci of concern in reflecting on our roles as researchers and on the ideas that we were bringing to the work of analysis. Looking first at our roles as researchers, we were positioned very differently in relation to the topic and to the student participants. As earlier sections have revealed, Pauline was very much an insider. As we have highlighted, during 'data-collection' she needed to engage with her role as tutor if she were to act in a morally responsible fashion. By contrast, Charles had no direct contact with the students until the stage of interview and had never acted in the role of tutor to secondary school teachers in training. While it might be conventional to see the insider role as one that is more likely to introduce bias into the analysis of data, it is important to note that disadvantages also inhere in the more distanced view of an 'outsider'. The outsider may lack the insider's refined ways of seeing that have been cultivated through practice and may be less able to read a context and the more subtle aspects of its meaning.

At the stage of analysis we were very alert to the advantages and disadvantages associated with our insider and outsider positions; the way in which we took the analysis ahead in effect served both to capitalise on their strengths and, to a degree, disrupt these positions. During the first stage of the analysis – that of close, interactive reading of the transcripts – we first read through and annotated each transcript independently before coming together to discuss our interpretations. For Pauline, this close reading drew on her insider knowledge of and perspective on the interactions in these sessions, but at the same time she attempted to adopt a more distanced and somewhat detached stance. When we came together, we set out to unpack and justify the grounds on which we were developing particular readings of the transcripts. An important element of this interaction around the transcripts involved Charles in effect interviewing Pauline concerning her motives for the focus, substance and form of specific interactional moves, her general purposes and the values that were actuating her conduct in these sessions. Questions included 'Why did you ask X this question in that particular way?' While these repeated interviews were necessary for the appropriate interpretation of individual transcripts, they can also be seen cumulatively to have served the purpose of unpacking, to some extent, Pauline's insider's assumptions and perspectives. At the same time, gaining greater insight into Pauline's insider views made Charles, to a limited but important degree, less of an outsider. This process proved both a challenging and a surprisingly enjoyable experience.

The unpacking and sharing of Pauline's insider stance was of course only one element of the analysis. It was important to balance attention to her actions with a detailed consideration of the students' discourse and actions. Here there was a need to consider not only the immediate contextual circumstances that occasioned their talk and the fact that their classroom performance was subject to assessment, but also a wider institutional context where, in relation to Pauline as tutor as well as to established classroom teachers, the students occupied an asymmetric position in terms of status and experience. While alert to the possible effect of these asymmetries in the discussion sessions, informed by studies of talk in institutional and work settings we did not assume that the asymmetries would necessarily play out in any straightforward fashion in the interactions within the sessions.

At the beginning of this chapter we highlighted the foundational assumptions concerning the nature of teacher formation that informed the study and we have described the work of unpacking Pauline's theory in action. During the analysis we also tried to think through what emerging interpretations revealed about our own assumptions about what becoming an accomplished teacher entails. We certainly could not claim that we could easily bracket these assumptions or that they were always the focus of our attention, but at least we were careful not to be wholly confined by them. It is worth adding that, in the analysis of sessions where student teachers were being encouraged to be more reflective about their practice, it would have been egregiously inconsistent of us as researchers not to examine our own theoretical understanding and everyday assumptions.

We will return to outline the ways in which theories featured in our interactions with the transcripts and how we thought through key methodological issues. For the moment, though, it is appropriate to draw out a central thrust of how we reflected on and attempted to take account of the effects of: our researcher roles; our positioning in relation to research participants; and our values and ideas. This central thrust is brought out more eloquently than we could achieve ourselves in the following discussion of self and reflexivity in literary studies by Hunt and Sampson:

> reflexivity . . . involves creating an internal space, distancing ourselves from ourselves, as it were, so that we are both 'inside and outside' ourselves simultaneously and able to switch back and forth fluidly and playfully from one position to the other, giving ourselves up to the experience of 'self as other' whilst also retaining a grounding in our familiar sense of self . . . Thus reflexivity involves not *getting rid* of the self, but *doubling* the self: distancing ourselves from ourselves to a greater or lesser extent, so that we have a sense of standing outside ourselves and observing what we are doing and thinking.
> (2006: 4)

The quotation resonates with our own experience of attempting to gain some distance from an unreflective 'grounding in our familiar sense of self' but not seeing it as either possible or desirable to get 'rid of' our own ways of thinking and being. While we would not at all claim to have achieved any 'doubling' of the self, gaining more of an observer's view on our thinking and activities was of distinct value to the project; we would claim that it is an objective that conscientious social researchers should aim towards. However, we would not see such actions as a straightforward answer to problems of bias, for our somewhat more detached observer view of ourselves is still a necessarily partial view from somewhere and does not give us a single, veridical perspective on the topic that we are investigating. We will return to questions concerning epistemology and validity.

An overview of analytical approaches and procedures

In considering our research roles, we have necessarily had to preview certain activities involved in the analysis. Moving now to focus centrally on the analysis itself, it can be seen to have involved three main phases: an initial phase of inter-active reading (see Dey, 1993); a phase which centered on thematic analysis of the transcripts; and a final phase which examined the transcripts through the lens of narrative. The processes that featured centrally within the initial phase of interactive reading have been described in some detail in the preceding section. Before we focus on the separate stages of thematic and narrative analyses, it is necessary first to point out commonalities in approach and in procedures that marked all phases of analytical work. Central questions that feature here are: How inductive was our analysis? What epistemological status did we give to our findings?

Analysis and findings: an interpretative, constructive stance

In addressing both these questions, it is appropriate to note the degree to which the first two stages of our analysis were influenced by recent reformulations of grounded theory (Charmaz, 2006; Dey, 1999; Pidgeon, 1996; Pidgeon and Henwood, 1996), as well as points of contrast with a grounded theory approach. Given that grounded theory itself has changed considerably over time and that different grounded theorists have been guided by differing epistemological assumptions, it is important to be precise about the exact points of influence on our own work. With Charmaz (2006: 131) we would wish to distance ourselves from the objectivist grounded theory to which its founders subscribed and which 'resides in the positivist tradition and thus attends to data as real in and of themselves and does not attend to the processes of their production' (ibid.). Rather, we would wish to align ourselves with the constructivist approach Charmaz advocates, an approach which 'assumes an obdurate, yet ever-changing world but recognizes diverse local worlds and multiple realities' (Charmaz, 2006: 132). At the same time it 'explicitly assumes that any theoretical rendering offers an *interpretive* portrayal of the studied world, not an exact picture of it . . . Research participants' implicit meanings, experiential views – and researchers' finished grounded theories are constructions of reality' (Charmaz, 2006: 10). Such an approach – where the researcher's own constructive efforts in analysis are foregrounded – would seem to point out the centrality of the matters regarding reflexivity that we have just addressed, including the effects of our own general values and our values concerning how school students and teachers in training should be treated. Viewing our efforts as an '*interpretive* portrayal' was a particularly salient concern in the narrative phase of our analysis.

How inductive was our analysis?

Reviewing the debates within grounded theory also enables us to frame the discussion of how our research questions and knowledge of particular bodies of literature informed our interactions with, and around, the transcripts of these sessions. How innocent were our eyes in scanning these transcripts? Reading in areas that we viewed as relevant to the topic (e.g. teacher development, reflective practice, studies of talk in educational and other institutional settings and politeness theory) meant that we were, in effect, approaching the analysis with what Blumer (1969) describes as 'sensitizing concepts' that could not but influence the questions and the issues to which we were alert. However, we did not view this as at all problematic, taking encouragement from Dey's pithily expressed judgement that 'there is a difference between an open mind and an empty head' (Dey, 1999: 251 cited by Charmaz, 2006: 48). What to us was key was that there had to be an appropriate meshing of concepts and perspectives from the literature with the particular patterns of meaning that were emerging from our analysis of this data set. We felt that this meshing was achieved, for example, in relation to our deployment of Ricoeur's concept of 'narrative time' – a matter that we discuss in the following section. In seeking this mesh between concepts brought to the data and the data themselves, we were in effect following Charmaz's cautionary note that:

> sensitizing concepts and disciplinary perspectives provide a place to *start*, not to *end*. Grounded theorists use sensitizing concepts as tentative tools for developing their ideas about processes that they define in their data. If particular sensitizing concepts prove to be irrelevant, then we dispense with them.
>
> (2006: 16)

A similar set of considerations applied to the role of our research questions. It will be seen from the listing in the section on our aims that these were not designed as hypotheses to be tested in a top–down fashion; rather, they acted to give focus to the research, including the stage of analysis. We felt that the particular way in which they were framed did not constrain our interaction with the data. Our actual practice, particularly in the thematic phase of our analysis, fits the more constructionist version of grounded theory that Pidgeon (1996) has formulated to a considerable degree. In particular, the following quotation from Pidgeon captures the interplay between concepts brought to our study, side-by-side with emerging ideas, in ongoing engagement with the data:

> a more satisfactory resolution of the problem of grounding in grounded theory is to recognize that it makes no sense to claim that research can proceed *either* from testing prior theory alone *or* from a 'pure' inductive analysis of data. In the case of grounded theory, in particular, what appears to be the 'discovery' or 'emergence' of concepts and theory is in reality the result of a constant interplay between data and the researcher's developing conceptualizations, a 'flip-flop' between ideas and research experience (Bulmer, 1979). This sort of process is better described as one of *theory generation* (rather than as one of discovery), something which is a central aspect of the social practice of science, as well as use of the grounded theory technique.
>
> (Pidgeon, 1996: 82)

Central processes in the analysis

A central matter in taking the interactive reading and subsequent phases of analysis of transcripts ahead was continuous comparison across the data set to assist us in the construction of patterns of meaning. Comparison took place both within individual transcripts and across the whole set of transcripts for an individual student, where a key matter was considering continuities and contrasts over the course of the year. (Indeed the whole study has been designed to make such an exercise of examining potential changes over time possible.) Comparison also took place between students, not only synoptically but also in relation to specific themes and forms of construction of their accounts. In making all these comparisons we had an eye for commonalities and contrasts, and were aware of the danger that one can readily fall into the set of being a lumper or a splitter. We have noted earlier how the interaction between us in work sessions served to clarify and refine our understanding of the transcripts and forced us to justify emerging interpretations. As interpretations began to firm up we tried to be alert to possibly disconfirming data; we readily fell into the enjoyable roles of bickering counsels for the prosecution.

Emerging themes and the move to a narrative focus

Among the themes which began to emerge as we took the analysis forward was the role the tutor played in the 'education of attention' (Gibson, 1979: 254). It was a role that entailed lending her attentiveness to particular aspects and patterns of classroom life and, in Bruner's phrase, providing a 'loan of consciousness' (Bruner, 1986: 76) to the students. Other matters on which attention came to centre in the analysis included:

- marking up key matters for students;
- fostering particular values and ways of being as teachers;
- teaching as performance;
- matters marked up for praise, revealing the tutor's implicit model of teaching and learning;
- variability in the tutor's interactions across students and over the year.

Identifying these general themes helped us to clarify what was happening in these sessions. It also seemed appropriate to report on these matters at this level of generalisation. One possibility at this stage would have been to have taken these emerging themes and develop them in a manner fully consistent with a grounded theory approach, constructing clearly defined individual analytical categories that would have coherence as a set and appropriately frame key patterns of meaning. However, at this point we chose not to take this road; we chose to move to a focus on narrative and to deploy narrative constructs in our analysis. Why?

Certain other themes in, and insights emerging from, the transcripts could not readily be captured in a thematic analysis. This was particularly true of the intricate ways in which Pauline was acting to position students' professional development in relation to time. This dynamic positioning could not be fitted in an appropriate fashion into a synoptic, analytical scheme of categorisation. Individual patterns of meaning would be ill served by being shoehorned into such a scheme, and we were forcibly struck by how the meanings created in these sessions hinged on the exact forms and structures deployed in the talk. Accordingly, we needed to take ahead a form of analysis that brought the form – the hows of interaction – to the foreground. What was happening in these sessions was not a simple recounting of events on which the tutor then provided feedback, but rather a more complex joint weaving of an account that brought meaning to the events of the lesson. What was happening is captured in the following quotation from Salmon as she notes that:

> A fundamental criterion of narrative is surely that of contingency. Whatever the content, stories demand the consequential linking of events or ideas. Narrative shaping entails imposing a meaningful pattern on what would otherwise be random and disconnected.
>
> (Salmon and Riesmann, 2008: 78).

Close attention to the forms that interaction was taking in these sessions revealed that they could be appropriately represented by deploying constructs from literary narrative analysis. Before we describe the particular constructs that centrally featured in this phase of our work, it is necessary to give a sense of how we also took account of insights from the extensive body of writing on the use of narrative methods in the social sciences. In common with writers such as Gubrium and Holstein (1995, 2009) we were alert to the fact that 'analysis needs to orient to the interactions and circumstances of narrative production as well as to the story that is produced' (2009: 42). In our particular setting, this entailed being alert to both the asymmetries between Pauline and the students and the fact that Pauline brought a particular set of audience requirements to the student. Attention was similarly given to what narrative resources and constraints operated in this setting, considering, as Chase indicates, how students' accounts were

> both enabled and constrained by a range of social resources and circumstances. These include the possibilities for self and reality construction that are intelligible within the narrator's community, local setting, organizational and social memberships, and cultural and historical location.
>
> (2005: 657)

While we shared this concern with how the accounts we were studying might be shaped by very immediate interactional and wider social factors, our focus of attention was somewhat different from that of studies which have employed narrative methods within life history studies. There, as Chase rightly observes, 'narrative is retrospective meaning making – the shaping or ordering of past experience' (2005: 656). In our own study, the sessions displayed a strong concern rather with prospective meaning making and professional development; time's arrow flew forwards and backwards within the narratives. Through experiment and reflection, it became clear that this work of prospective meaning making could be captured by means of the central devices that are customarily employed in analysing literary narratives. Focusing on these devices also made us very alert to our own narrative moves in progressing the analysis and in reporting.

Structures, narrators, characters and themes

Moving from these general considerations to give a more detailed sense of which literary narrative constructs proved to be productive in our analysis, our efforts focused on examining: narrative structure; narrative perspective; story and emplotment; characterisation; setting; tone; themes; and discourses. Reviewing briefly in turn how we deployed these constructs, under narrative structure we examined the precise ways in which students earlier in the year were assisted to construct a chronological, analytical account of the lesson which they had just planned and delivered. We also recognised how such a chronological, analytical structure was regarded as a foundational, framing device in this setting. A key matter that emerged from the close consideration of the structure of students' accounts was the differential shift over the year in the degree to which students could wholly structure their own narratives rather than have these scaffolded by the tutor. We also compared the nature of these narrative structures over the course of the year, noting how they tended to become more complex. In particular, we noted that they were not confined to straightforward chronological accounts but could move with some flexibility between the recent past, the present and the envisaged future. Attending to narrative perspective, we categorised whether the student teachers were telling a story wholly from their viewpoint or bringing school students' voices and perceptions more centrally into the narrative. Examining narrative perspective entailed identifying the stance that they were adopting towards the school students and the ways in which, and the degree to which, they could shift perspectives.

In looking at story and emplotment, we charted how events were simply recounted or presented in a more cohesive fashion, revealing how interconnections were perceived and constructed. Part of our concern here was to explore the emplotment of their own role in their accounts (i.e. how did they order and establish connections between classroom actions, draw events and activities together into an account and place themselves within this account?). This included the extent to which they presented connections as occurring as the result of their own agency or as happening outside their own control. Our analysis revealed how the unfolding of the plots of teacher students' narratives was shaped by the ways in which they characterised themselves and their school students both explicitly and implicitly. For example, there were marked differences in the plots of lessons given by students who characterised themselves as lacking agency and who did not present themselves as centrally responsible for how events unfolded in the classroom versus those who presented themselves as more powerful agents who could both influence and have responsibility for classroom events.

Close attention was paid to variations across an individual student's transcripts and across the whole data set to see how they characterised their motivations and themselves in relation to other actors. This provided insights into students' professional formation. Most students could be seen over time to move from portraying themselves as more detached individuals to talking about themselves as part of a community of teachers. Changes over time were also noted in how these trainee teachers characterised their school students – changes that were associated with their increasing capacity to deploy different narrative perspectives. In addition, we noted whether individual students confined their accounts to the immediate setting of the classroom where they were teaching or also invoked future settings for professional action. Variations in the tone created by students – as their narratives developed, as they characterised themselves and their school students, as they established settings and as they adopted different narrative perspectives – were compared and contrasted.

In identifying the themes that featured in the sessions, we were concerned with tracking any changes in the matters to which they attended and in the weighting given to different themes. Who introduced and controlled the themes – tutor or student – and possible changes here over time also merited attention. In examining themes, it was important to be alert to the questions of themes from whose perspective there was clear evidence of student and tutor directly surfacing and orienting to a particular theme. Or, at the stage of analysis, were we inferring the existence of certain themes? At the same time, we noted the discourses within which these themes (and indeed all of the students' talk about teaching) were framed. In particular, we noted whether or not the students shared a common professional and academic discourse about teaching with Pauline.

Developmental narratives

The preceding paragraphs have foregrounded the devices around which students' narratives were analysed. In pursuing this analysis of student narratives, we were very conscious of the fact that these were in effect co-constructed with Pauline. Accordingly, a central concern was to delineate Pauline's shaping of these narratives and to identify the types of narratives that she was facilitating and promoting. Pauline's actions, including how she encouraged students to characterise themselves, could be viewed as giving students a disciplinary gaze on the world, which, in Gubrium and Holstein's words:

is not only a way of viewing the world, but also a way of understanding, describing, and controlling it. Such disciplinary discourses result in characteristic narratives, leading participants to story things in special ways.

(2009: 162 and see Sheridan, 1980)

Analysis of Pauline's actions across all of the sessions revealed that the way in which she provided students with a particular perspective on time and the relationship of this perspective to students' development were central matters. Here we found Ricoeur's concept of narrative time (Muldoon, 2002, 2006; Ricoeur, 1990), which explores how 'our experience of time is embedded in the textuality of our existence . . . [and] is refashioned by its passage through the grid of narrative' (Muldoon, 2002: 65–66) to be a valuable theoretical lens. It provided an apposite way in which to frame the tutor's activities in intricately positioning the students in relation to time in ways which foregrounded development. This particular emplotment of students' activities in relation to time was coupled with other narrative moves. Taken together, these narrative actions could be viewed as assisting students to gain a sense of coherence and meaningful pattern to their experiences and to construct a developmental narrative of their actions and being as teachers, marked by: orientating towards the future; treating the immediate past as a resource for learning; positioning themselves within the community of teachers; and presenting themselves as active, potentially powerful agents. These sessions could thus be seen as not simply occasions for giving students feedback on their teaching, but as being settings for interactively creating particular narratives of professional formation that refigured experience.

Questions of trustworthiness

Although not fully persuaded by reader response theories of literary analysis (e.g. Rosenblatt, 1995; Karolides, 2000), we recognise that a listener or reader does not simply decode a literary or social text, but that narratives reside at least in part in the processes of reading and the pre-understandings that are brought to them. While we were alert to the elements of co-construction of narratives in these sessions by the students and Pauline, we also need to acknowledge that the account we have produced as analysts is itself a co-construction between ourselves in this role and the original participants.

Clearly, other researchers approaching these sessions with different analytical lenses and personal investments and values concerning this topic might have constructed a markedly different account. Recognising this possibility does not mean, however, that we would see these transcripts, or indeed any text, as susceptible to any reading whatsoever or that qualitative judgements cannot be made in comparing different interpretations. What was key for us was to ensure that the particular reading we produced – and the reporting narrative we then wove from this analytical reading – was well grounded in the details of interaction in the session, with points of interpretation being clearly and consistently linked to supporting passages in the session texts. As we have stated earlier in the chapter, there was also an attempt to be as alert as possible to disconfirming evidence.

Interpretations had to be argued, both as a point of principle and as a productive part of the dynamics of our research relationship. Moving away from our own practice for a moment to the wider discussion of validity in the social sciences, it might be productive if more attention were focused on the role of argumentation in creating a trustworthy account. For Ricoeur this was one of the central matters in the validation of the meaning of a text. In Kaplan's explication of Ricoeur's position, this entails:

> attention to the other possible meanings that could affect the meaning of text that presents a range of possible interpretations. A guess is always putative, fallible, open to further revision and interpretation, and validated against the horizon of possible meanings by showing that one interpretation is more probable than another in light of what we already know. Validation is not verification but an argumentative practice similar to juridical procedures used in legal interpretation. It follows a 'logic of subjective probability' like Popper's procedures for falsifiability. One can argue for the relative superiority of a conflicting interpretation by showing how one interpretation is false or invalid, or that one interpretation is more probable than another.
>
> (Kaplan, 2003: 68)

Kaplan goes on to derive from Ricoeur's writings the position that 'truth claims raised about human actions are interpretations, configured into narratives, open to rational argumentation' (Kaplan, 2003: 73). Staying with wider debates on validation within the social sciences, one main perspective within the last two decades – spearheaded by writers such as Mishler (1990) – has involved reformulating 'validation as the social construction of knowledge. With this reformulation, the key issue becomes whether the relevant community of scientists evaluates reported findings as sufficiently trustworthy to rely on them for their own work' (Mishler, 1990: 427). Such a view of validation as an essentially social process concomitantly foregrounds the importance of transparency in reporting. In Mishler's own words:

> The view of validation that I have advanced suggests that the questions to be asked about my study, and of any study within any research tradition, are: What are the warrants for my claims? Could other investigators make a reasonable judgment of their adequacy? Would they be able to determine how my findings and interpretations were 'produced' and, on that basis, decide whether they were trustworthy enough to be relied upon for their own work? I believe these questions have affirmative answers. The primary reason is the visibility of the work: of the data in the form of the texts used in the analysis, with full transcripts and tapes that can be made available to other researchers;

of the methods that transformed the texts into findings; and of the direct linkages shown between data, findings, and interpretation.

(1990: 429)

Commenting on Mishler's advocacy of the display of 'direct linkages' between 'data, findings, and interpretation', such linkages would seem to entail both the construction of chains of evidence and argument and the display of these chains of argumentation within an account that calls for a particularly open narrative form. There is a resonance here with Kaplan's statement.

Within this chapter we have set out to make our research work in this study sufficiently visible so that others can judge its adequacy. At the same time we recognise that there are obviously clear limits on the extent to which visibility of the work can be achieved and represented to others. There also may be a distinct conflict between the need to warrant and make procedures visible and the need in any narrative – be it a chapter in a methods book such as this one or a fairy story – to tell a clear, coherent story which is not encumbered with too much detail. We leave the reader to judge how well we have handled these (to a degree) competing claims.

References

Alger, A. (2006) 'What went well, what didn't go so well': growth of reflection in pre-service teachers, *Reflective Practice*, 7(3): 287–301.

Atkinson, P. (1992) *Understanding Ethnographic Texts*, Newbury Park, CA/London: SAGE.

Barnett, R. and Coate, K. (2005) *Engaging the Curriculum in Higher Education*, Buckingham: Society for Research into Higher Education and Open University Press.

Blumer, H. (1969) *Symbolic Interactionism*, Englewood Cliffs, NJ: Prentice-Hall.

Bruner, J. (1986) *Actual Minds, Possible Worlds*, Cambridge, MA/London: Harvard University Press.

Charmaz, K. (2006) *Constructing Grounded Theory: A Practical Guide Through Qualitative Analysis*. London/Thousand Oaks, CA/ New Delhi: Sage.

Chase, S. E. (2005) 'Narrative inquiry: multiple lenses, approaches, voices', in N. K. Denzin and Y.S. Lincoln (eds) *The Sage Handbook of Qualitative Research*, Third edition, Thousand Oaks, CA/London: Sage.

Dey, I. (1993) *Qualitative Data Analysis: A User-Friendly Guide for Social Scientists*, London: Routledge.

Dey, I. (1999) *Grounding Grounded Theory: Guidelines for Qualitative Inquiry*, San Diego, CA/London: Academic Press.

Forde, C., McMahon, M., McPhee, A., Patrick, F. (2006) *Professional Development, Reflection and Enquiry*, London: Paul Sage Publishing.

Gibson, J. J. (1979) *The Ecological Approach to Visual Perception*, Boston: Houghton Mifflin.

Gubrium, J. F. and Holstein, J. A. (1995) 'Biographical work and new ethnography', in R. Josselson and A. Lieblich (eds) *Interpreting Experience: The Narrative Study of Lives*, (pp. 45–58) Thousand Oaks, CA/London: Sage.

Gubrium, J. F. and Holstein, J. A. (2009) *Analyzing Narrative Reality*, Los Angeles/London: SAGE.

Hunt, C. and Sampson, F. (2006) *Writing: Self and Reflexivity*, Third edition, Basingstoke/New York: Palgrave.

Kaplan, D. M. (2003) *Ricoeur's Critical Theory*, Albany, NY: State University of New York Press.

Karolides, N. J. (2000) 'The transactional theory of literature', in N. J. Karolides (ed.) *Reader Response in Secondary and College Classrooms*, Mahwah, NJ: Lawrence Erlbaum Associates.

Langdridge, D. (2007) *Phenomenological Psychology*, Harlow: Pearson Education Ltd.

Lynch, M. (2000) 'Against reflexivity as an academic virtue and source of privileged knowledge', *Theory, Culture and Society*, 17(3): 26–54.

Macfarlane, B. (2004) *Teaching with Integrity: The Ethics of Higher Education Practice*, London/New York: Routledge Falmer.

Macfarlane, B. (2008) *Researching with Integrity: The Ethics of Academic Inquiry*, New York/London: Routledge.

MacIntyre, A. (1981) *After Virtue*, London: Duckworth.

Mishler, E. G. (1990) 'Validation in inquiry-guided research: the role of exemplars in narrative studies', *Harvard Educational Review*, 60 (4): 415–442.

Muldoon, M. (2002) *On Ricoeur*, Belmont, CA: Wadsworth.

Muldoon, M. S. (2006) *Tricks of Time: Bergson, Merleau-Ponty and Ricoeur in Search of Time, Self and Meaning*, Pittsburgh, PA: Duquesne University Press.

Nussbaum, M. C. (1986) *The Fragility of Goodness: Luck and Ethics in Greek Tragedy and Philosophy*, Cambridge: Cambridge University Press.

Nussbaum, M. C. (1990) *Love's Knowledge: Essays on Philosophy and Literature*, New York/Oxford: Oxford University Press.

Ottesen, E. (2007) 'Reflection in teacher education', *Reflective Practice*, 8 (1): 31–46.

Pidgeon, N. (1996) 'Grounded theory: theoretical background', in J. T. E. Richardson (ed.) *Handbook of Qualitative Research Methods for Psychology and the Social Sciences*, Leicester: BPS Books.

Pidgeon, N. and Henwood, K. (1996) 'Grounded theory: practical implementation', in J. T. E. Richardson (ed.) *Handbook of Qualitative Research Methods for Psychology and the Social Sciences*, Leicester: BPS Books.

Pollard, A. with Anderson, J., Maddock, M. Swaffield, S., Warin, J. and Warwick, P. (2008) *Reflective Teaching: Evidence-informed Professional Practice*, Third edition, London/New York: Continuum International Publishing Group.

Ricoeur, P. (1990) *Time and Narrative*, vols 1, 2 and 3, paperback edition, Chicago/London: Chicago University Press.

Riesmann, C. K. (1993) *Narrative Analysis*, Newbury Park, CA/London: Sage.

Rosenblatt, L. M. (1995) 'Continuing the conversation: a clarification', *Research in the Teaching of English*, 29: 349–354.

Salmon, P. and Riesmann, C. K. (2008) 'Looking back on narrative research: an exchange', in M. Andrews, C. Squire and M. Tamboukou (eds) *Doing Narrative Research* (pp. 78–85), Los Angeles/London/New Delhi/Singapore: Sage.

Schwandt, T. A. (2003) 'Three epistemological stances for qualitative inquiry: interpretivism, hermeneutics, and social constructionism', in N. K. Denzin and Y. S. Lincoln (eds) *The Landscape of Qualitative Research: Theories and Issues*, Second edition, Thousand Oaks, CA/London/New Dehli: Sage.

Sheridan, A. (1980) *Michel Foucault: The Will to Truth*, New York: Tavistock.

Stevens, D. and Lowing, K. (2008) 'Observed, observer and observations: initial teacher education English tutors' feedback on lessons taught by student teachers of English', *English in Education*, 42(2): 182–198.

Wilkinson, S. (1988) 'The role of reflexivity in feminist psychology', *Women's Studies International Forum*, 11: 493–502.

Chapter 9

Exploring talk

Identifying register, coherence and cohesion

Susan Rodrigues

As a researcher keen to explore the nature of language found within classroom communities, whether it be initiated, supported or mediated by the pupils or teachers, I look for approaches that support ways of exploring and analysing the nature of language in a classroom setting. I am not alone in this quest to improve classroom education by increasingly focusing on the role of language in the learning environment (see for example, Yore, 2003).

As most of my research is based in the science classroom and predominantly involves either observation or interviews, I have tended to rely on the analysis of language to look at how students negotiate meaning through verbal interaction during their science lessons. The analysis techniques that I use for this exploration depend upon the nature of the complex layers and intricate interactions to be explored.

Analysing classroom talk in order to identify the negotiation of meaning is challenging. For a start, there are numerous variables, many of which researchers cannot govern in a natural classroom setting. In addition, given the diverse nature of our student population, many of these variables will combine to different extents at different times.

In recent times I have used facets of Halliday's systemic functional linguistics (SFL) to study the language layers and look at the networks of related systems found in classroom talk. In this chapter I provide a brief overview of the strategies that I have found useful when analysing science classroom transcripts or 'text' (i.e. transcribed discourse) in order to capture and explain verbal science classroom interaction. 'Text' refers to any spoken or written passage that constitutes a cohesive entity (Halliday and Hasan, 1976). As such, it is essentially a unit of language in use, where that unit of language expresses specific meaning.

Introduction

While investigating teaching and learning in context, not simply in terms of student engagement with familiar topics, but in terms of how language generated relevant contexts, I encountered literature discussing SFL. The edited collections by Hasan, Matthiessen and Webster (2005a, 2005b) were extremely useful starting points.

They show how talk is semiotic (i.e. how meaning is created through negotiation) before it becomes semantic (i.e. a word with meaning in given context): thus talk involves meaning making. Not surprisingly, Vygotsky thought that language in social and contextual environments might be the key to learning (Williams, 2005). Given the positions adopted by both Vygotsky and Halliday, Wells (1999) notes a synergy between Halliday's observations on language and some of Vygotsky's research.

Hasan, Matthiessen and Webster (2005a, 2005b) signal that the work of Halliday and Hasan provides a defensible linguistic position for the analysis of classroom dialogue and talk. Facets of SFL have helped me to document and interpret data I have collected in the form of talk generated during science lessons or retro-, intro-, pre-, inter- and post-lesson interview conversations. The literature shows that language and talk in science classrooms can be studied and typified in many different ways. Language can be considered in terms of where it happens, who is responsible for generating it and how it is done. It may involve teacher and/or pupil engagement and written and/or spoken language. It may take place in the school or in an environment beyond the school walls. Not surprisingly, given this broad scope, researchers have sought and used a range of strategies, tools and techniques to ensure rich data collection when studying particular elements of language in science classrooms.

Some researchers have analysed text found in articles, books or multimedia. Some studies recorded pre- and post-interviews which were on an individual basis or in focus groups. Some researchers recorded classroom conversation and/or retrospective or stimulated recall. Nowadays it is not uncommon to record talk digitally rather than solely rely on notes made when observing classroom practice. As we have read in the chapter by Paul Denley and Keith Bishop (Chapter 7), this has led some researchers to use video stimulated recall to establish relational understanding, to verify concept development and to substantiate inferred meaning ascribed to actions and behaviours. Video stimulated recall studies generate data that is often rich, dense and usually complex in terms of dialogue and interpretation. The challenge lies in attempting to interpret this data. In reality, identifying strategies, tools and techniques for data collection is often the most straightforward aspect of any methodological consideration, providing the researcher has carefully considered the theory underpinning the analytical approach.

Analysing classroom talk

Communication in science classrooms, in terms of the balance of power, exchange of ideas and the pattern of talk, have been studied through an analysis of language from different theoretical perspectives. For example, Barnes and Todd (1977) reported how effective participants were making meaning explicit in discussion. They described a continuum of group talk, which included what they called the 'intimate' to the 'public'. The work of Barnes and Todd (1977), together with the work of Edwards and Mercer (1987), probably led to an expansion of the interpretive research approach for researching language in classrooms. This resulted in a 'flow of discourse' framework. Mortimer and Scott (2000) wrote that the flow of discourse framework provides a structure to consider the nature and pattern of classroom talk (i.e. teacher and student utterances) through a continuous timeline (e.g. a lesson or sequence of lessons).

Sinclair and Coulthard (1975, 1992) looked at the structure of discourse in classrooms and identified widespread, often rigid, patterns of turn-taking in many classrooms. They noticed that students and teachers took turns to speak according to a perception of their roles. This perception within the classroom generated the 'initiate, respond and follow up' paradigm. The teacher asks a question, the student responds and the teacher evaluates the response and follows with closure or another question. More recently, Hsu Roth and Mazumder (2009) reported on a pattern of talk that was similar to that observed by Sinclair and Coulthard but was observed when school students participated in an environmental science laboratory. Rodrigues and Thompson (2001) analysed datasets of teachers working in 'context'. They linguistically illustrated how teachers and students differed in their interpretation of set tasks. Chin (2006) looked at patterns of teacher questioning. The Barnes and Todd (1977, 1995), Edwards and Mercer (1987), Sinclair and Coulthard (1975), Rodrigues and Thompson (2001) and Chin (2006) research largely concentrated on patterns of talk and behaviour in classrooms. However, turn-taking is just one facet of classroom behaviour that can be explored through the analysis of classroom talk.

In science, Johnstone's work shows how other facets of classroom interaction can be explored. Johnstone (1991) considered the nature of language in science lessons from another perspective. Johnstone (1991) identified three forms of 'language' found in science lessons, which he labelled 'microscopic', 'macroscopic' and 'symbolic'. For example, teachers may refer to the macroscopic entity of water (we pour water), mention 'H two O' (H_2O) or draw symbols on the board to represent the water molecule when they are teaching a topic involving water. Teachers with their experience and familiarity of these macroscopic, microscopic and symbolic views of chemicals might also move between these forms of language interchangeably. Rodrigues and Bell (1995) suggest that this may be problematic for some students who are, in essence, novices and therefore may have difficulty moving between the three forms because they do not grasp the implications and significance of the macro, micro or symbolic representations. Some of these difficulties can be better illustrated when we consider the use of the English language in science classrooms in more detail.

The English language brings with it rules and conventions that dictate how particular words can be chained together to produce sentences or phrases. For some of those who explore linguistics, there are four systems in the language structure. These systems include phonology (i.e. how something sounds), semantics (i.e. the meaning), lexicon (i.e. the word and fixed expressions of the language) and grammar (i.e. morphology and syntax). Morphology dictates word formation and inflexion, while syntax dictates the rules governing sequencing words. Therefore, in essence, syntax generates rules that determine how words should be chained collectively to form accepted sentence or speech patterns. At an even smaller level, morphemes (i.e. a combination of phonemes to form larger units) are the smallest combination of sounds. So, for example, the words 'car' and 'bar' have different meanings because of the different initial sound/phoneme. But the sounds 'c' or 'b' are meaningless in themselves. 'Car' is one morpheme – it is a combination of sounds that form the smallest unit with any particular meaning – whereas the word 'carpet' contains two morphemes (i.e. 'car' and 'pet').

In science, the same morpheme can have different meanings. Some words may have the same morpheme because their combination of phonemes is identical, but these words, when used in various science disciplines (as well as within everyday settings), have altered meanings. For example, the word 'cell' is one morpheme, but it has a distinct and different meaning in biology, chemistry and everyday life. In biology we may talk about a single cell organism, while in chemistry we may discuss an electrochemical cell and in our everyday life we may refer to a jail cell. Thus the milieu in which these morphemes are used make a difference to the intended meaning. In addition, in science lessons it is not only the combination of sounds or morphemes that result in difference. Sometimes, as Rodrigues (1999) showed, common everyday words are used in chemistry to mean different things, and sometimes these meanings are at odds with the everyday use. For example, for most students 'reduction' would imply that something was getting smaller. Yet in chemistry, we define 'reduction' as 'the gain of'.

Language in science lessons may be tri-lingual – some have even suggested quad-lingual, adding mathematical to the macroscopic, microscopic and symbolic strands. In addition, it would appear that in science lessons, some of the mainstream English language rules and principles are abandoned, some of the everyday meanings are discarded and some of the words are used in a contradictory fashion when developing meaning for science concepts. It is hardly surprising then that many students find science challenging.

Given the potential for confusion as a consequence of language use in science classrooms, many researchers interested in strategies to encourage concept development in science are looking at the role of language and/or techniques that involve language. For example, Jarman and McClune (2007) wrote about the use of newspaper articles to explore science ideas in classrooms. Rodrigues (1999) described the use of role play and debate. Young and Nguyen (2002) looked at modes of meaning in science teaching and learning, while Keogh and Naylor (1999) considered concept cartoons. Many of these strategies blend the need for a change in the blueprint of the character of communication often found in science classrooms with an increase in awareness of language and science concept development. Our quest to explore language usually results in a search for methodologies that allow us to focus on specific aspects of communication.

The preceding paragraphs illustrate the breadth and depth of research exploring talk and discourse in science classrooms. Given my interest in the use of language to negotiate meaning, I have chosen to focus this chapter on a methodology that considers the impact of register, coherence and cohesion in science classroom talk.

Setting the scene

As a teacher of chemistry I have always been interested in the way students make sense of chemistry during their lessons; as a researcher my focus has been on the role of context on learning science. These interests led me to look more closely at the language found in the classroom and to consider methodologies that allow me to inspect language. When I stumbled upon Halliday's work while searching for literature on 'relevant contexts', I began to view teaching in context as more than simply bringing into the classroom student familiar objects, topics or themes. For me, Halliday's work (in particular SFL) suggests that 'relevant context' is a linguistic construct. For me, Halliday's work identifies the essential role of language in establishing authentic relationships between students and their learning environment. SFL is of interest to me because I accept that talk is a semantic activity and that it involves meaning making. SFL depends on the context in which the language occurs and it describes 'meaning potential' (Unsworth, 2000).

Over the last decade I have reviewed classroom data through various aspects of the SFL window. I have contemplated how I could employ SFL to explore different elements of talk (i.e. group, dyad, teacher–pupil, pupil–pupil, didactic, discussion and retrospective) within primary and secondary science classrooms. As I am not a linguist this was, and continues to be, quite a challenge. I addressed this challenge by working with colleagues who are linguists or are involved in researching language. This chapter provides some insight into how, with the help of these colleagues (see for example, Rodrigues and Thompson, 2001), I have used aspects of SFL to explore science classroom talk and activity. The challenge for me is finding out how students come 'to know' and how language in a science classroom comes 'to mean' something to the student. So, assuming that SFL describes meaning making within specific contexts, I took it to be a useful analytical approach to explore classroom talk. It allows me to explore what language does and how it does it in the context of a science classroom.

Systemic functional linguistics

Halliday suggests that through interaction children are able to create language with 'acculturated others' (Hasan, 2005: 42). That is my starting point. In a science classroom students attempt to buy into relevant, appropriate and expected language when interacting with their teacher and peers. It is through this interaction within science classrooms that students determine whether they are going to gain access to this science classroom community, or in some cases they use this interaction to determine whether they even want to be part of this community.

To a certain extent, for many students learning science in schools is akin to a toddler learning new words. In most cases, like a toddler, a student can refer to an informed other (e.g. a parent or teacher), but unlike a toddler, a student can also refer to a dictionary. A student can also develop their understandings for the new words they encounter *in situ*. Hasan (2005) pointed out that Malinowski (1935) looked at the context of the situation and the context of culture, and suggested that sometimes language becomes a vehicle for action rather than reflection. So, for example, as a toddler uses words within an everyday pursuit or activity, they establish a more transparent link between saying and meaning. Likewise, in science lessons it is possible that the students engaged in practical work establish meaning for particular utterances *in situ* and through active or purposeful engagement in that situation. Most do not rely on a dictionary to figure out the meaning, instead they learn what it means through association with a given task, a given action or as part of a particular behaviour. The context of the situation and the context of culture are important in scaffolding their learning (Unsworth, 2000). According to Hasan (2005), a relevant context can be actual, imaginary or virtual. Hasan (2005) suggests that 'actual' refers to aspects for discourse for a precise instant in time, while 'imaginary' need not pertain to that particular moment and 'virtual' could be conditional, hypothetical or simply some form of generalisation.

Some of the ideas from systemic functional linguistics

The SFL theory/model was developed by Michael Halliday and colleagues (see Halliday, 1993, 1994; Halliday and Hasan, 1985). It looks at the grammatical description and the series of choices that a speaker or writer makes dependent on intention and context. Halliday considers language to be social-semiotic, functional and context dependent (Hasan, 2005). Not surprisingly, SFL sees language as a source people use to articulate and derive meanings in context. When it comes to exploring dialogue in the classroom, SFL has plenty to offer, for, as Halliday, McIntosh and Strevens (1964) suggested, language is not abstract; it involves specific people and situations, using a distinct register and dialect for a unique activity.

The immediate context in which language is deployed is the context of situation (Unsworth, 2000). Of course, the context of situation (i.e. the environment in which verbal interaction occurs) can vary between cultures. For example, consider a context of situation that involves buying groceries. In some countries this might involve paying the set price, but in another country bargaining is an option, and/or expected.

The context of the situation is often described in terms of field, tenor and mode. 'Field' is the topic or content of the social activity. 'Tenor' describes the relationship between the participants. 'Mode' reflects the medium (written/spoken/other) and role of language. The field, tenor and mode are related to what Halliday described as metafunctions: the experiential, interpersonal and textual (Christie and Unsworth, 2000).

For Halliday (1994) language serves the three following metafunctions (meaning) simultaneously:

- *experiential* metafunction (the representation);
- *interpersonal* metafunction (the exchange);
- *textual* metafunction (the message).

The field contextual variable has an experiential metafunction. It represents our experience of reality. How speakers signify what is going on generates the experiential metafunction (Halliday, 1994). The tenor contextual variable has an interpersonal metafunction. It represents the generation and establishment of our social relationships. The mode contextual variable has a textual metafunction. It depicts messages in various forms (text/icons) within a given context.

A statement by Hasan (2005) influenced my interest in the role of language in teaching and learning in context in science classrooms. Hasan signalled the importance of social practices and the relationship between field and tenor in maintaining cultural activities. Halliday proposed that language varied as function varied and he suggested that language would be different in different situations. The term given to language distinguished according to use is 'register'. The three contextual variables (i.e. field, tenor and mode) are usually clustered beneath this heading of register. Register is based on what Hasan (2005) described as an awareness and appreciation for the patterns in language use. We can look at register by exploring contextual and metafunctions. Consider for example someone making one of the three following remarks:

'Susan Rodrigues stood at the front when she spoke to the children.'

'Professor Rodrigues stood at the front when she spoke to the children.'

'Did Professor Rodrigues stand at the front when she spoke to the children?'

The meanings are essentially the same. The statements contain the same process (talking), the same people (Rodrigues and the children) and the same circumstances (standing at the front). However, by subtly altering some of the words, we change the register. For example, by changing the terms of address, the speaker changes the interpersonal meaning. The use of 'Professor' makes it a more formal relationship. The person relating the event is putting some distance between them and Susan Rodrigues. It could be argued that by introducing a title they are introducing a degree of formality. The difference between the question and the two statements also signals a difference in interpersonal meaning because, as is to be expected, the question brings with it an enquiry. The interpersonal meaning can change when the mood of the tenor changes. So by changing something to a query, we change the mood and hence the interpersonal meaning.

According to Eggins (2004), speakers draw on what is called the 'transitivity system' or 'meaning potential' in order to grasp experiential meanings. The transitivity system includes the participants, the circumstance and the process. For examples, see Table 9.1.

The changes in participant, circumstance and process can result in changes in experiential meaning and, as a consequence, change the register. The phrase as a

Table 9.1 The participants, the circumstance and the process

Participant	Circumstance	Process	Participant
Professor Rodrigues	stood in front when	she spoke to the	children.
Professor Rodrigues	stood in front when	she questioned the	children.
Professor Rodrigues	mingled when	she spoke to the	children.
Ann Other	stood in front when	she spoke to the	children.

message or communicative event forms the textual metafunction (Halliday, 1994). So by changing the position of the words within the phrase, we may well change the textual meaning. This is because the focus of the statements or question will have shifted. For example, if the speaker said, 'Standing in front of the room, Professor Rodrigues then spoke to the class', the person (Rodrigues) is no longer central, but her position in the room now takes centre stage. So while the experiential and interpersonal meanings remained the same, the textual meaning changes.

We can also use register, to look at cohesion in talk. Cohesive elements are clues; they are guides to coherence. Coherence is really about how the text knits together (Halliday and Hasan, 1976). Coherence tries to ensure that talk is more than just a jumble of words. If we said, 'Charlotte likes science. She danced in Dundee.', the sentences are cohesive (i.e. 'Charlotte' and 'She' provide the cohesive ties), but the sentences are not coherent (i.e. linking science and dancing in Dundee). A method described by Hasan (1984) and Halliday and Hasan (1976) can be used to generate a measure of cohesion when analysing text. We look at this in more detail later when we consider some data in the form of transcripts.

In essence, text must show continuity of topic and reference, and cohesion contributes to this continuity. Cohesion is deemed to occur when the interpretation of a precise element within the discourse is dependent on that of a different element (Halliday and Hasan, 1976). Cohesion can be determined by considering the ties or links in talk that internally relate clauses and sentences cohesively. If ties or links are weak, then the listener may experience some difficulty in discovering the speaker's intention. This may result in the boundaries for a topic losing a degree of definition. However, in general, casual conversation between speakers talking on or about a familiar topic may include few cohesive links or ties because those doing the talking are familiar with each other and the topic. According to Hasan (1984), conversational, informal speakers say about half of what they mean, which would suggest that the dialogue partner infers the other half. Unfortunately, as Rodrigues and Thompson (2001) showed, in a science classroom setting, saying half of what is meant may result in confusion, as the cohesive ties may be insufficient, and as a result neither dialogue partner is successful in inferring appropriate meanings.

In a science classroom, if teacher talk has weak links then students may have difficulty in determining the teacher's intention. The students may have to rely on inferences. Similarly, if the student's response has weak links then the teacher has to rely on inferences. In both cases these inferences may result in further confusion.

To further complicate matters, we should also signal that if links are dense then the talk may appear pedantic. So in a science classroom there is a need for a balancing act between trying to ensure that the ties are not dense and trying to ensure that there are sufficient cohesive ties to enable everyone to make sense of the dialogue.

In addition to looking at register and coherence, we can also conduct a comparison of word frequency. Counting the frequency of word occurrence could show which words are commonly used in particular lessons or how the frequency of the scientific words (or macroscopic, microscopic, symbolic and mathematical terms) vary between different classrooms or different teachers or different year levels.

However, before we look at the nature of the insights generated as a consequence of these different approaches, we should consider the craft of data collection and transcription.

Data collection and transcription: issues to consider

It is worthwhile taking time to consider the nature and scope of data collection and transcribing techniques as these will have an influence on the unit of text available for analysis when studying the data. The following are important and worth bearing in mind before any data are transcribed. Is it imperative that you:

1   include local ways of speaking, or include the dialect, the parlance and idiom of the culture or situation;
2   capture intonation and rhythm (every time or only for specific elements and for particular circumstances);
3   include timed pauses, silence, overlaps or interruptions between speakers;
4   take account of stammers (i.e. the 'ers' and 'ehms') or repetitions;
5   consider ways to record gestures, body language and character differences in the nature of response (e.g. if someone laughs during a conversation, does it matter if it was cynical, restrained, boisterous or another emotion-driven form of laughter?).

These issues need to be considered before the data are collected and well before the data are transcribed because these issues could potentially influence the way clauses and texts are constructed and consequently interpreted.

How SFL is used during data analysis will depend on the research objectives and the research questions. In my experience, particular aspects of SFL are useful because I am interested in exploring talk in terms of the negotiation of meaning in school science classrooms. I am interested in mapping the relationships across language levels (i.e. macroscopic, microscopic, symbolic and mathematical levels) because these different alignments and relationships provide degrees of semantic consequences. In the sections that follow, I hope to illustrate the types of mapping that I have used and that rely on particular SFL assumptions and techniques. The examples provided in this chapter are taken from an earlier research project completed some years ago.

Analysing science classroom data

As indicated earlier in this chapter, there are different ways to quantifiably analyse talk, ranging from counting word frequency to mapping coherence. Various technologies now make it easy to ascertain and document the frequency of words. If we consider the text transcript that follows, we can log the frequency of a given word:

> I'd like you to circle those seven questions, very easy, very quick to answer. At the bottom of page 5 I'd like you to put question 8, question 8 and could you say PTO, for turn over. If you turn over to page 8, there's a table that you will need to copy and, oh, sorry, page 6, question 8, you'll need to copy and do. Now throughout this book, there are a series you virtually have to have together, a number of research questions of this, of which this forms the first eight. Fairly easy, and there's really not much that you should have any trouble with at all. Ok? There's just one, question 3, about the only thing that might, question 3, underline the word 'husks'. The other thing is they ask you to write up a full practical report for a number of pracs. I'd be quite happy for you to write up the first one in full detail, which means you've got to write the method out. If you do a really good job of that, I won't ask you to write up the next prac. For those of you who do not write p, the first one up properly, I will be asking you to write it up, every prac up until you actually give me a really good prac. So if you do the first one really thoroughly and well, then I'll just ask for the short method during lesson time.

We could analyse the above text for the number of times this particular teacher used the word 'prac' in context. Our findings would show the following:

- . . . for a number of pracs . . .
- . . . you to write up the next prac. For those of you . . .
- . . . actually give me a really good prac. So if you do . . .
- . . . to write it up , every prac up until you actually give . . .

Counting word occurrence may tell us whether a particular word in a particular lesson is common. It is a simple strategy and is useful if we want to draw comparisons. For example, if we decided to compare different classrooms or different teachers, we could in theory compare the use of that word (or indeed other words). This may be a useful strategy for comparing the frequency of words used to describe the macroscopic, microscopic or symbolic elements used in science to represent the same concept. An analysis of the use of these terms from the students' and teachers' perspectives could help us determine their familiarity and, to a certain extent, how comfortable they are in using these terms. For example, how many times does a pupil talk about 'water' and/or use the formula 'H_2O'? We could compare cross-class, -pupil and -teacher frequency. In addition, from a flow of discourse analysis perspective (rather than an SFL perspective), if we were interested in classifying utterances, these types of frequency approaches are valuable. So if the correlation between student utterance(s) and the teacher's learning intention for any given lesson or part of any given lesson were of interest, these frequency approaches are helpful. Again, from a flow of discourse framework perspective, searching for utterance frequency might also lend itself to helping to illustrate the flow of discourse categories such as description, explanation and generalisation.

Counting words is a useful, simple mechanism to explore familiarity with terms and language. However, for me, simply counting the frequency (as in our example of the notion of the word 'prac') does not provide much insight into the way the teacher talk (i.e. text) helped or hindered the student when it came to them determining what was needed for this 'prac'. Counting words does not provide an insight into the nature of exchange or the degree of cohesion between the teacher's instruction and the student's interpretation or the student's explanation and the teacher's response. So, for example, the various studies that have reported on the patterns of talk could be further explored in terms of the nature and scope of cohesion and coherence. Halliday and Hasan (1989) consider reference, ellipsis, substitution, conjunction and lexical relationships to be the mechanisms that sustain cohesion and this cohesion is directly related to coherence of a text. They also suggest a mechanism to measure cohesion in talk.

The Halliday and Hasan (1989) cohesive harmony index (CHI) enables researchers to subjectively explore the nature of cohesion in classrooms. They suggest that clusters of words (chains) that are related to other clusters in a given text provide cohesive harmony. So if one is interested in placing the interaction in the perspective of the total text then chain interaction analysis – better known as 'cohesive harmony analysis' – is useful.

In essence, cohesive harmony analysis tries to determine how closely and how often clusters of words (which are sometimes called 'chains') interact with each other. If we take the percentage of words that interact together and divide that by the number of total words rendered from the original text, we can generate the CHI. In effect, cohesive harmony index is a percentage measure of the cohesive links or ties in a text. Hasan (1985) advocated a 50 per cent criterion level as being necessary for textual coherence.

Identifying the CHI involves a process with several steps. You begin with a transcript (text) and convert it into clauses. Later on in this chapter, with the help of my colleague, Thompson, we show how a text can be analysed from a CHI perspective. We start by identifying clauses according to Halliday's (1985) principles of clause delineation. Once the clauses are identified, they have to be pared down to what are called 'tokens'; some refer to this in terms of the text being 'lexically rendered'. The tokens (i.e. pared down clauses) have grammatical and lexical significance. The total tokens for the text are the sum of these words. The tokens are entered into clusters of words (or as we said before, chains), which are semantically related through either classification or reference. If a token does not enter the chain, it is deemed to be a peripheral token. If it does enter the chain, it is deemed to be a relevant token. At least two words in any given chain must have the same semantic relationship with at least another two words in another chain. There should also be at least two words in any given chain. Otherwise, we would have to allow for each and every word being responsible for coherence!

Some key steps

- Transcribe the speech dialogue or monologue (and make a note of the participants, their relationship to each other, the purpose of the discussion and the nature of the shared knowledge between the speakers).
- Divide the transcript sample into clauses. (Look for a verb to identify the clause and include incomplete clauses as long as a verb is present (e.g. 'it's a. . .'). Any stammers or false starts that do not contain a verb should be grouped together until the verb appears (e.g. 'they, er, he, no we, said yes'). Make sure there is one verb per clause.)
- Note gestures and have notation for unintelligible speech.
- Extract all the tokens. Tokens are lexical items carrying content. They are elements within the discourse. Keep the tokens within the clauses.
- Total the number of tokens in the text. (Call this the 'total tokens'.)
- Total the number of relevant tokens in chains.
- Look for the grammatical relationships between the tokens in chains.
- Count the number of tokens in the chain interaction. (Call this 'central tokens'.)
- Calculate the percentage of central tokens over total tokens. (This gives the CHI.)
- Build in inter-observer reliability measures to increase reliability with regard to clause and token analysis.

What follows is Thompson's list of clauses for the text provided earlier in the chapter (Thompson, telephone call, May 2009). There were 247 words in the original text (transcript segment):

1　students circle (seven questions)
2　easy/quick (to answer) (seven questions)
3　put (question 8) bottom (page 5)
4　say PTO
5　(page 8) table (copy and complete)

6   Book series research questions
7   (eight questions) first series
8   easy
9   (question 3) trouble students
10 underline 'husks'
11 write-up (one full practical report in a number of pracs)
12 students write (first prac) (detailed method)
13 student (good write)
14 student (not do) (next prac)
15 student (bad write) (first prac)
16 student write every (until good prac)
17 (first prac) (good write)
18 student write (short method) (in lesson)

There are 84 words or 52 tokens (when words are bracketed). Of these 52 tokens, 38 are repeated or link to each other in topics (so 14 do not and are peripheral to the text) and 32 of the tokens relate to each other across the topics. The (32) chaining tokens divided by the (52) total tokens and converted into a percentage is approximately 62 per cent. As a general rule 50–60 per cent is normal, but it is usually higher when giving specific information, which is what this teacher is doing.

There are nine topics: 'you students', pages, series, questions, hard/easy, work completion (circle/answer), write-up, pracs and method. So in essence the teacher is saying:

> You students are to circle the first 7 questions, and it's easy. Do question 8 at the bottom of page 5 and PTO it. The textbook has research questions in series, the first series is easy, but question 3 might trouble you, here is how you fix it. Write up the first prac report fully with a detailed method. If you do it well, you won't have to do the rest. If you do it badly you'll do them all until you get it right. If you can do that, you can also do a shortened method in lesson time.

The problem is that the teacher in their original monologue was very wordy. The teacher was constantly repeating aspects or repairing what was said. In effect, approximately 38 per cent of the teacher's conversation adds nothing to the core message. But what is left is powerful. Thirteen of the teacher's sentences have linking chains across the discourse. Six of those are two-word chains (which is usual for this number of words (82)), six are three-word chains (which is unusual in 82 words) and one is a four-word chain (which is quite unusual): 'you students have to write up these pracs and include a detailed method'.

From this CHI analysis we can gain some insight into the challenge the students face in trying to determine the teacher's meaning. However, despite the fact that we can use CHI to illustrate the cohesiveness of particular discourse texts, it is neither ethical nor reliable to suggest difficulty in the negotiation of meaning unless we adopt some form of triangulation. Some may even suggest that conversation modification does not equate, necessarily, with negotiation of meaning, so we should be cautious when we seek to interpret classroom talk. However, if analysis is supported with and by triangulated data, aspects of SFL provide an extremely powerful analytical tool to explore classroom talk.

Apart from CHI, other aspects of SFL allow us to explore various language levels in order to look at the expressed meanings in context. We can look at semantics, lexicogrammar or context. Semantics includes the propositional content, interpersonal semantics and textual semantics. As stated earlier, Halliday (1977) suggested there were three general functions of language (i.e. experiential, interpersonal and textual) that were the organising basis for the semantic level. Not surprisingly, therefore, semantics is a key facet in SFL. Lexicogrammar usually warrants analysis in terms of roles, so we can use it more broadly to explore communicative competence through the engagement of people. In essence, grammar is the resource that helps us understand the way knowledge is coded. We can explore context by considering the register. Register differs in terms of its lexis and grammar – in other words, its form (Hasan, 2005).

As previously stated, Halliday and his colleagues initially identified three aspects regarding register: field, mode and style. The following transcript from a lesson where pupils were learning about materials in a chemistry lesson was taken from an earlier research project completed some years ago. The transcript involving the teacher and students was obtained when the teacher was working with the whole class. The teacher wanted the pupils to underline key words that might be of use to them when the pupils start to revise the topic:

Teacher:	Yep, I'd underline 'clothing industry' and the word 'use'. And the other bit might be 'demands of different clothes'. OK, the next one, Joanne, should be pretty easy for number five.
Joanne:	Define?
Teacher:	Sorry?
Joanne:	Define.
Teacher:	Yes, but define what?
Joanne:	Um, polymer.
Teacher:	Yeah, polymer and?
Joanne:	And monomy.
Teacher:	Monomer.
Joanne:	Monomer.
Teacher:	Yeah, monomer. OK, number six please, Steve?

We can probably summarise the field, tenor and mode because the pattern and setting suggest that this is a science classroom and that the teacher is trying to elicit information through a fairly common (see for example Barnes and Todd, 1977; Sinclair and Coulthard, 1975) pattern of talk. Talk in classrooms conforms to rules. The teacher initiates, the pupils respond and the teacher follows up. From an SFL perspective, the field is the science lesson on materials, more particularly polymers and monomers. Lesser and Milroy (1993) provide a review of the application of sociolingual rules for constructing conversations. However, the structure of the classroom talk as seen in the transcript, in terms of commands, questions, responses, statements and other pedagogical moves, falls into what Sinclair and Coulthard (1975) described as 'Soliciting', 'Reacting', 'Responding' and 'Structuring'. The tenor of the lesson suggests that the teacher has (and is exercising her) power by using fairly closed questions to maintain control of the class and to steer the dialogue in the direction she wants. In addition, it is likely that the pupils address her formally, while the transcript shows that she uses their first names. The mode is aural and involves face-to-face interaction. Though the transcript provided was collected during whole class (involving teacher and class dialogue and activity), in this particular transcript segment individual pupils are identified by the teacher and asked to contribute and respond. There is immediate feedback, whether it is in the form of teacher soliciting, reacting, responding or structuring within the dialogue.

It is worth noting that upon closer inspection of the transcript segment, we can recognise what Martin (1993) would distinguish as schematic structures. There are several stages in the transcript. These stages and schematic structures illustrate that in addition to register, there is a cultural purpose that informs and shapes this particular talk text. The transcript had a start. The teacher provided an example and then posed an invitation that was directed at a particular student. Once this student responded, the teacher sought clarification and the pupil again responded and the teacher again prompted for fuller detail. Once this detail was secured, the teacher confirmed their response and then sought a response from another student.

Many of us would recognise this pattern of behaviour and deem it to be common to many science classrooms. In essence, the genre network – in our case the classroom – signals that particular systematic combinations are possible within that cultural situation. In our context and cultural situation (i.e. the data was collected in the classroom), the students knew that their participation in the initiate, respond and follow-up pattern of talk was a requirement at this stage of the lesson. They have, to a certain extent, been conditioned to take part in dialogue that is teacher-led; they know that they may well be called upon to provide a response to a teacher soliciting information or recognising their input.

The students might not be clear about the field, but they are aware of the schematic structure required at this stage of the lesson. The students adhered to this schematic structure, taking their cues from the teacher, either in terms of language or gesture.

From a data analysis perspective, determining schematic structures and the lexicogrammar for a given genre requires a degree of objectivity. It also needs objective justification for the classifications that are used. For more detailed information with regard to how to examine lexicogrammar patterns in various genre stages, see Hasan (1996).

Various forms of coding can be used to examine the patterns and nature of talk. As a researcher, I can attempt to describe meaning features in a transcript documenting the conversation between the teacher and students. For example, by reviewing a classroom transcript we could look at the nature of the options favoured by the teacher or the students. We could start by analysing the transcripts in terms of semantic unit messages.

Consider the transcript excerpt that follows. In this transcript each of the square bracketed numbers suggests the beginning of a message:

Teacher: [1] Yep, I'd underline 'clothing industry' [2] and the word 'use.' [3] And the other bit might be 'demands of different clothes'. [4] OK, [5] the next one, [6] Joanne, [7] should be pretty easy for number five.

Joanne: [8] Define?

Teacher: [9] Sorry?

Joanne: [10] Define.

Teacher: [11] Yes, [12] but define what?

Joanne: [13] Um, [14] polymer.

Teacher: [15] Yeah, polymer [16] and?

Joanne: [17] And monomy.

Teacher: [18] Monomer.

Joanne: [19] Monomer.

Teacher: [20] Yeah, monomer. [21] OK, [22] number six please, [23] Steve?

In this analysis I have also allowed for punctuation and progression messages. So, for example, '[4] OK, [5] the next one', the message '[4] OK' is punctuation whereas, '[5] the next one' is progression. Hence we can see in the transcript that the teacher's talk is both instructive (i.e. trying to establish knowledge and skills by, for example, correcting 'monomer' and trying to apprentice Joanne into using specialist language) and regulative (i.e. keeping moral order by, for example, using Joanne's name to engage her in the dialogue). This type of analysis, in terms of the semantic message, allows us to make comparisons in terms of the balance between regulative and instructive across different types of science lesson styles or strategies (e.g. demonstrations, practicals, didactic, etc.).

By considering the various clauses, we can explore the transcript in terms of how propositional knowledge evolves and we can look at the social and semiotic ways that govern these developments. In our previous transcript example the teacher was trying to develop fairly specialised, scientifically accepted, precise meanings (monomer and polymer) within a specific domain (chemistry). The teacher was trying to help students to construct new knowledge. Therefore, by using this type of analysis, we can explore the socially (in our case, classroom-) mediated meanings and key principles that govern the production of propositional knowledge.

Caution

Though SFL has tremendous potential, we also need to bear in mind that while it provides insights with regard to how talk can influence or mediate meaning making, it does have two limitations.

First, if we engage with SFL in its fullest sense, we see that SFL is very complex. The vocabulary used for coding is extensive and technical. Consequently, it is challenging. To further complicate matters, coding reliability is problematic. For example, during my discussions with Thompson, as we analysed the transcript independently, we batted our analysis of the transcript to and fro as we compared our coding and sought coding reliability. Coding difficulties may also arise because different interpretations of SFL terminology can result in more ambiguous clauses. These ambiguous clauses can locate themselves within overlapping categories. However, even when coding vocabulary has been mastered, one should still bear in mind the fact that the coding process is subjective. Second, to a certain extent, if clauses are too fragmented, they are often not really suitable for SFL.

Nevertheless, even with these caveats, if we want to study how teacher and student talk influences meaning making in the science classroom then SFL has potential. Applying the SFL framework to teacher's and students' talk also provides an opportunity to ascertain what works and what does not work in terms of promoting engagement, skill acquisition and concept development.

Conclusion

Systemic functional linguistics theory provides many tools that can be used to analyse classroom transcripts. In this chapter I have shown how facets of SFL can be used to analyse science classroom talk. Other researchers have used it to consider other modalities. For example, Lemke (1998) looked at scientific texts to show how symbols, graphical figures and written language could be described using SFL descriptions of logical relations (i.e. 'enhancement', 'elaboration' and 'extension'). My chapter does not discuss the application of the full spectrum of SFL as this would require several books. More detailed guidance with regard to the use of SFL can be found in Eggins (2004), Unsworth (2000) and Hasan *et al.* (2005).

My aim with this chapter was to signal the variety of SFL elements that lend themselves to informing the analysis of classroom talk. The preceding paragraphs were intended to simply highlight the scope of these various elements of SFL for those interested in the role of language in lessons. SFL can help us to explore aspects such as register and coherence in classroom talk. It can be used to examine frame, relevance and negotiation. Attempting to show, within one chapter, the scope of SFL and potential research options with regard to classroom data analysis was challenging. Nevertheless, I hope that this chapter has shown how SFL can be used to explore how students in school are apprenticed in education.

References

Barnes, D. and Todd, F. (1977) *Communication and Learning in Small Groups*, London: Routledge and Kegan Paul.

Barnes, D. and Todd, F. (1995) *Communication and Learning Revisited: Making Meaning Through Talk*, Portsmouth: Boynton/Cook.

Chin, C. (2006) 'Classroom interaction in science: teacher questioning and feedback to students' responses', *International Journal of Science Education*, 28(11): 1315–1346

Christie, F. and Unsworth, L. (2000) 'Developing socially responsible language research', in L Unsworth (ed.) *Researching Language in Schools and Communities* (pp. 1–26), London and Washington: Cassell.

Edwards, D. and Mercer, N. M. (1987) *Common Knowledge: The Development of Understanding in the Classroom*, London: Methuen.

Eggins, S. (2004) *An Introduction to Systemic Functional Linguistics*, Second edition, London and New York: Continuum Publishing Group.

Halliday, M. A. K. (1977) 'Text as semantic choice in social contexts', in van T. S. Dijk and J. S.Petofi (eds) *Grammars and Descriptions*, Berlin: Walter de Gruyter.

Halliday, M. A. K. (1985) *Spoken and Written Language*, Victoria: Deakin University.

Halliday, M. A. K. (1993) 'Towards a language based theory of learning', *Linguistics and Education*, 5: 93–116.

Halliday, M. A. K. (1994) *An Introduction to Functional Grammar*, Second edition, London: Edward Arnold.

Halliday, M. A. K. and Hasan, R. (1976) *Cohesion in English* (English Language Series 9), London: Longman.

Halliday, M. A. K. and Hasan, R. (1985) *Language, Context and Text: Aspects of Language in a Social Semiotic Perspective*, Geelong, Vic.: Deakin University Press.

Halliday, M. A. K. and Hasan, R. (1989) *Language, Context and Text: Aspects of Language in a Social Semiotic Perspective*, Second edition, Oxford: Oxford University Press.

Halliday, M. A. K., McIntosh, A. and Strevens, P. (1964) *The Linguistic Sciences and Language Teaching*, London: Longman.

Hasan, R. (1984) 'Coherence and cohesive harmony', in J. Flood (ed.) *Understanding Reading Comprehension*, Newark Delaware: International Reading Association.

Hasan, R. (1985) 'The texture of a text', in M. A. K. Halliday and R. Hasan (eds) *Language, Context and Text: Aspects of Language in a Social Semiotic Perspective*, Geelong, Vic.: Deakin University Press.

Hasan, R. (1996) 'Literacy, every day talk and society', in C. Cloran, D. Butt and G. Williams (eds) *Ways of Saying: Ways of Meaning: Selected Papers of Ruqaiya Hasan*, London: Cassell.

Hasan, R. (2005) 'Language and society in a system functional perspective', in R. Hasan, C. Matthiessen and J. J. Webster (eds) *Continuing Discourse on Language: A Functional Perspective*, Volume 1, London: Equinox.

Hasan, R., Matthiessen, C. and Webster, J. J. (eds) (2005a) *Continuing Discourse on Language: A Functional Perspective*, Volume 1, London: Equinox.

Hasan, R., Matthiessen, C. and Webster, J. J. (eds) (2005b) *Continuing Discourse on Language: A Functional Perspective*, Volume 2, London: Equinox.

Hsu, P.-L., Roth, W.-M. and Mazumder, A. (2009) 'Natural pedagogical conversations in high school students' internship', *Journal of Research in Science Teaching*, 46(5): 481–505.

Jarman, R. and McCLune, B. (2007) *Developing Scientific Literacy: Using News Media in the Classroom*, Maidenhead: Open University Press.

Johnstone, A. H. (1991) 'Why is science difficult to learn? Things are seldom what they seem', *Journal of Computer Assisted Learning*, 7(2): 75–83.

Keogh, B. and Naylor, S. (1999) 'Concept cartoons, teaching and learning in science: an evaluation', *International Journal of Science Education*, 21(4): 431–446

Lemke, J. (1998) 'Multiplying meaning: visual and verbal semiotics in scientific text', in J.R. Martin and R. Veel (eds) *Reading Science: Critical and Functional Perspectives on Discourses of Science*, London: Routledge.

Lesser, R. and Milroy, L. (1993) *Linguistics and Aphasia: Psycholinguistics and pragmatic Aspects of Intervention*, London: Longman.

Malinowski, B. (1935) 'An ethnographic theory of language', in *Coral Gardens and their Magic*, Volume II, Part IV, London: Allen and Unwin.

Martin, J. R. (1993) 'Genre and Literacy: modelling context in educational linguistics', *Annual review of applied linguistics*, 13: 141–172.

Mortimer, E. and Scott, P. (2000) 'Analysing discourse in the science classroom', in R. Millar, J. Leach and J. Osborne (eds) *Improving Science Education: The Contribution of Research*, (pp. 126–142). Maidenhead: Open University Press.

Rodrigues, S. (1999) 'Teaching science in context: a case study from the Classroom Learning Project'. Australasian science education research association conference, Rotorua, New Zealand, July.

Rodrigues, S. and Bell, B. (1995) 'Chemically speaking: students' talk during chemistry lessons', *International Journal of Science Education*, 17(6): 797–809.

Rodrigues, S. and Thompson. I. (2001) 'Cohesion in science lesson discourse: clarity, relevance and sufficient information', *International Journal of Science Education*, 23(9): 929–940.

Sinclair, J. and Coulthard, M. (1975) *Toward an Analysis of Discourse: The English Used by Teachers and Pupils*, Oxford: Oxford University Press.

Sinclair, J. and Coulthard, M. (1992) 'Toward an analysis of discourse', in M. Coulthard (ed.) *Advances in Spoken Discourse Analysis*, London: Routledge.

Unsworth, L. (2000) *Researching Language in Schools and Communities: Functional Linguistic Perspectives*, London and New York: Continuum International Publishing Group.

Wells, G. (1999) 'Dialogic inquiry: toward a sociocultural practice and theory of education', in R. Pea, J. Seely Brown and J. Hawkins (series eds) *Learning in Doing: Social, Cognitive and Computational Perspectives*, Cambridge: Cambridge University Press.

Williams, G. (2005) 'Grammatics in schools', in R. Hasan, C. Matthiessen and J. J. Webster (eds) *Continuing Discourse on Language: A Functional Perspective*, Volume 1, London: Equinox.

Yore, L. D. (2003) 'Examining the literacy component of science literacy: 25 years of language arts and science research', *International Journal of Science Education*, 25: 689–725.

Young, R. F., and Nguyen, H. T. (2002) 'Modes of meaning in high school science', *Applied Linguistics*, 23(3): 348–372

How to use pronoun grammar analysis as a methodological tool for understanding the dynamic lived space of people

Christine Redman and Rod Fawns

This chapter aims to outline a research approach to illuminate the ways that people use their understanding of their rights and duties to effect change in social behaviour and enact their agency. The chapter describes techniques by which the researcher may psychologically locate and analyse the ways people interpret their own and others' rights and duties in a particular social episode and perceive the values held in their particular community of practice or institutional setting.

Overview of positioning theory

Wyn exclaimed, 'But with . . . we've got so much . . ., we've got Water, we've got Aborigines, we've got this, we've got that, it's ridiculous!'

The above statement was made with great intensity to colleagues meeting in a primary school staffroom. The purpose of the statement, it seemed to us, was to seek agreement or support from colleagues that 'too much' was being put on them for the group to accept any other obligations. Does such a statement have any impact on future events? Will this statement alter or change future events because this specific concern was signalled in a public space?

A person can understand their own agency, their rights and duties in a particular social hierarchy and institutional structure only by recognising what they are permitted to say and do in the context of the semiotic interactions occurring in conversations. Moghaddam *et al.* (2008) observed in conversation and other discursive conventions that people will point to, draw on or align themselves with or against the community's values, often using these values as reasons to justify or strengthen their statement, argument and position. People make sense of these discursive conventions in the moment. Positions are contestable, by the person and by others, and challenges to positions may occur in conversation minute by minute. The ways that a person shapes, accepts or denies any attempts to re-position them contributes to their personal sense of identity and formation and their sense of 'who I am' in this particular place, at this particular time and in this particular context.

A 'position' is a metaphorical term that describes a psychological location (Phillips and Hayes, 2008) which a person publicly occupies in a workplace or other conversation. A position is expressed in language or gesture in a moment in conversation when a person perceives the conversation impinges on their place in the local moral order. A position publicly adopted is likely to influence what they subsequently say and do.

Positioning theory takes conversation to be the basic human social entity because it is in conversation that moral structures and personal identity are made potentially determinate as rights and duties are distributed and confirmed. To study personal identity formation and organisational transformation in any workplace, it is often necessary to first understand the complex life spaces a person occupies in different conversations in diverse institutional practices and societal rhetoric of the workplace.

Phillips (2002, 2006, 2008) demonstrated the value of positioning theory in the education of midwives, to both understand the factors that seemed to impact progressively on personal identity formation throughout the post-graduate academic year and how to better support and transform learning and professional practice in clinical settings. Webb (2004) used positioning theory to reveal how past socio-cultural understandings impacted differently on the professional identity formation of student physiotherapists of different ethnic origins in clinical conversations with Australian clinical supervisors. Arkoudis (2005, 2006) high-lighted the linguistic complexity of collaborative conversations between two long-time colleagues – one a teacher of chemistry and the other a teacher of English as a second language – as they sought to establish a language-across-the-curriculum literacy programme for migrant children in an inner urban school. Watkinson (2007) and Ashton-Smith (2009) used positioning theory to codify and track the socialisation of new learning technologies in different school settings.

Positioning theory has been used with both young children and teachers to make better sense of primary science classrooms and staffroom conversations (Redman, 2004; Redman and Jones, 2007; Redman and Coyle, 2008). The Theory supported the Redman and Rodrigues (2008) and Ashton-Smith (2009) enquiries into Foucault's technologies of self that allow teachers to transform themselves to meet different socio-cultural challenges associated with the introduction of new learning technologies imposed on their professional identities within their schools. Positioning theory informed the study of the interdependence of professional identity formation of teachers and organisational transformation in a new 'lighthouse' school for teaching science with new learning technologies (O'Mara and Redman, 2007; Redman, 2005) and how communities of practice mediate between personal claims of fulfilment of social duties and personal claims of responsibility for agential acts, including self-improvement and using new learning technologies (Redman, 2008).

It is often important to understand how people in particular communities are functioning in terms of accepted or denied positions. Challenges to positions can be associated with learning and change or with conflict and disharmony. Discourse analysis is useful to help 'comprehend exactly what it is people are doing with and through language as they speak' (Bartlett, 2008: 169). Positioning theory has provided an analytic tool to understand how, what and/or who is positioning and re-positioning members in the dynamic of social episodes.

Introduction to positioning theory

Positioning theory applies to 'the study of local moral orders as ever-shifting patterns of mutual and contestable rights and obligations of speaking and acting' (Harré and van Langenhøve, 1999: 1). It is an informing analytic tool that can assist the development of a deeper understanding of a community's values and practices and, importantly, people's relations with these values and practices. This offers a useful approach for the researcher who needs to make sense of the dynamic and complex inter-relationships that individuals have with others in a community of practice. It may provide a more informed base from which to consider the values and practices of group members and the success of any changes to an institution's beliefs or practices.

Positioning theory is associated with the work of Rom Harré and has its roots in the earlier work of the ordinary language philosophy of Austin, Vygotsky and Wittgenstein. It can be seen as a development of Vygotsky's premise that language is a tool that develops from, and in its use, in the culture (Howie and Peters, 1996; Moghaddam *et al.*, 2008). Harré suggests that as meanings and values are exchanged and communicated between members of a community, they are also being continually defined and challenged. Linehan and McCarthy (2000) describe positioning theory as an analytic tool that can be flexibly used to describe the shifting multiple relations in a community of practice.

Harré and van Langenhøve (1999) suggest that positioning theory provides for a more dynamic consideration of events in social settings than has been possible using the role theory approach to understanding the social behaviour of individuals in institutions. In role theory the individual is defined as a bundle of behaviours they are expected to exhibit and personal agency is typically ignored. Moghaddam *et al.*, observe that:

> Positioning Theory is seen as complementary to the older framework of Role Theory, rather than an alternative. Roles are relatively long lasting norms determining what a person in a role is able to do . . . Positioning Theory concerns conventions of speech and action that are labile, contestable and ephemeral.
>
> (2008: 9)

Role theory could be conceptually seen to be more aligned to the idea of institutional 'climate' in that it is concerned with relatively stable, long-lasting and predictable behaviour. Positioning theory, in contrast, is more aligned to our understanding of the 'weather' in that it is changeable, more reflective of the moment and not as reliably predictable as climate.

Positioning theory both examines and reveals the local distribution and allocation of people's rights and duties (Redman, 2008: 96). A right is what a person expects others may be reasonably held to be accountable for and to provide and protect for them. A duty is what others can expect a person to be providing and to be accountable to, and responsible for, in a particular setting and social world. The researcher records (in the form of dialogue or interview) accounts of personal positioning in the context of storylines they or others present in everyday discursive practice.

In coming to better understand people's discursive practices – evident in their speech and actions and their interpretation of their rights and duties – we gain a better sense of the lived space of individuals as members of specific local communities. Positioning theory aids researchers to understand how social knowledge is being dynamically, institutionally and socially constructed and how it may be frequently re-constructed and negotiated.

Positioning in the social dynamic moment of the local moral order

Positioning theory takes a micro-sociological perspective and a social psychological view that holds both the person and the context in focus. It examines people's discursive practices in social episodes in light of the distribution, adoption or appropriation of people's rights and duties, and thus the local moral order. This social realist approach proposes that the local moral order forms and arises as an outcome of people's interpretations and discursive expression of their rights and duties. The local moral order is what members may assume or expect will accompany certain roles in certain institutional settings and is explicable to observers who attend to how people interpret and act out their interpretation of their rights and duties in everyday conversation.

The local moral order becomes established and maintained in and through its members' storylines, positions and strategic discursive acts/actions, and these need to be considered and documented as they are enacted. The storyline can highlight tacit (Polanyi, 1967) practices that are habituated or ritualised and no longer overtly discussed. They are most likely acquired and identified by observing and listening to others. As a researcher attends more to these tacit behaviours, they may gain a greater awareness of which (and how) past social episodes may be contributing to and consciously and unconsciously influencing the current storylines.

Social episodes are best considered and analysed from data sets that are gathered in the lived moments. Data that are gathered after the social episode (typically in interview) are not a first-hand experience, as von Uexküll (1982) argues, and should be understood to be a reflexive version of events. Reflexive accounts allow a person to position and re-position themselves in their narrative. Re-positioning can occur as a person acts to accept or reject any challenges to their allotted or assumed position. These data are useful as they may illuminate the possible positions that are available to members.

With a deeper understanding of the rights and duties that are assumed in the local moral order, there exists for members of a community a sense and perception of 'what we do here and how we do it' and so 'what is expected of us' as we conduct our practices. These studies of moral expectations about what 'we should do' are usefully described as investigations of 'oughtness' by Linehan and McCarthy (2004). This concept of oughtness helps us to attend to the moral forces that positioning theory proposes are constantly impinging on and shaping why and how people eventually sense what amongst competing grammars (Harré, 1997a) they *should* chose to adopt. In the semiotic existence of institutional life, members come to assume and know what is expected of them in their particular situation. These assumptions are drawn from both official role descriptions and people's interpretation of these roles. As people attempt to fulfil institutional roles or social expectations, members of a practice community often discover that tensions exist in and between their roles and their rights and duties, which they commonly describe as their 'responsibilities'. These personal responsibilities, or internalised roles, are often aligned in dialogue with accepted social and cultural norms. Members' personal and professional values may conflict with aspects others identify with the role. By attending to institutional talk and action and focusing on individual community members as they rationally and emotionally process their behaviours, we come to better understand what members value, assume and expect, and so what influences their sense of personal commitment and intent. 'Positioning Theory aims to analyse an individual's voice(s) within the institutional structures in which they engage in conversations' (Arkoudis, 2005: 175). According to Phillips, Fawns and Hayes (2002: 243) 'The discursive act of positioning requires reconstructing the speaker's biography in relation to the individual being positioned and adopting positions that may be subject to rhetorical re-descriptions'. Feelings are significant to consider when analysing a person's position, how effectual or influential they feel and are and when they are positioning themselves or being positioned. These will be evident in gesture, words and actions and can be coded in events.

Coding, tracking and analysing the transition from good advice to a committed grammar

Positioning theory has informed the development of pronoun grammar analysis (PGA) as an objective coding tool for the fine-grained analysis of conversational data (Mühlhäusler and Harré, 1990). PGA supports a researcher to identify the relationship a speaker has with the topic, object or artefact at hand from the notion of the umwelt (von Uexküll, 1982). Coding of pronoun grammar in conversation analysis has a Vygotskian emphasis on the way in which socio-psychological tools and signs (Vygotsky, 1987) act in the mediation of social factors, but it allows more success in addressing the pressing issue of how the collective representation may be being actively interpreted by the individual (Daniels, 2004) at particular moments.

In the 'saying' . . .

A word develops and sustains its meaning in use. Others hear our words and interpret our intended meaning based on numerous factors. The context of the spoken word combines with the interplay between the extent of the listener's prior knowledge and the assumptions and expectations made by the speaker of the listener. The interpretations of words are assumed by listeners to have meaning. This is limited to how the listener understands the significance of the immediate context, past events and associated ideas. The meaning of a word can be located in its use and in the context of its use, and sometimes may be only used and useful in that context.

Not surprisingly, the meanings of our conversations are connected to and will be interpreted by others according to the setting, time and place (temporal and spatial). The meanings of words become representative of the social constructions that are shaped and influenced by the location, as well as the immediate and past events. Practices, location, time and place of spoken words will influence and impact upon the interpretations that others make of conversations. So 'How are you today?' when asked in the privacy of a hospital consultancy room may return a different response than if the question is asked of you by a friendly passer-by in an unfamiliar street.

Contextual and procedural language for one hospital will be much the same as another. But there may have been changes in the nuances of practices that have steadily developed a localised shared lexicon. These may be no longer noticed by participants and are unlikely to be signalled or realised until the doings are accompanied by the sayings. For example, back in the hospital setting, when a person is described as 'throwing up' it incurs a particular colloquial interpretation of vomiting. When used in the local post office, it might refer to the practice of taking handfuls of mail, packed tightly into mailbags, and lightly tossing letters up to free up and sort the mail for the local postal route.

In the 'doing' . . .

If colleagues suggest 'Let's go for coffee', it may mean simply walking to a staffroom and making instant coffee, leaving the building and ordering tea and a slice of cake or, if it is very late in the day, it might mean a glass of wine. Only when embedded in the everyday lived reality does the action come to be realised in the doing.

A word or phrase may not reveal its particular meaning until it is in use. When members of an institution enact their words then the meanings are made clearer, but until those actions are seen, interpretations of the word may remain hidden or misinterpreted. In the daily actions and long-standing practices of communities, the meanings of words become better illuminated and the hermeneutic of an individual becomes disclosed. Sometimes, until the words are seen in action, outsiders may make inadvertent assumptions about what is being said. A researcher needs to consider both the sayings and doings against the lived practices as they are enacted and against the social rhetoric of how people perceive we do things here.

The discursive practices of people doing and saying should be considered alongside the overt societal rhetoric and any specific institutional rhetoric. The societal rhetoric may differ to the institutional rhetoric that may be stated in the institution's written policy documents. Variations in the interpretations of the institutional rhetoric may develop. For example, schools in the same town have the same state-level guidelines, but they have developed localised, institutional variations.

The sayings include what members of the community say about themselves and their practices. These practices need to be closely examined and aligned with their doings. It may be naïvely anticipated that there would be an agreement between institutional sayings and doings (Davies and Harré, 1991), but members rarely experience this. People exercise their choices and their agency. If there is a mismatch between some of the sayings and doings then perhaps there is also a degree of tension. If there is a match between the official and public sayings and doings then there could be parity in the institution.

In research that uses positioning theory, it is important to ascertain and identify whether there is a match between individuals' doings and sayings and the institutional rhetoric. Institutional words may be accompanied by habits, actions and practices that are specific, significant and valued in various degrees by its members. In people's ontologies, in their discursive practices and in their adaptations, people's interpretations reveal the values, beliefs, attitudes and desires of the members and their institution.

Institutions document their desired practices in their public statements and documents. These are assumed to shape and influence the discursive practices of the members. So the expected priorities of members should align with and be evident in the institutional documentation, yet they sometimes may not be evident in their practices. When seeking to identify and locate these matches between people's doings and sayings, we may be distinguishing which daily practices or aspects of them are valued. Any discrepancies between an institution's documented policies and the members' practices may indicate that potential tensions may exist between the doings and sayings. Everyday practices exist both overtly and tacitly, and the tacit practices are as significant in helping to understand daily events as the overt ones. Positioning theory helps to elucidate these relationships between the stated values of their institution, and people's commitment and willingness to enact and embrace the documented practices.

Local moral order and habitus

Rights and duties will be referred to in conversation but perhaps only drawn upon as needed as generally these lie just quietly in the background of the everyday clatter of the busy lived space. In this system of rights and duties, located in the institutional settings, members enact their interpretations of their rights and duties. Tacit and overt rights and duties can be aligned to a person's place in the institution's local moral order and societies accepted codes. Herein lays the struggle of power, the daily battle of living with others, which is heard in expressions like, 'That's not fair' or statements like 'I won't be doing that!' Many rights and duties of institutional life are constantly being redefined and reconstructed in conversations and practices. These challenges and affirmations can be found to occur in silent, unspoken acts and gestures, as well as in the verbal conversations.

The rights and duties of an institution contribute to the habitus or the way people know that things are done in this particular institution. This knowledge is documented, perceptual and enacted and could be assumed to be influencing people's everyday sayings and doings. The habitus influences members' discursive practices and what people will accept and or reject and so become indicative of their shared and personal values. The habitus arises from what is known from previous practices and influences members' current practices and can be seen to generate 'actions that are appropriate given the demands of the current situation and a person's past activity' (Schatzki, 2002: 698).

Using positioning theory as a research methodology

People enact their agency and they act intentionally and unintentionally. The outcomes of people's doings and sayings indicate the moral authority that is available to an individual's position. This moral authority is the strategic or illocutionary force aligned to the individual's position.

Position, storylines and illocutionary force are mutually determinate entities in discursive psychology. The researcher presents an account of the speaker's agency through their self and others' positioning practice in descriptions of the storylines they choose to introduce about institutional practices or societal rhetoric, in which they claim or deny responsibility for their doings and sayings, using speech acts of different social force.

Introducing pronoun grammar analysis

As previously stated, pronoun grammar analysis (PGA) (Mühlhäusler and Harré, 1990) can be used to assist in the fine-grained analysis of textual data. In the analysis of conversations between groups, pairs or with individuals, it becomes apparent when people feel confident, hesitant or committed to the content under discussion. The use of the pronoun 'I' is a key indicator of a person's moral commitment.

> The selfhood of autobiographical telling is expressed predominantly in the uses of first and second (indexical) pronouns and in the choice of narrative conventions within which to tell the story. Pronouns are used to index what

is said with the various locations of the speaker as a person among persons in several patterns of relations. The uses of 'I' with the tenses of verbs, together with local narrative conventions, expresses the shapes of the many stories we can tell about ourselves.

(Harré, 1997b: 99)

Bearing this in mind, conversational or interview data can be coded. Coding will support tracking of the shifts in the multiple relations or positions a person may have, 'or access deliberately' (Louis 2008: 23), with a range of elements in an institution or society. Not only can people assume different positions, but individuals can move fluidly between positions in seconds, shifting perhaps between speaking from a leadership position that provides the professional representative voice of and for others to stating their own personal values and desires.

In this sample piece of dialogue, we hear one teacher move from talking about a personal perspective to signalling that they also represent, and speak for, the professional perspectives of others.

Dot in the meeting with Wyn and her primary teacher colleagues says:

So as **I** trial run (a new teaching strategy which is not embraced by Wyn and others), only from **my** point of view, as well, pop it into grade four, **I**, probably, it would be good practice to have a look at it for next year. It would, yeah, but also **we** are also looking at the water challenge too.

The use of the pronoun 'I' indicates that this statement reflects a personal commitment. This is further qualified by using 'my' and then inserting the personal pronoun 'I' again. This ensures this is not a statement to be taken as representative of the group. The use of the personal pronoun may indicate that this person, who has a leadership role, is being extremely cautious to ensure that listeners understand from whose position in the local moral order a statement is being made.

Someone who did not know or understand the significance of Dot's formal leadership role would understand the content of what was being said, but not what the statement potentially means in terms of outcomes. Dot acted cautiously and expressed a guarded commitment to the suggestion by an esteemed visitor that the technical innovation would be professionally and strategically worthwhile. Dot confirmed in the visitor's presence that the idea was 'good'. The 'we' was the team Dot led, the team was already busy, and the rhetoric of busyness was strengthened and emphasised by the use of the words 'also' (twice) and 'too'. The implication was that we will be too busy next year. Although Dot acknowledged that valuable professional learning was a likely outcome and staff professional development was part of her role, she did not have the moral authority to impose this self-improvement on her colleagues. She had responsibility to protect them from additional burdens that would distract from their core duties as primary teachers of language and number. It was this latter perception of Dot's role that Wyn addressed.

In the following utterance later in the same staff meeting, Joi, who is a mid-level team leader, used the indexical 'I' to propose a highly compromised settlement: 'But **I** suppose if **it** fits in with the topic **we** could, sort of, um integrate **it**, somehow, **you know** . . .'

From life in the mental space of reason, Joi reduces the threat of the new to an object, 'it', where it is less threatening. She offers, on behalf of the others, to integrate the problem away, to socialise it into daily practice in a way familiar to all present. The phrase 'you know' has several uses here.

Qualifying and quantifying words strengthen or weaken statements

In the study of speech patterns and the use of personal pronouns it becomes apparent that individuals may be (intentionally and unintentionally) using certain phrases or particular words to qualify and quantify what they are saying. These phrases and words act to indicate the strength or lack of personal conviction that they have about the content under discussion. In the previous quote, the speaker qualifies their thoughts with words like 'suppose', 'sort of' and 'somehow'. These words act to quantify and qualify a speaker's words to listeners. These words may imply a weakening or strengthening in the speaker's commitment.

So words like 'perhaps', 'maybe' or 'possibly' will position a speaker as uncertain, hesitant or unsure about the content or ideas under discussion. These words may also imply that the speaker is thinking and weighing up prospects and finding potential opportunities in an idea. Other words may act to imply that the speaker is confident and certain, and these words can include 'really', 'actually' or 'basically'. There are phrases and words that arise at specific moments in history. These may be culturally located and specific, so they need to be examined within the context of a setting, while cognizant of temporal and spatial colloquial turns of phrase. The phrase 'sort of' and the word 'like' appear to have currency in today's spoken language. 'Sort of' can act to diminish the vision and 'like' can act to punctuate sentences, but without defining the commitment: '**We**, like, always try to get some information (about a task) for the others (colleagues) to share in groups, like, **we** usually do that.'

Positioning others: challenging or affirming practices

Joi said: 'But **I** suppose if **it** fits in with the topic **we** could, sort of, um integrate **it**, somehow, **you know**.'

Joi used the phrase 'you know' to coax or position her teaching colleagues to agree with her compromise proposal. From her position of moral authority she offers parity. It also appeals here to the virtue of vagueness, shared lived experience or reverence for ritual. She says, in effect, 'we know how to handle this and no further detail is needed at this time'.

The phrase 'you know' may be used to punctuate statements that are seeking to be explanatory and to position listeners to be in agreement. Once a speaker thinks that they have adequately explained and referenced enough important background details, listeners are reminded of past agreements or events and the speaker inserts 'you know'. This means 'you know what I am talking about, and you most likely agree with me'. If listeners nod in agreement, the speaker may assume that all listeners understand, but listeners may not publicly assert their disagreement for a range of reasons.

If 'you know' is used with the word 'we', it could imply that it represents a group's point of view. If 'I' is used, it is likely to be a more personal statement and represent the speaker's point of view. The use of 'you know' to position listeners can be both an effective and ineffective strategy depending on whether the listeners recall and perceive the event the same way as the speaker. But if there is disagreement, the speaker's argument may have been weakened, reducing their influence on events. If the listeners do not accept the speaker's attempt to position them into agreeing, a challenge to the speaker's position can arise.

In the statement below we see Joi provide a reason for an alternative use of the computers. Joi explains how she has devised half-class access to computers:

No, well, when **they** . . . our kids come in half, half the class come, just, just from a lesson with X (the computer aide) so . . . **you know, they** haven't really done a lot of work, on websites, **you know**, for research, and that sort of thing.

Joi positions herself as morally responsive to our kids' needs. She points to and draws on what she has presumed is the agreed educational virtues of the half class, small group, teaching and a sense that perhaps they have been neglecting the development of website research practices. She sought to position others to agree with her using 'you know', but she has employed a risky strategy as the phrase 'you know' points here to two assumptions that are not necessarily connected in others' minds, particularly if they are not familiar with the practices to which she refers.

Comments are better understood and interpreted for their power and influence in the outcomes of later actions. The institution will have placed values on the practices of the small group and website research; these relative values will become evident in the doing and saying of the group's members. Previous discursive practices may influence what and how these particular group members might weight the values of certain practices as part of their institutional rhetoric. To know how effective this phrase has been, it will be necessary to examine what was said next. It can also be assessed for its eventual outcome and effect by considering what happened in subsequent events. The response to Joi's statement from Wyn was 'mmm, mmm, but how would **you** organize that though, because . . . would **you** still bring them in half groups, but then **you** wouldn't be doing the (same work) . . .'

There has been a challenge. The challenge from Wyn is to Joi, who is addressed as 'you' and not by name. If Joi had been personally addressed, the challenge may have seemed more personally confronting. The challenge is to Joi's team, but it seemed to be addressed to her personally, as the representative of an absent group. It is sometimes important to consider to whom a challenge is being made and how the challenger is positioning them. This may indicate the status the challenger perceives the speaker to have in the local moral order as well as the value of the proposed institutional reforms.

The paraverbals, 'mmm mmm' indicated that the new speaker had been publicly deciding to challenge and was contemplative. The challenge was directed at the alternative organisational structure and the element that focused this challenge was in the unfinished statement. A moral and ethical dilemma had been raised and it had focused on the alternative organisational structure: 'but then you wouldn't be doing the . . .'. Wyn's sentence could have been finished with one word: 'same'.

The idea of 'same' is an embedded tacit practice. 'Same' refers to equity and it was apparent that all students should have the same opportunities. Wyn's challenge here may lie in what had not been said and the absent word 'same' would pose a moral challenge that had been laid alongside this alternative way of organising classroom groups. The tension arose between the value of the moral and the ethical expectations of the same practices being provided for all and the pedagogical virtue of a more personalised teaching approach that used small groups and web research for independent learning. The institutional rhetoric of past conversations and actions contributes to the degree of support that the speaker and challenger may receive now from their listeners.

Any evaluation of Joi's choice to make her lessons half groups and to position others to support this idea will become evident only by tracking the subsequent conversations and the events. The response to Wyn's challenge to Joi indicated that she knew that Wyn had taken a moral viewpoint and had referred to the concept of same, but Joi too did not use the word 'same': 'No, **I** wouldn't be but . . . um . . . I mean . . . it's better that they come in half groups, than, **you know**, a whole grade, so . . . half groups are good . . . **you know**.'

Here were references to the broader ongoing moral debate between the concept of personalised learning and the concept of equity and equal access for all, within which judgements of practical epistemologies are likely to be made.

It is only by examining the outcome of speech acts that it becomes possible to determine the illocutionary force of a speech act. 'You know' can be used to position listeners or to show that the listeners are already positioned to be simultaneously agreeing with the content of a statement. The phrase 'you know' acts like a rhetorical question. It does not always seek or require an answer. It may simply signal that there is no need for more details or explanations, showing that the speaker has perhaps avoided providing listeners with an unnecessary lengthy description or explanation. This phrase positions listeners, who can/may choose to accept or reject this attempt to position them.

The teachers in this conversation have adapted their classroom practices according to their interpretation of a range of ethogenic episodes in their institutional life. These speakers attempted to position and re-position each other against their perspective on the relative values of their embedded and embodied practices. Through attending more seriously to everyday workplace conversations in research and the positioning and repositioning occurring in them, we gain a better sense of human agency (i.e. the status of different practices and their relative values) and how structural change may be achieved.

Recognising position shifts

Because personal pronouns are often interchangeable in an utterance, they can be used to index shifts in psychological position. By tracking the use of pronouns in conversations, the researcher can recognise where in the conversation the position of a person in the local moral order has been appropriated or been assigned. Positioning theory supports the understanding of the possible positions that may be available and or appropriated by individuals. It reveals the options that are available to members to enact their positions and where and when they seek to be influential by drawing upon specific reified practices.

> As the occupant of a role a person has certain prescribed relatively long term rights and duties, known to and generally accepted as legitimate by other members of the social order in which the role has an established place. In contrast, by establishing a position in the course of a then-and-there conversational manoeuvre, a person takes on or has thrust upon them a repertoire of rights and duties that are ephemeral. They rarely hold good, that is are taken up by others involved, for more than the course of the episode in which they are created.
>
> (Redman, 2008: 96)

Initially, coding of dialogue can begin with consideration of the personal pronouns. This is often helpful as it helps to isolate the range of positions people may be assuming or adopting during different moments of a conversation. These positions are often made explicit early in a conversation. This begins to show how a person is asserting themselves and adopting a particular position. This indicates if they can/may speak for and be representative of others. For example, a person who speaks using the word 'we' will bring the invisible faces of their team into the conversation. The team materialises behind the speaker. The speaker signals that they are speaking on behalf of other people. In the following example, a leading teacher, Wyn, represents her Grade 4 teaching colleagues in discussion of the Grade 4 curriculum with a researcher: 'Whereas next term, **we'll** be doing more the physical side of things. So, with the water topic, **we** have . . . got next week, the Water Watch Week, whether **we** can . . .'

Here Wyn provided information about future events, before hypothesising other possibilities. Wyn used the pronoun 'we' three times, strongly asserting her leadership position. Wyn's authority exists as part of her rights and duties in the institutional moral order of their school. It is Wyn's role to speak for the others in her team. The absent colleagues may assume they have the right to be represented by Wyn in any justification of their activities that may impinge upon their roles and possibly protect their rights and duties to make such curricular decisions. In the dynamic conversations between people, personal pronouns may change frequently. A person may use the word 'we' to claim greater authority for what they are saying, but they may alternatively elect to change pronouns and use 'I' or 'you'. This can be significant and PGA can indicate a possible and significant shift in the emphasis, commitment or confidence within the context of the conversational action. On the one hand, to substitute 'I' for 'we', for example, would indicate that they are claiming personal responsibility for an action or discursive act. To substitute 'you' for 'we' or 'I', on the other hand, would probably communicate that they were distancing themselves from an action or discursive act.

Later in the conversation, Wyn negotiates the timing of a task in a collaborative project with the researcher: 'So **it's** going to be after that isn't it, basically, because **we're** really into reports at the moment (student) reports at the moment, so it would suit **me** after . . .'

This comment shifts from representing the activities and commitments of others (shown in the use of the word 'we') and moves the focus to the individual's needs (evident in the use of 'me'). So as well as expressing their concern about the imminent and immediate demands on their team, there is also a focus on me and who I am understood to be in this project. 'Me' is a very interesting pronoun. It makes the content being referred to more personally located to the speaker's story. There is an assumption that significant components of a person's life story are being drawn into the moment. If the speaker states 'that would not seem fair to me' then the addition of 'me' is a reference to the speaker's values. So again knowledge of to whom the use of the word 'me' refers is important to understand. With or to whom are they contriving, affirming or asserting that they are at that moment in the conversation?

Further consideration of the place of the pronoun 'we' in the conversation

As indicated above, if a statement includes the personal pronoun 'we', it can indicate that it is positional and its relational position. Hypothetically, it could be implied and usually taken to be that it represents the views of others. The 'we' may indicate that the speaker has access to the values, beliefs and ideas of others. Importantly, it signals that the person also has the duty and a right to speak on behalf of these others.

It is important to consider and ask, who does 'we' represent? Does this person have the local moral authority to speak on behalf of the others? Do they have the right to represent these ideas? Do they have a duty to speak on behalf of others? Consider the following question asked by a teacher of a senior staff member: 'Do you mean this particular thing that **we're** going to do, or in . . .?'

This 'we' could refer to the 'we' in this particular meeting. But this 'we' could be the speaker's team or the speaker's class, the 'we' of all the students in the team's classes or the 'we' of all the teachers in this school. It could refer to 'we' being all the people who teach grade two students or all the teachers in our region of schools or all the teachers in the state of Victoria, the country Australia or the world. In this case, the speaker was referring to the class that was to have a different structure that they had described earlier. The issue had remained unresolved in this conversation and was revisited. In the end the half-groups were used by one teacher, who therefore successfully used the reified practices of small group teaching and thwarted the pressure to not do so because of the tacit practice of the need to be providing all the children with the same experience.

If a speaker represents the absent others outside their moral authority, outside the bounds of the borders of their duty to do so, then problems can arise. It is elucidating to identify the 'we' and who the 'we' references. Then there is a need to consider whether this person have the authority to speak on behalf of people. Is this their duty and responsibility? Do others see this as their right to be represented on certain matters by this person?

Wyn's objection is to an extra imposition on an already crowded role. This outburst is safe as there is hardly anyone in this setting who is going to say that there is not enough happening in the school curriculum: 'But with . . . **we've** got so much in one term, **we've** got, **we've** got Aborigines, **we've** got this, **we've** got that, **it's** ridiculous!'

The answer to these questions about who this 'we' represents is important as it frames the 'who' that is being represented and this is often important to know. If they are speaking without the moral authority being allocated to them, their statement could be considered to be presumptuous and the effect of their statement could be weakened. If the position was inappropriately adopted then their statements may be ineffectual in this conversation or have no significance or weight to change or influence practices. If they have had the position assigned to them and accepted in the local moral order then their authority and power will most likely be respected and, as a consequence, they may have more influence and weight behind their statement.

An allotted position is not enough to affirm an individual's authority and effectiveness as other related storylines also have to be considered. A person may have been assigned the position, but the community's members may not accept it. It can be challenged and there can be attempts to reposition the speakers and to reduce their authority and reduce or remove their obligation to enact their duty, thus impacting on the rights of the group that the person leads.

This aspect is the illocutionary force of the statement. How much effect do the statements have on the community's practices? The illocutionary force indicates the strength or power in an utterance to influence a group's decisions and actions.

A person can have moral authority by appointment or other election to a particular position but may not speak with illocutionary force. This may be a choice exercised in a particular conversation or they may, for various reasons, lack moral capacity to strategically undertake duties and responsibilities or rights.

So when considering a single pronoun in a statement, it needs to be aligned against the storylines, a person's position in the local moral order and the illocutionary force in order to understand a person's agency in relation to a particular area of social action. This fine-grained analysis of the personal pronouns used in textual data needs to be juxtaposed against the context, the culture, an understanding of people's perceptions of their rights and duties and how individuals are being positioned by these elements.

The use of 'you' in a conversational dialogue

A pronoun can be used by a speaker to achieve a positional or relational effect. To take a position or position others is always a relational act with humans or other entities. The use of the pronoun 'you' in a conversation, like 'we', needs to be considered for its effect. 'You' used in place of 'I' can index a distancing or detachment from personal responsibility or agency between the speaker and the action in the conversation. However, 'you' may form a vision of future agency. When the speaker uses 'you' they may be projecting themselves into future and anticipated practices and be imagining or structuring a range of possibilities beyond those currently being rehearsed. Both indexes are not necessarily addressed to a present second person but often to a vague other person. 'You' replaces 'one' in previous conversational use, as in 'one' can or 'one' could do this or imagine that.

The word 'you' isolates a speaker from the content. The pronoun 'I' immerses the speaker into the content. In the following examples children's statements have been considered using PGA. They indicate the usefulness of applying the tool to consider the degree of confidence the child has with the aspect of the content under discussion.

This example is from a ten-year old child, Indiah. She is perceiving, for the first time, real-time pictures of the Earth in space. She looks at the Earth rotating and the Earth's shadow moves over its surface and is asked by Redman (2004) to describe what she thinks she is seeing:

> Oh **I** think that's really interesting, that **you** can be looking at **it** at that very time and if it's night time **you** can see lights from the cities that are going on at that time. **I** think that's really cool.

There were shifts between the pronouns 'I' and 'you'. Indiah uses 'I' to communicate her personal engagement with the image on the monitor. The use of 'you' objectifies what she is envisioning, implying that humanity in general would see these things and it is not just in her imagination.

She was also positioning the researcher, from her position as good student. Her heuristically grounded storyline, her agentially dynamic positioning and the illocutionary force of her final existential exultation proclaim her high place in the local moral order.

In contrast, Frank, aged eight, sounded confident about the science content as he inserted the pronoun 'I': 'Well, I think, well, I think I know the reason we have (night) . . . is because, the Earth . . . spins round this way . . . the sun's in the middle.' But when Frank considered the technology aspects of the event, he was less confident, as is indicated by his choice of 'you'. The 'you' was used when Frank did not have confidence and moved between pronouns fluidly:

> I think . . . it depends what **you** loaded on to the CD. If **you** didn't load all of it on I reckon it would be best to use the website. But if **you** did, it would be quicker to put the, um, or **you** could use the Internet, but I don't know how **you** would get onto this, **I'm** not sure if it takes a long time to set up, I would reckon on the CD because that's quicker to set up.

He uses the 'I' to communicate his technical reasoning and the 'you' in the realm of possibilities that others are managing.

An adult speaker, like Joi, talking about her vision for using web-based research in her classroom, shifts between pronouns, beginning with 'I' to convey her personal commitment and using 'you' to introduce elements not yet owned as part of her overall vision. Joi moves between the two pronouns fluently:

> Um, Oh I was hoping to (do web-based research), but it is just too difficult to try and fit it in and yeah . . . I was going to try and fit **it** in as part of a reading thing . . . like just make **it** a whole guided reading session that each group would have **their** own . . . something based at **their** own level, which is something, **you, you'd, it** would really be a great thing to do, **you know**, **you** could use big books at the same time, and um, and **you** could use a whole heap of things, but, just the time, I, **you'd** have to plan something like that, very well, so that **you** could have **your** groups working on things that **they** were capable of doing, and the other, and then the kids at the other end, the extension kids, could really go ahead and, I mean research things, **you** know, using this site, so yeah, that would be a great way to use it, I reckon.

Conclusion

The socialisation of artefacts like the web or an object or equipment in a science experiment can only be achieved through language and there are two social codes at work. In the interaction with the material artefacts, including concepts, there is the language code of management and there is the language code of expression. As the conversations above show, the latter dominates in most cases. In their doings and saying, whilst engaging in the ritualised and reified socio-cultural practices of an institution, individuals shape their own agency in the context of social dominance, using the various forms of reason described as 'technologies of self' by Foucault. Positioning theory assists researchers to study work on themselves in everyday discourse in the process of constructing their social identity at the intersection of their intentions and contingent necessities, while they simultaneously transform or maintain the social rules of their organisational structure. Positioning theory is concerned with conventions of social practice and assists us to better understand how 'human agency develops and functions within particular social episodes in the interactional nexus of local community settings' (Harvey, 2002: 184) by anticipating the expectations of others. Understanding people's perceptions of their responsibilities and duties reveals the ways that certain institutional factors may be enabling and disabling people's commitments. The position is a metaphor for understanding the social actions of the person that is conceptualised by ethogenics (Harré and Secord, 1972) in the local moral order of the discourse community.

As Davies and Harré point out:

> 'Positioning' and 'subject position' . . . permit us to think of ourselves as a choosing subject, locating ourselves in conversations according to those narrative forms with which we are familiar and bringing to those narratives our own subjective lived histories through which we have learnt metaphors, characters and plots.
>
> (1991: 41)

References

Arkoudis, S. (2006) 'Negotiating the rough ground between ESL and mainstream teachers', *International Journal of Bilingual Education and Bilingualism*, 9(4): 415–433.

Arkoudis, S. (2005) 'Fusing pedagogic horizons: language and content teaching in the mainstream', *Linguistics and Education*, 16(2): 1973–187.

Ashton-Smith, N. (2009) 'Prensky's digital images: the life of science and English teachers with digital learning', unpublished D.Ed. Thesis, University of Melbourne.

Bainbridge, J. (2008) 'Educational accountability and organizational capacity in school science departments: a material critique of management models of mandated curriculum reforms', unpublished D.Ed. Thesis, University of Melbourne.

Bartlett, T. (2008) 'Wheels within wheels, or triangles within triangles: time and context in positioning theory', in F.M. Moghaddam, R. Harré and N. Lee (eds) *Global Conflict Resolution Through Positioning Analysis* (pp. 169–187), New York: Springer.

Bourdieu, P. (1990) *The Logic of Practice*, Cambridge: Polity Press.

Bainbridge, J. (2008) 'Educational accountability and organizational capacity in school science departments: a material critique of management models of mandated curriculum reforms', unpublished D.Ed. Thesis, University of Melbourne.

Daniels, H. (2004) 'Activity theory, discourse and Bernstein', *Educational Review*, 56, (2): 121–132.

Davies, B. and Harré, R. (1991) 'Positioning; The discursive production of selves', *Journal for the Theory of Social Behaviour*, 20 (1): 43–63.

Foucault, M. (1983) 'Afterword: the subject and power', in H. Dreyfus and P. Rabinow, (eds) *Michel Foucault: Beyond Structuralism and Hermeneutics*, Chicago: University of Chicago Press.

Harré, R. (1983) 'Commentary from an ethnographic standpoint', *Journal for the theory of Social Behaviour*, 13(1): 173–191

Harré, R. (1997a) 'Forward to Aristotle: the case for a hybrid ontology', *Journal for the Theory of Social Behaviour*, 27(1): 173–192.

Harré, R. (1997b) 'Pathological autobiographies', *Philosophy, Psychiatry, and Psychology*, 4(2): 99–109.

Harré, R. and Secord, P. (1972) *The Explanation of Social Behaviour*, Oxford: Blackwell.

Harré, R. and van Langenhøve, L. (1999) *Positioning theory: Moral contexts of intentional action*, Malden: Blackwell.

Harvey, D. (2002) 'Agency and community: a critical realist paradigm', *Journal for the Theory of Social Behaviour*, 32(2): 164–194.

Howie, D. and Peters, M. (1996) 'Positioning theory: Vygotsky, Wittgenstein and social constructionist psychology', *Journal for the Theory of Social Behaviour*, 26(1): 51–64.

Johnson, M. and Kerper, R. M. (1996) 'Positioning ourselves: parity and power in collaborative work', *Curriculum Inquiry*, 26(1) 5–24.

Linehan, C. and McCarthy, J. (2000) 'Positioning in practice: understanding participation in the social world', *Journal for the Theory of Social Behaviour*, 30(4): 435–451.

Louis, W. R. (2008) 'Intergroup positioning and power: an introduction', in F. M. Moghaddam, R. Harré and N. Lee (eds) *Global Conflict Resolution Through Positioning Analysis* (pp. 21–40), New York: Springer.

Miettinen, R. (2006) 'Epistemology of transformative material activity: John Dewey's pragmatism and cultural-historical activity', *Journal for the Theory of Social Behaviour*, 36(4): 389–408.

Moghaddam, F. M., Harré, R. and Lee, N. (2008) 'Positioning and conflict: an introduction', in F. M. Moghaddam, R. Harré and N. Lee (eds) *Global Conflict Resolution Through Positioning Analysis* (pp. 3–21), New York: Springer.

Mühlhäusler, P. and Harré, R. (1990) *Pronouns and People: The Linguistic Construction of Social and Personal Identity*, Oxford: Blackwell.

O'Mara, L. and Redman, C. (2007) 'Primary teachers' practices in a demonstration school; the pedagogical uses of websites', Australian Association for Research in Education (AARE), Notre Dame University, Fremantle, Western Australia, November.

Phillips, D., Fawns, R. and Hayes, B. (2002) 'From personal reflection to social positioning: the development of a transformation model of professional education in midwifery', *Nursing Inquiry*, 9: 239–249.

Phillips, D. and Hayes, B. (2006) 'Moving towards a model of professional identity formation in midwifery through conversations and positioning theory', *Australian Journal of Adult Learning*, 46 (July 2): 224–242.

Phillips, D. and Hayes, B. (2008) 'Securing the oral tradition: reflective positioning and professional conversations in midwifery education', *Collegian*, 15: 109–114.

Polanyi, M. (1967) *The Tacit Dimension*, New York: Anchor Books.

Redman, C. (2008) 'The research planning meeting', in F. M. Moghaddam, R. Harré, and N. Lee (eds) *Global Conflict Resolution Through Positioning Analysis* (pp. 95–112), New York: Springer.

Redman, C. (2004) 'Meaning making with real time images of earth in space', unpublished PhD Thesis, The University of Melbourne, Melbourne.

Redman, C. and Coyle, D. (2008) 'The place of the social, cultural and affective domains in supporting the uptake of new technologies, International Federation for Information Processing (IFIP), WG 3.5 Informatics and Elementary Education', Valuing Individual and Shared Learning: the role of ICT conference, Charles University, Prague, Czech Republic, 23–26 June.

Redman, C. and Rodrigues, S. G. (2008) 'Researching the relationships in the technologies of self: habitus and capacities', Australian Association of Research in Education (AARE) Queensland University of Technology, Kelvin Grove Campus, Brisbane, 30 Nov.–4 Dec.

Redman, C. and Jones, T. (2007) 'Conflict in practice: metacognitive behaviours in a science lesson using ICT', Redesigning Pedagogy; Culture, Knowledge and Understandings Conference, National Institute of Education, Nanyang Technological University, Singapore, 28–30 May.

Schatzki, T. R. (2002) *The Site of the Social: A Philosophical Account of the Constitution of Social Life and Change*, University Park, PA: Penn State University Press.

Schmidle, R. (2008) 'Positioning and military leadership', in F. M. Moghaddam, R. Harré and N. Lee (eds) *Global Conflict Resolution Through Positioning Analysis* (pp. 189–206), New York: Springer.

Van Langenhøve, L. and Harré, R. (1999) 'Introducing positioning theory', in R. Harré and L. van Langenhøve (eds) *Positioning Theory* (pp. 14–31).

Von Uexküll, J. (1982) 'The theory of meaning', *Semiotica*, 42(1), 25–82.

Vygotsky, L. S. (1987) 'Thinking and speech', in R. W. Rieber and A. S. Carton (eds), *The Collected Works of Vygotsky, L.S.: Vol. 1. Problems of General Psychology*, New York: Plenum.

Watkinson, A. R. (2007) 'Uneasy lies the head: the repositioning of heads of English in independent schools in Victoria in the age of new learning technologies', unpublished D.Ed. Thesis, University of Melbourne, Melbourne.

Webb, G. (2004) 'Clinical education in physiotherapy: a discursive model', unpublished D.Ed. Thesis, University of Melbourne, Melbourne.

Chapter 11

Conclusion
What next?

Susan Rodrigues

When I was teaching in a school in New Zealand I was interested in finding ways to make chemistry more interesting and relevant. After a period of trial and error, I realised that familiar themes and contexts engaged the children I taught, but I wanted to know how the use of these themes and contexts influenced the children's ability to learn chemistry. I explored the potential of teaching a conceptually difficult chemistry topic through the use of various contexts. I had my research questions mapped out fairly early. After reading various journal articles and texts, I identified data collection strategies that involve pre-, post-, retrospective and introspective interviews, classroom observation, pre- and post-surveys and tests, materials and class work analysis. Despite having those data collection strategies in place, I was still in a quandary when it came to how to analyse this data. And as a scientist, I was used to collecting and analysing data and then sharing my analysis and conclusions with the scientific community, holding up my analysis and findings for peer scrutiny. So if I were to collect and analyse classroom data, what would I need to do to ensure that my findings were valid, trustworthy and stood up to scrutiny?

When I started my doctoral study I began what might be described as an apprenticeship within my immediate community of educational researchers. Within this community we discussed and shared understandings of theoretical perspectives that supported particular types of research approaches and I drew on the expertise and experiences of colleagues. I read numerous articles and used these to validate and justify the general approach, the tools and the strategies that I adopted.

This book has drawn on research expertise and experience of a number of my international colleagues. It is intended to provide the reader with an apprenticeship with access to an international community. The chapters outline specific issues, challenges and considerations that will be of interest to researchers who are considering an exploration within educational research. As each chapter has shown, if research is to be productive, a good theoretical and pragmatic foundation – one that allows the researcher to establish a good fit between the milieu they wish to research, their research question and the data they wish to analyse – is helpful.

At the start, researchers need to ask four key questions:

1 What is my research question?
2 What sort of analysis will help me address this question?
3 What sort of data do I need for this analysis?
4 How do I collect and record these data?

For many of us however, once the research question has been identified we tend to concentrate our energies on data collection: What strategies/tools to deploy? Who to involve? How often? The sort of analysis and the theoretical nature of the approach that we will need to address the question and provide credibility tend to assume a lower priority as we become engrossed in the practicalities of collecting data. Of course, it is important to select appropriate tools to use if we want our analysis to be trustworthy. As Table 11.1 shows, our contributing chapter authors used a variety of research tools when conducting their research.

The previous chapters detail the sort of analysis that is possible when data are collected with these tools and the nature of the data (i.e. the what, who and how) that are required for the type of analysis that is being advocated.

As this book has shown, there is a broad range of analytical tools and strategies informed by various theoretically-informed approaches that are widely used in social research. These approaches have distinct epistemological and ontological assumptions. These assumptions could – and we would suggest should – be used to inform the selection of strategies in order to ensure that the choice is trustworthy and well principled and that the fit is appropriate.

In the following sections of this chapter we first revisit some of the key ideas presented by my colleagues and then we consider elements that help to ensure that the data are trustworthy. All ten chapters described validity (in terms of plausibility, credibility and empirical evidence) and they showed how they

Table 11.1 Tools and strategies described in this book's chapters

Chapter	Interviews	Surveys/ Questionnaires/ Tests	Observation	Analytical monitoring technology
Ainley and Buckley		x		x
Jindal-Snape and Topping	x	x	x	
Shin, Stevens and Krajcik	x	x		
Valanides		x	x	
Conner	x	x	x	
France	x			
Denley and Bishop	x		x	x
Anderson and Sangster	x		x	
Rodrigues	x		x	x
Redman and Fawns	x		x	

generated trustworthiness in the findings and results. We look at the issue of trustworthiness later in this chapter.

A brief review of the chapters

Mary Ainley and Sarah Buckley, in Chapter 1, described the use of social network analysis to investigate the influence of students' multiple peer networks on what happens in classrooms. Mary and Sarah demonstrated how approaches such as person-centred clustering techniques and social network analysis could be used to identify complex interactive associations that vary within groups of students and trajectories of educational development. They also advocated caution when it comes to interpretation. As they suggested, an answer based on 'all other things being equal' affords valuable information with regard to the dynamics of educational achievement, but it may disregard intricacies and complications related to the variety of combinations and/or patterning of these variables given that they involve an assortment of students.

Divya Jindal-Snape and Keith Topping, in Chapter 2, discussed case study approaches. A single case design is usually used to observe the impact of any intervention on the participant's behaviour. By comparing the participant's performance or behaviour during different intervention conditions encountered by the participant, one can make inferences about the effectiveness of the intervention. Multiple baseline designs collect baseline data across either different settings or different behaviours for the same individual and/or across different participants being trained at the same time. The intervention is applied to one setting/behaviour/participant while the others continue in baseline, then the intervention is applied to the other settings/behaviours/participants. The graphs of observational data are examined to see if improvement is notable when the intervention is started in those particular settings/participants/behaviours.

Chapter 3, by Namsoo Shin, Shawn Stevens and Joseph Krajcik illustrated learning progressions, which is a strategy for longitudinal studies that allows researchers to collect and analyse data that would be akin to a video documentary rather than a collection of photographs. Namsoo, Shawn and Joseph proposed using construct-centred design as a methodology because it focused on the construct that students are expected to learn and that the researchers and teachers want to measure. As an example, Namsoo, Shawn and Joseph illustrated how the construct-centred design process provided a systematic research methodology for learning research using the development of learning progressions, which is a new and complex research field in science education.

The first three chapters showed how data collated from various sources over short and long durations can be analysed and interpreted when exploring the dynamics of educational achievement.

Chapter 4, by Nicos Valanides, will be of interest to those researchers contemplating quantifying qualitative data for statistical analysis. Nicos described how the constant comparative analysis method (CCAM) or grounded theory (GT) can be used to review interview data. Perhaps what is noteworthy is the fact that, unlike most other research studies where the participants constitute the unit of analysis, in CCAM/GT the unit of analysis is the incident. Nicos described how the CCAM involved inductive category coding and an assessment of observed behaviours across groupings. He also showed how using the CCAM/GT scoring rubrics were produced for specified variables and component factors. Nicos described the different coding process steps, as well as ways of quantifying qualitative data for statistical analyses.

For the most part, many qualitative projects involve multiple data collection techniques that are predominantly observational in some form and usually in

Table 11.2 Mapping analysis requirements to theoretical approaches

Once research questions are identified and the questions suggest predominant interest in:	*Then it is likely that:*
Observing the impact of an intervention on a participant's behaviour	Single case design techniques may be useful. By comparing the participant's performance or behaviour during different intervention conditions, researchers can make inferences about the effectiveness of an intervention.
Collecting baseline data across either different settings or different behaviours for the same individual and/or across different participants being trained at the same time	Multiple baseline designs may be useful as an intervention is applied to one setting/ behaviour/participant while the others continue in baseline. The intervention is applied to the other settings/behaviours/ participants with a lag of time between them. Inferences can be made by observing the graphs that are compiled to see if the graphs reflect improvement only when the intervention is in place.
Interactive associations within particular groups	Person-centred clustering techniques and social network analysis may be useful. Researchers could use person-centred clustering techniques and social network analysis to identify composite and intricate associations that vary within groups of students and variable educational development pathways.
Collecting longitudinal data to track development of particular concepts or knowledge	Construct-centred design (CCD) may be useful as it focuses on the construct that students are expected to learn and researchers want to measure.
Thinking aloud protocols and having collected pre- and post-product or outcome information	Constant comparative analysis method or grounded theory (GT) provides a convenient way to quantify qualitative data and prepare it for statistical analyses.

significant detail to reflect a specific context. Lindsey Conner, in Chapter 5, described a research framework that showed how analytic tools, called 'meta-matrices', enabled multiple sources of data to be triangulated when analysing students' learning processes. Lindsey described how the matrices provided a convenient and visual method for triangulating multiple sources of data, such as interviews, classroom materials produced by students, classroom observations, journal entries and student assessment information.

The three chapters that followed Lindsey's chapter focused on the analysis of narrative. Many researchers collect narrative data. For them the challenge lies in providing trustworthy interpretation when they analyse and report on the narrative data. Chapter 6, by Bev France, described a particular form of narrative inquiry. Bev described the use of connective stories as an outcome of a research activity in order to illustrate the merit of narrative research methodology. She suggested that narrative enquiry is not simply an account of what happened; the focus of narrative enquiry is on how people make sense of what happened. To illustrate this concept, Bev described this process in terms of the co-construction of teachers' parallel stories when they explored their pedagogy.

Paul Denley and Keith Bishop, in Chapter 7, described a qualitative approach using video stimulated recall (VSR) to analyse the practice of a group of highly accomplished science teachers. Paul and Keith suggested that, unlike VSR, conventional post-lesson interviews, direct classroom observation and interaction analysis methods may not provide real insight into thought process and decision making. Paul and Keith discussed reliability and validity issues, such as whether accounts generated through a stimulated recall interview are a reconstruction of the events drawing on stored memory relating only to that event or a re-interpretation of the event drawing on a variety of stored memories. However, they suggested that the point is really an epistemological one as it pertains to the knowledge claims a researcher intends to make from the recall data.

In Chapter 8, Charles Anderson and Pauline Sangster talked about how they analysed data collected during one-to-one sessions in which Pauline and student teachers discussed and reflected on episodes of teaching. What their chapter showed is the need to adopt an approach that is founded on specific research questions and consonant with the nature of the data generated. They also reviewed other methodological related matters, such as the issues that arise if one of the researchers has an 'insider' role (as in Pauline's case, where she was a tutor and an observer). Charles and Pauline addressed questions concerning the validity of the analysis.

Chapter 9 will be of interest to those contemplating analysing dialogue or exploring the nature of talk. In Chapter 9 I showed how particular analytical strategies have the potential to help researchers explore how socio-cultural and linguistic knowledge is linked in the negotiation and communication of meaning during classroom lessons. I drew largely on the work of Halliday and Hasan to show how language can be analysed. I focused on the notions of register and coherence to illustrate the potential of Halliday and Hasan's work when it comes

Table 11.3 Triangulating data to promote reliability and validity

Once research questions are identified and the questions suggest predominant interest in:	Then:
Collating multiple data sets and involving a range of data sources (e.g. interviews, materials, observations, journals, diaries and assessment information)	Metamatrices provide a visual method for triangulating these multiple sources of data in terms of various themes.
Collecting data to reveal the issues found at intersections where practitioner knowledge meets knowledge constructed by others	Narrative interrogation can be used as it allows for member checks through the co-construction of a parallel story when the subjects explore their actions or pedagogy in action.
Collecting practitioner data in which they talk about their actions and the process of decision making underpinning these actions	Video stimulated recall technique involving qualitative data analysis software provides the practitioner with a way of explaining his or her own actions and the process of decision making underpinning them.

to analysing classroom talk, if a researcher wants to do more than analyse data from a turn-taking perspective.

Chapter 10, by Christine Redman and Rod Fawns, will be of interest to those contemplating analysing personal identity formation and organisational transformation in any workplace. They suggested that it is often necessary to first understand the complex life spaces a person occupies in different conversations in diverse institutional practices and societal rhetoric of the workplace if one wants to analyse identity formation or transformation. Christine and Rod also showed how positioning theory can be utilised as an analytic tool as the theory provides a way to examine the notion of 'oughtness' in every day practices. In essence, Christine and Rod's chapter takes us full circle as they explore person–process–context, an aspect Mary and Sarah introduced to us in Chapter 1.

Each of the ten chapters has shown how they were informed by approaches with clearly stated epistemological and ontological assumptions. Each of the ten chapters has also included elements of techniques, strategies, tools and protocols that differ. Nevertheless, as the chapters have shown (see Tables 11.2, 11.3 and 11.4), educational researchers have developed rigorous strategies that are sufficiently meticulous and suitably trustworthy.

Quality measures

Periodically, naturalistic enquiry is attacked as untrustworthy. These challenges are voiced primarily because the subjective nature of the data collected makes quality monitors of reliability and validity problematic when researchers attempt

Table 11.4 Analysing talk at the grammar or position level

If the research questions identify a reliance on collecting dialogue or talk and the research questions are interested in:	Then:
The negotiation of meaning	Analysis of register, cohesion and coherence provide a method to explore talk in order to investigate the development of socio-cultural knowledge.
The relationships that exist in a community of practice	Positioning theory can be utilised as an analytic tool by considering the development of pronoun grammar analysis as an objective coding tool for fine-grained analysis of conversational data.

to apply them to qualitative research. In Chapter 1, Mary and Sarah suggested that researchers must clearly specify the character of the participant group; in Chapter 2, Divya and Keith suggested that researchers must define behaviours as specifically as possible if researchers are to promote trustworthiness in terms of the reliability and validity of observational analysis and intervention gains. Lincoln and Guba (1986, 1989) suggest that internal validity, external validity, dependability and confirmability should be considered when ascertaining trustworthiness in qualitative research. They also suggest that in qualitative research internal and external validity are analogous to the quality monitors of validity and transferability that are often applied in quantitative research, while dependability and confirmability are analogous to reliability and objectivity. So when educational researchers are deciding on the analytical approach to use, it is important that they pay due attention to credibility, transferability, dependability and confirmability.

There are many factors that influence the concept of credibility. For example, credibility is influenced by the duration of participant observation, as well as persistent observation. The approaches described in Chapters 1 through 4 illustrated the concept of duration and persistence. For example, Divya and Keith advocated conducting observation more than once, and in more than one setting/context, to encourage data reliability when using case studies. Notably, they also intimated that some researchers considered multiple case designs to be more robust, possibly as a consequence of the duration and persistence strategies deployed when collecting data over a long period. The chapters by Divya and Keith and Namsoo, Shawn and Joseph also showed how duration of participant observation and persistent observation could be used to provide a degree of triangulation.

Triangulation (i.e. using many perceptions to clarify findings) and peer consultation (i.e. extensive discussions with peers who are not directly involved) also have significant influence on determining credibility. The approaches described in all the chapters showed how triangulation and peer consultation worked within particular approaches. For example, all the authors showed how a researcher has to define behaviours as specifically as possible to promote reliability and validity.

All the authors also suggested that the reliability of data analysis could be ascertained using inter-observer reliability measures. However, as Chapters 5 through 8, by Lindsey, Bev, Paul and Keith and Charles and Pauline, showed, peer consultation can be used to promote credibility.

Credibility (see Figure 11.1) is also influenced by what is sometimes called 'progressive subjectivity' (i.e. researcher rapport and researcher awareness of their impact in terms of objectivity/subjectivity or their research) and member checks (i.e. testing assertions and interpretations with the original source).

All ten chapters described their approach to triangulation. But Chapter 1, by Mary and Sarah, Chapter 4, by Nicos, Chapter 5 by Lindsey, Chapter 6, by Bev, Chapter 7, by Paul and Keith, and Chapter 8, by Charles and Pauline, in particular, report on approaches they have used to help capture multiple meanings that their participants attach to personal experiences. Likewise, the research approach described by Christine and Rod, as well as my own research, showed how we used particular opportunities and specific approaches to analyse data and construct explicit cultural knowledge about the project milieu and the project participants. Analysis of the data the authors generated usually enabled them to draw conclusions. Several of the authors showed how member checks, progressive subjectivity and peer consultation helped support triangulation. The authors also showed how they used multiple perceptions to verify repeatability and inter-pretation or to clarify meaning and as a consequence triangulate their data.

From a dependability perspective (see Figure 11.2), the ten chapters provided insight into different dependability audits (see Figure 11.3). In particular, Chapter 3, by Namsoo, Shawn and Joseph, Chapter 2 by Divya and Keith, Chapter 1, by Mary and Sarah, Chapter 10, by Christine and Rod, and my own chapter, Chapter 9, explicitly showed how we tracked changes and shifts to enable readers and reviewers to explore and judge our decisions and interpretations. All of the authors documented the factors in the project that led them to particular decisions, conclusions and assertions. This form of transparency is important as it enables others to confirm the stability of the data, or what is commonly called 'dependability'.

All of the authors showed that a researcher has to define behaviours as specifically as possible to promote reliability and validity of observational analysis and inter-vention gains. So, for example, some suggested that the reliability of data analysis could be ascertained using inter-observer reliability measures. They advocated conducting observation more than once, and in more than one setting/context, to encourage data reliability. In qualitative educational research, it is often difficult to include random sampling procedures, but as the chapters in this book show, it is possible to address representativity through alternatives, such as comparing elements with those of the larger population or through the collation of studies. Most of the chapters showed how interpretations, conclusions, assertions and

Credibility

'The match between the constructed realities of respondents (or stakeholders) and those realities as represented by the evaluator and attributed to various stakeholders' (Guba and Lincoln, 1989: 237).

Triangulation and confirmability

Use multiple perceptions to verify repeatability, interpretation or to clarify meaning. So data is triangulated.

Ensure data can be tracked to original source and show how the conclusions were drawn from the data.

All ten chapters in this book involved one or more of these elements.

| Duration of participant observation | Persistent observation | Peer consultation | Progressive subjectivity | Member checks |

Figure 11.1 An overview of credibility

Dependability

The stability of data over time (Lincoln and Guba, 1989).

All ten chapters illustrate how their approach has a dependability audit.

Show the method to document the logic of process and method decision.

Track the changes and shifts so that external reviewers can explore and judge decisions and interpretations.

Document the factors in the project that lead you to particular decisions.

Document the factors in the project that lead you to particular conclusions/assertions.

Figure 11.2 Facets of dependability

All ten chapters illustrate elements of trustworthiness.

Transferability	Confirmability	Authenticity		

Transferability	Confirmability	Fairness	Ontological authenticity	Educative authenticity
'An empirical process for checking the degree of similarity between sending and receiving contexts' (Guba and Lincoln, 1989: 241).	Assuring that data, interpretations and conclusions are not simply constructs of researcher imagination!	Fairness: 'the extent to which different constructions and their underlying value structures are solicited and honoured within the evaluation process' (Guba and Lincoln, 1989: 245–246).	Ontological authenticity: 'improvement in the individual's (or group's) conscious experiencing of the world' (Lincoln, and Guba 1986: 81).	Educative authenticity: 'extent to which individual respondents' understanding of and appreciation for the constructions of others outside their stake holding group are enhanced' (Guba and Lincoln, 1989: 248).
Ensure that the descriptions are rich and thick. Provide clarity with regard to the milieu, time, duration and place.	Ensure that conclusions can be traced to the data and information provided by participants.	Look for participant constructions of particular experiences and look for differences or issues that exist between them and you as the researcher with regard to that particular experience.	What this is basically suggesting is that you as the researcher can show that the participants were gaining an advantage or learning.	Keep all participants informed about, and at, all stages of the research. Inform the participants about the intention of the project from various perspectives to encourage them to be better informed about these perspectives.

Figure 11.3 Facets of trustworthiness

assumptions could be tested by triangulating data and/or methods or through respondent validation.

Approaching your research

Start by writing a brief introduction to the research question.

Before you start to think about how you want to analyse the data you collect during your research project, you will probably have to put some thought into what it is that you specifically hope to study. With that in mind, you might want to start by identifying the project's principal aims and objectives, making sure they are clearly and explicitly expressed. These will determine what it is you hope to study and will help provide a basis for more detailed planning.

Before you decide on the approach you wish to adopt when you come to analyse the data, try to brainstorm the likely nature of both the short-term data and findings and long-term consequences or implications of the project. This will help you make decisions when it comes to choosing an appropriate approach.

Question: Given your research aim and objectives, what sort of data are you hoping to collect?

Try to identify and highlight key activities, timeframes, critical dates and key people. Use these to determine the type and nature of the data you hope to collect. When you are thinking about your project, reflect specifically on how it will be managed. Try to be explicit about the management structure. It might make a difference if you anticipated a particular style of data, but generated data of a different nature because insufficient attention was paid to managing your data collection.

Question: How will you show trustworthiness?

Which elements of trustworthiness will you be able to use and which elements are restricted by the nature of the milieu, the tools you hope to use and the data that is generated? Given these limitations with regard to elements of trustworthiness, which approach offers best fit?

Having identified the approach you hope to use, try to provide a more detailed analysis of the context in which your project will operate. Cost may be a factor. The approach you have opted to use may be time- or cost-intensive. By carefully considering the process you hope to use and the nature of the data you hope collect, you will be better informed.

Question: Will this approach work?

Does the context/milieu suit the level of detail you need? Having revisited the approach, revisit your project aims and start to create a more detailed project plan which demonstrates how the project's findings and data collection will be sought for your given situation. Put some careful thought into how you hope to monitor whether your progress and your data still lend themselves to the approach you have chosen.

The sequence in Figure 11.4 is common to much classroom-based research.

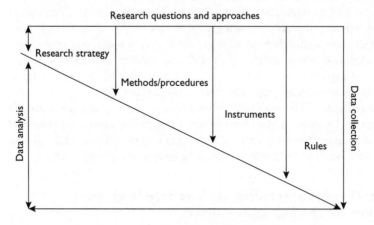

Figure 11.4 A common classroom-based research approach

In reality, we often identify the research question and launch into a research strategy with limited awareness of the theoretical approach until we are well into our research. This may be because many of us come to educational research without formal training and find ourselves learning *in situ* as we try to find trustworthy strategies to support informed data collection and data analysis. Intuitively and sensibly, many researchers often generate lots of data, but being systematic may help researchers obtain richer data or make us, as researchers, more aware of the possibilities. We hope that the chapters in this book will afford some insight into the nature of trustworthy theoretical approaches to help govern and inform research strategies chosen by potential researchers.

References

Guba, G. and Lincoln, S. (1989) *Fourth Generation Evaluation*, Newbury Park, CA: Sage.
Lincoln, Y. and Guba, G. (1986) 'But is it rigourous? Trustworthiness and authenticity in naturalistic evaluation', in D. D. Williams (ed.) *Naturalistic Evaluation* (pp. 73–84), San Francisco, CA: Jossey-Bass.

Index

Note: 't' after a page number refers to a table.